FREEDOM
AND
COMMUNITY

FREEDOM AND COMMUNITY

The Ethics of Interdependence

ERICH H. LOEWY

State University
of New York
Press

Published by
State University of New York Press, Albany

Printed in the United States of America

Production by Susan Geraghty
Marketing by Bernadette LaManna

For information, address State University of New York
Press, State University Plaza, Albany, NY 12246

Library of Congress Cataloging-in-Publication Data

Loewy, Erich H.
    Freedom and community : the ethics of interdependence / Erich H.
Loewy.
      p.   cm.
    Includes bibliographical references and index.
    ISBN 0–7914–1513–9 (hc : acid free). — ISBN 0–7914–1514–7 (pb. :
acid free)
      1. Solidarity. 2. Community. 3. Social contract. 4. Social
justice. 5. Liberty. 6. Individualism. I. Title.
HM126.L595   1993
303.3'72—dc20   92–24773
                                                                   CIP

10 9 8 7 6 5 4 3 2 1

This work is dedicated to the memory of
Ernst Hudik
without whose early friendship little else
would have been possible.

CONTENTS

ACKNOWLEDGMENTS

This book must, first of all, acknowledge the role played by my students: by asking critical questions, by raising troubling issues and often by making pertinent suggestings they have been instrumental in shaping my thoughts. This work began to take shape during a seminar held in 1991 (and repeated in 1992) at Philips Universität in Marburg, Germany, under the leadership of Dr. Friedrich Heubel. Dr. Heubel and his students were (and continue to be) instrumental in helping me think through problems. Arguing, and often disagreeing with them (and then reflecting on the areas of disagreement), has been of immense help. They are deserving of all the thanks I can give them. My students in the United States have played a very similar constructive and ongoing role. Many have read and freely criticized this manuscript in its early and later stages.

There are a large number of others to whom thanks are due. Dr. Larry Churchill of Chapel Hill, South Carolina, and Dr. Jonathan Moreno of SUNY in New York painstakingly read the manuscript and must be thanked for many first-rate criticisms and suggestions. Many of my ideas were developed or sharpened in conversations with these colleagues as well as with Dr. David Thomasma, to whom continuing and ongoing thanks are due. Besides my students at this university, thanks are due to Dr. Jean Aldag to whose understanding and unflagging interest much is owed. Likewise, I must thank Ms. Carola Sautter, my editor at SUNY Press, who not only guided this book's development but suggested the title (the original title *Community, Communities, and Suffering* was clumsy and awful; I was stymied until she suggested what has become the current title).

Above all, I must thank my wife, Roberta Springer Loewy. As a philosopher she served as a daily sounding board, and as a wife and compassionate human being, her patient understanding of the problems of authorship and of the not-rare moodiness of the author was essential to the work. What she has so generously shared about the fundamental work that she is doing on relationships has profoundly influenced what I am trying to do. Furthermore and above all, her work has served as an ongoing example.

PREFACE

For there is neither East nor West
Border nor breed nor birth,
When two strong men stand face to face,
Though they come from the ends of the earth.
                                        —R. Kipling

In *All Quiet on the Western Front* Erich Maria Remarque sketches
a close community of men united by a common purpose, a purpose which is not so much of defeating "the enemy" as it is the
desperate purpose of staying alive.[1] Staying alive, however, necessitates not only a great deal of luck in not being torn apart by
shrapnel, hit by machine-gun fire, or gassed, but likewise requires
solidarity and mutual help. In that desperate purpose the soldiers
form a close-knit community as do the soldiers on the other side
of the front whose purpose to stay alive is much the same. These
communities are close-knit and their solidarity is powerful not
because they know that others within their own group have
undertaken not to harm them but for two reasons: they are, first
of all, threatened by external circumstances (the opposing forces)
largely beyond their own control and they are, secondly, united by
mutual caring and benevolence. Veterans of trench warfare have
often pointed to this sense of community and solidarity as
enabling their physical and emotional survival. The experience,
for those who have themselves experienced it, seems to have been
one of the most powerful ones of their lives.
   Both opposing groups have been manipulated, forced into
and maintained in their position by forces they conceive to be
beyond their control. The opposing groups can see no way of
achieving their purpose without eliminating each other: they are
locked in a seemingly endless and purposeless battle not of their
willing, choosing, or making. The interrelationship of these two
communities is one which requires them to destroy each other

without reason, without hate, often even with regret and with no
ultimate profit beyond bare survival. It is the story of war as it
has been waged since war began. Men have become objects: the
disposable weapons of a war conducted by forces beyond their
understanding and control. Their only hope for individual survival lies in their communal cohesiveness, in their ability to
defend themselves not only against the forces opposed to them
but likewise to resist as far as possible the forces which manipulated and continue to control them.

Remarque's work shows more than the cohesiveness and solidarity of a small and intensely threatened community. It is a community which on the one hand is actively attacked and on the
other is manipulated by its larger "home community" so as to
make such attack and such attacking inevitable. There is thus a
total breakdown of communications and each of these small communities no longer feels itself, or truly is, part of another and
larger community. The immediate survival of each of these smaller
communities depends on the destruction of the other and yet such
destruction in itself would not form the basis of long-term survival. Communities, just as individuals, ultimately depend on each
other.

The experiences of this century, while especially concentrated
in their ferocity are scarcely unique to it. Such experiences have
recurred from antiquity onward. Whether one thinks of Hebrew
slaves fleeing Egypt, of slaves in the Roman Empire, of the terror
following the French Revolution, or of slavery in the United
States, the story has been the same. Humans have needed community to survive or to eventually overcome their oppressors. Without such community individual survival for any length of time is
impossible; without integration into and support by a larger community, smaller communities likewise cannot and do not survive.
When solidarity is lost, communities and the individuals within
them perish. This sense of community and solidarity is like the
concentric waves formed when a pebble is dropped into a pond: it
extends from the innermost core to the outermost reaches.

Examples of such human tragedy are hardly limited to the
past. Inevitably such events involve a breakdown of community at
some level. Whether one looks at the crass examples of hordes of
refugees who have and are wandering across the earth throughout
this century or at the poverty in the ghetto areas in the United

States, the picture is the same. It is of the dispossessed and disadvantaged (persons and groups dispossessed and disadvantaged so that another individual or group of individuals may ultimately draw profit from their misery) who have only their small community of fellow sufferers to rely upon. They have lost or they have been denied the fellowship of and with larger communities. It is the story of the ghetto dweller or of the illegal refugee seeking to escape; it is the story of third world nations, first exploited and then left to their own devices: invariably it is a story which involves the breakdown of community and consequently a denial of mutual human obligation.

The relationship of persons with and in their community is critical to their survival. Persons cannot survive or even be conceived without community. In turn, the survival of communities is dependent upon the relationship of smaller to larger communities. When the smaller community is isolated from friendly contact with other communities or when it is manipulated by other, more powerful communities it may, as the price for immediate survival, lash out at whatever other groups are immediately in its way. Examples of such lashing out in desperation can be seen not only under the conditions of warfare, but are a phenomenon likewise observable in Suweto, in the ghettos of America, and elsewhere across the world. Desperate German and French forces manipulated by powers they believed to be beyond their control, along with American forces in Viet Nam, did just that. They had lost meaningful contact with other communities, were isolated and imperiled. While lashing out at the immediate threat has short-term survival value, it is ultimately destructive. Just as individuals cannot conceive of their own existence, let alone survival, without community, isolated communities, as the German and French troops were, cannot ultimately survive without re-establishing meaningful and orderly communication with other larger communities. And often, as the Viet Nam experience, as well as the German experience after World War I, have shown, re-establishing meaningful and orderly communication remains incredibly difficult.

Individualism, presaged in the eleventh century but growing especially since the Reformation and one of the cornerstones of capitalist societies, has been seen as opposed to this sense of community and solidarity.[2] Indeed, capitalism (predicated as it is

on a philosophy of individual competition and finding its caricature in a misunderstood interpretation of Darwin which would
extend Darwinism uncritically and unthinkingly to the social
realm) is opposed to a sense of community.

Many persons who in theory would embrace the concept of
community shrink from it for personal reasons: they fear that
community would force undesired, close and even intimate association with others whose values, interests, and goals they do not
share and, thereby, would dilute their own capacity to pursue
their own values, interests and goals so as to lead their lives in
their own way. Such forced association, it is feared, might exact a
uniformity of values, interests, and goals, homogenize society
and, ultimately, stifle the expression of individuality and progress.
There are at least two objections that can be made to this misper-
ception: the first is that close association is unlikely; homogeneity
of values is not a necessary result of a sense of community. The
second is that not wanting to eat dinner with someone is a dis-
tinctly different matter than being deeply concerned that others
with whom we may not necessarily wish to eat do have a dinner
to eat. Community is not about sameness but about cooperation
and mutual aid.

The desire to thrive as individuals is a goal common to all of
us even if our understanding of what thriving means may be quite
different; the desire for developing our unique culture, likewise, is
a common goal of all cultures even when their idea of culture
may be quite different. We may not wish to associate socially
with another person or culture whose interests, values and goals
we do not share; but having said that we nevertheless must
acknowledge that by virtue of our basic common humanity we
do, in fact, share some common interests, values, and goals with
them. At the very least these basic goals consist of fair access to
those things necessary to sustain life as well as to those things
which enable us to pursue our individual freely chosen and mutually respected differing interests, values, and goals. In order to
accomplish this we, no matter how we may otherwise differ,
share at least one other interest, value, and goal: the goal of community itself. A proper and, therefore, lasting community, lasting
because solidarity cements it together, is one which holds community as one of the goals of its association.[3,4]

In this book I want to (1) briefly explore the notions sketched in my previous work (*Suffering and the Beneficient Community*) and then (2) develop and move beyond them. I will start by giving a brief summary of a philosophy which grounds moral worth on the shared capacity for suffering. Such a philosophy seeks the answer to the question of what gives objects moral worth and what, therefore, changes them from objects to subjects, in their capacity to suffer. Such a point of view accepts suffering as the starting point of moral concern. Causing direct or indirect suffering is a prima-facie wrong—prima facie because causing suffering may at times be unavoidable or even morally necessary. The moral worth of objects lacking the capacity to suffer depends upon the valuing or disvaluing of such objects by others.[4] Our moral sense, that which makes us not only question the rightness or wrongness of our actions but that which makes us realize the concept of rightness and wrongness in the first place, is held to be very similar to Rousseau's "primitive sense of pity."[5] The "primitive sense of pity" is akin to the moral sense (or "sentiment") of benevolence. Hume considers benevolence to be the one sentiment "bestowing the most merit." The merit of benevolence resides in its tendency to promote the interest and happiness of mankind.[6,7]

Rousseau's "primitive sense of pity" (or, perhaps, sense of compassion which makes it not possible to look with total indifference upon the suffering of another) is, in my view, not only what makes ethics operative and powers our ethical feelings but is the capacity which enables us to recognize ethical concerns in the first place. It is the basis of benevolent feeling and, eventually, of beneficent action. Such a "sense of pity," like other emotions in biological organisms, is an evolutionary development whose continuation and expansion is made possible by its survival value for individual and species alike.[8] A "sense of pity" or compassion can certainly be suppressed but without it and without the recognition that others, even others arraigned against us, can and do suffer, an ethical ought does not present itself. Such a "primitive sense of pity" (even, as Remarque shows, towards an individual enemy) can be suppressed but not entirely eliminated. Even when we desire to make another suffer (or even when we take pleasure in the suffering of another as the German word *Schadenfreude* illustrates so well), it is this primitive sense of pity which allows us to recognize the suffering of another. The desire to make another suffer and the pleasure in that suffering is a perverted sense of pity. Our question of moral rightness or wrongness as well as our sense of compassion (or pity) occurs and is unthinkable without a community which, in the first place, must shape and define who and what we are.

Social contract and the structure of community are critical to our sense of mutual obligation. In order to understand the sense of communal relations here, I will briefly examine historical ways of looking at social contract and community and especially review the notion of community.[4] Community can be conceived as solitary individuals who come together to form associations, or as primordial realities which spawn the individual. The problem, when posed in this manner, is a largely non-biological chicken-and-egg question which ignores evolutionary process and insists that, somewhere along the line, a chicken or an egg must have developed *de novo* and started the whole thing. Such a question, and, therefore, arguments as to what the answer to it might be, can get us nowhere. Nonsense questions cannot have meaningful answers. When one looks at the evolutionary process, it is evident that most newborn beings and certainly all human infants are born into communities and are critically dependent on nurture and caring. Human infants as well as those of other higher species are born without a psychological (or immunological) knowledge of themselves as selves and distinguish their selfness only after some time. Without nurture and caring such beings can never attain self-differentiation, let alone develop a sense of self and of autonomy. Autonomy, therefore, necessarily and inevitably occurs in the embrace of communal nurture.

Communities constituted in this fashion take on tacit obligations of nurture. Individuals cannot otherwise survive. Community and communal nurturing of the young has communal and ultimately species survival value just as does thinking. Nurturing individuals to allow them to develop and thrive, however, is not enough. To survive, communities must develop their members' individual talents, must help them survive, thrive, and grow so that the community itself may survive and thrive. Fostering autonomy, just as nurturing infants, has communal and ultimately species survival value.

Communities take on obligations of beneficence towards their members who, likewise, are obligated to others in this way. I shall claim that such an obligation is grounded in the necessary nurture of infants, in the communal fostering of their autonomy and in a "primitive sense of pity" (or compassion) which sees the strong as necessarily obligated to the weak by virtue of such a difference of power.[9-11] Beneficence, however, while it forms the initial embrace in which the infant develops and beneficence, while it is called upon in many ways to provide the necessary conditions enabling individual survival in a community, is insufficient unless it sees as part of its obligation the fostering of individual autonomy. Indeed, as Pellegrino and Thomasma have pointed out, beneficence which does not do this can hardly be called beneficence.[12] However, beneficence, whether it is the individual beneficence of parents or the communal beneficence of the state, can smother instead of embrace individuals and their individuality and autonomy. When that happens, beneficence becomes a caricature of itself. One can, therefore, as I have done in the past, argue that beneficence and the striving for autonomy are in conflict, that they form a dialectic relationship from which a synthesis emerges. The way particular relationships or the communal ethos are conceived at a particular time and under particular circumstances is the result of such a dialectic.[4]

In this book, I want to go beyond such a dialectic relationship. The dialectic relationship as it is usually conceived is one of internal conflict in which two opposites (thesis and antithesis) struggle to finally emerge with a compromise (synthesis) between them. Such a compromise, then, becomes a new thesis to which an antithesis forms. What I propose here is that in the relationship between community (beneficence or, as it can be translated "social justice") and individual freedom (autonomy or "human rights") a struggle of a dialectic type may constitute an incomplete model. When one looks at an organism's mechanism for maintaining its biological equilibrium a tension between various forces exists: but it is a tension which is not the same sort of struggle as the dialectic would offer. The forces are not, in the same sense at least, opposed to each other; they are, even if at first glance opposed, mutually supportive for the common end of keeping the organism functioning and alive. In this book I shall claim that the relationship between community and the individual (between beneficence or "social justice" and autonomy or "human rights") is quite similar to biological homeostasis: means and ends become largely if not entirely enmeshed. Such a relationship between individuals and their community (as well as the relationship between smaller, larger, and ever larger communities) likewise is one in which these forces, even when seemingly opposed, are mutually supportive for the common end of keeping each of these communities functioning and alive.

This homeostatic relationship between individuals and their community, is reflected in the relationship of smaller to larger communities and, ultimately, in the relationship of various cultures with each other. In a world in which all cultures impinge on each other, the development and thriving of any culture requires the support and cooperation of others. Smaller and larger communities and various cultures are inextricably enmeshed in and with each other. For their own survival they have obligations of mutual nurture. Community and communal nurturing of each other has communal and ultimately cultural survival value. Nurturing smaller communities and diverse cultures so that they can develop and thrive, however, is not enough. To survive, larger communities and cultures must develop and respect smaller communities and cultures, must help those weaker and smaller to survive and thrive so that the community itself may survive and thrive. Fostering cultural diversity, just as fostering the autonomy of individuals, has communal and ultimately species survival value.

In a work of this sort one cannot do more than sketch out some of the considerations which must inform individuals as well as communities if the species and the earth we inhabit is to flourish. Interdependence is progressively more a fact of life. This interdependence is bound to increase as our scientific knowledge and the technology based on such knowledge develops. In this book I shall claim that this interdependence is a fact of life which has bio-psycho-social underpinnings as well as having philosophical necessity. While a work of this sort cannot hope (and is not written) to give definitive answers, I feel that practical examples are needed if philosophy is to interconnect with the daily lives of all of us. Those of us interested and working in the field of ethics, whatever our background, must channel and test our abstract theories in the real world, where, ultimately, their truth will be tested. Such a "truth" is not immutable but rather is testable and tested in praxis.[13] In this book I hope to provide a possible conceptual framework, to offer a few thoughts on how such a framework might be useful in conceptualizing a reconstruction of our interpersonal and intercommunal relationships, and to leave it to others as well as to later efforts to test its possibilities and to adapt its structure.

REFERENCES

1. Remarque EM: *Im Westen Nichts Neues.* Frankfurt/M, Deutschland: Verlag Ullstein; 1962.

2. Tawney RH: *Religion and the Rise of Capitalism.* New York, NY: Mentor; 1926.

3. Oakshott M: *On Human Conduct.* Oxford, England: Clarendon Press; 1975.

4. Loewy EH: *Suffering and the Beneficent Community: Beyond Libertarianism.* Albany, NY: SUNY Press; 1991.

5. Rousseau JJ: *Du Contrat Social* (R. Grimsley, ed.). Oxford, England: Oxford University Press; 1972.

6. Mossner EC: *The Life of David Hume.* Oxford, England: Oxford University Press; 1980.

7. Hume D: *An Enquiry Concerning the Principles of Morals.* (E. Freeman, ed.). La Salle, IL: Open Court Publishing Co; 1966.

8. Darwin CR: *The Expression of the Emotions in Man and Animals.* New York, NY: D. Appleton and Co.; 1873.

9. Jensen UJ: *Practice and Progress: A Theory for the Modern Health-Care System.* Oxford, England: Blackwell Scientific Publications; 1987.

10. Jensen UJ: Are Selves Real? In: *Harré and His Critics.* (Roy Shaskar, ed.). Oxford, England: Basic Blackwell; 1990.

11. Jonas H: *Das Prinzip Verantwortung.* Frankfurt a/M, Deutschland: Suhrkamp; 1984.

12. Pellegrino ED and Thomasma DC: *For the Patient's Good: The Restoration of Beneficence to Health Care.* New York, NY: Oxford University Press; 1988.

13. Dewey J. *Reconstruction in Philosophy.* In *John Dewey: The Middle Works.* Vol. XII (JoAnn Boydston and BA Walsh, eds.) Carbondale, IL: Southern Illinois University Press; 1988.

INTRODUCTION

This book extends (and in many respects revises) the work done in a previous work entitled *Suffering and the Beneficent Community*. In this new work I begin to grapple with a problem I believe basic to all ethics today: the role that our ever greater interdependence plays and ought by rights to play in our understanding of ethical problems. Interdependence, despite what some would argue, has always been a fact of life, but interdependence was interdependence on a much smaller scale. Ethics until fairly modern times was predominantly "personal" in the sense of dealing with the relationship between and among individuals. Persons, however, were interdependent with others as well as with their community. The interdependence of persons with each other as well as the interdependence of communities with each other, while a fact of life since the beginning of history, has become a far more critical fact of life today. Many have seen a clash between the obligations of personal and the obligations of communal life. The allegedly unresolvable conflict between a Kantian and a utilitarian ethic has its roots in the inability of seeing both social and individual problems as inevitably related. Dewey, whose conception of individual ethics and of reasoning was predominantly communally based can, I think, be understood as grappling with community and experience and with their role in shaping our actions and thoughts. Although he does not speak directly to the conflict between the two forms of ethical thought, his approach to human problems goes a long way toward understanding and reconciling this rift. His thoughts and ideas are fundamental to what this work is about.

Like most works this work has its roots not only in theory and reflection about theoretical considerations but also in personal experience and reflection on such personal experience. Some would argue that one's personal history ought not to play a decisive role in the way one looks at ethical problems, that one ought to set such experiences aside and limit oneself to a careful, dispassionate, and "objective" analysis of ethical problems. Personalizing such problems, they would argue, is "unscientific" and risks an emotional approach. I happen to think that this belief is ill-founded: it is one's experience and reflecting on one's experience that, in the first place, gives the impetus to the search. Beyond this, I would argue that how one chooses the particular problem one devotes oneself to (what "one is interested in"), why one accepts or rejects a given theoretical point of view, the analysis itself, the examples one chooses, and, not least of all, the way one reflects cannot escape being grounded in one's experience and in one's reflection on such experience. To argue otherwise is to argue that history has (or ought to have) little influence.

Since I believe that one's personal history, one's experience, and one's reflection on one's history and experience are critical to the way one chooses, envisions, and then deals with problems, it may be helpful for readers to have some insight into this experience. A person's "own" experience begins, I think, long before one's actual birth and extends backward for at least a part of the previous generation. As one moves backward, what one looks at as "personal history" (even though it was not personally experienced) dims and becomes more and more simply "history." When one loses such a history (when, for example, one is an orphan without close kin or when one's parents and other relatives were forcefully and early separated from one), one inevitably loses a part of one's roots. It is not surprising that many, later in life, will spend a good deal of time searching for their roots. But even when one discovers one's personal history by such a method it is still less vivid and in that sense less personal. Furthermore, when the importance of community and of the community's history is downplayed, there is no communal history to replace what has been lost. This is one of the differences between having been born to a black mother sold into American slavery and separated from her at an early age and having been born an orphan in white America. Many black persons born into today's ghetto and poverty area are a product of such a lack of personal as well as of communal history. From slavery on, their family was disrupted, their history denied, and, therefore, their future distorted and maimed. Such a person's personal and communal history is perforce fragmentary and such a person's roots are often shallow and tenuous.

In my own case, as a child of the 1920s and as a child very close to his parents, my "own" history starts somewhere with theirs. My father's stories of the first world war in which, as a medical student, he served as a physician in the Austrian army first on the Russian and later on the Italian front, as well as my mother's stories of civilian life during that period, are vivid enough so that they form a part of what I tacitly assume to be "my own" history. His training as a pediatrician, his early interest in social problems and in social medicine (stimulated by a man named Gregorek who was his orderly during the war and who gave him some insight into the problems of the worker), his work in the socialist party, his sense of justice, and his fervid belief in the fundamental equality of men had a profound influence on me. I remember the Austrian revolution of the 30s, the clerical fascism that followed and the eventual German take-over in Austria. I remember the ever-increasing anti-semitism (at first regarded and justified as "moderate"—as though racism could ever be "moderate" or could ever be "justified"!) and its eventuating in howling mobs pelting one with refuse and of brown-shirted thugs lustily singing of killing Jews before attacking. And I remember the West's hypocrisy: the closed doors, the American visas refused under false pretexts by anit-semitic consuls and the many and hypocritically couched refusals of help. I remember how the Catholic churches (and many of the Protestant churches as well) closed their eyes to what they well knew was in progress: and the churches could, had they so wished and at almost any point in time, easily stopped Hitler, the war, and the atrocities. But they refrained. But I also and with equal force remember the other side of the coin: the often incredible risks persons took who intervened to help, the generous word, the compassionate gesture or deed that sustained one along the way. In my case, I particularly remember my boyhood friend Ernst Hudik (to whom this work is dedicated) who single-handedly and persistently stood by me when the others attacked; he, and the experience of others with persons like him, went far to convince me that decency could, even under incredible pressure to the contrary, persist.

My experiences under the Nazis, my experiences in emigration first in England and later in America, as well as my experience as one never entirely accepted in contemporary America but also, and with equal force, the many kindnesses shown are critical to the way I think, argue, and envision problems and solutions. These experiences again were a mixture of what one might, simplistically perhaps, call "good" and "bad." One would have to be an unfeeling and, in a sense, irresponsible person if one did not see parallels between the way life was viewed under fascism or in Nazi Germany and the way life is viewed in capitalist and still very much racist America today. Racism and institutionalized and avoidable or ameliorable poverty that is deliberately not avoided or ameliorated, the exploitation of a given class for the benefit of another that considers itself to be superior by virtue of its racial, social, or gender status is, unfortunately, not unique to Nazi Germany.

Some would argue that these different experiences and these different cultural backgrounds are apt to produce "moral strangers": persons who have starkly different cultural and personal backgrounds and who do not share common ways of looking at things, common interests, and, for that reason, a common moral framework. In such a way of looking at things, the only common denominator persons who come from vastly different cultural and personal backgrounds can share is the shared desire to pursue their own starkly different interests; to be left alone (except when one wishes otherwise) hampered only by the restriction that one must grant the same interest (and right) to others. From such a vantage point, "moral strangers" would see problems of value so differently that no other common ethic except one allowing for maximal freedom for all is possible. What, one could argue, does the howling brown-shirted mob have in common with its victims? What conceivable interests could unite a Bantu tribesman and a Norwegian attorney? What possible moral framework can and do they share?

This book argues against the notion of "moral strangers." If we consider ourselves to be "moral strangers" the notion of being "moral enemies" is not far behind. The assumption, as Primo Levi has pointed out, that the stranger is an enemy is an assumption leading inexorably to Auschwitz. And the assumption that we are "moral strangers" and quite possibly on the road to being "moral enemies" hedged only by obligations of mutual nonharm is flawed. Although all sentient creatures wish to pursue their own particular and peculiar interests as unhampered as possible, I argue that all sentient creatures share far more than merely such an interest. These shared interests provide a much richer moral framework and, therefore, imply far more than merely minimalist obligations of mutual nonharm and noninterference. We may not be "moral friends" but, at the very least, we are "moral aquaintances."

In today's world, the ethics of interrelationship and interdependence (not only how individuals relate to and depend on each other but how different collectives do) is of profound importance. If humans are to survive, an ethic beyond a minimalist and largely individualistic ethic and an ehtic that also avoids the pitfalls of communal regimentation must be found. An accommodation between individualist ethics, which regards interpersonal relationships as all important, and a communal ethics, which puts the interests of the community into the first place, is possible. Individuals as well as collectives (I hesitate to use the word "community" here since later in this book I will differentiate between various collectives of which community is but one) are interdependent and their relationship cannot be reduced to a minimalist point of view without seriously, and with today's possibilities perhaps irrevocably, endangering our existence on earth. If we are to survive, neither a starkly individualistic nor a blindly communitarian approach will do. Understanding the dependence of individuals on each other, understanding the dependence of individuals on their community and the way various collectives depend on each other ultimately results in a point of view in which individualism and communitarianism itself are seen as interdependent.

This book attempts to sketch out this point of view: if it provokes dialogue and stimulates discussion it will have achieved its purpose, for dialogue and discussion implies at least some framework in which such discussion and such dialogue can proceed. It is a dialogue that, to be carried on, already and by that fact concedes that we are more than "moral strangers": if we only shared a framework of mutual nonharm in which we wished to be left alone to pursue our own self-interests unhampered by the needs of others, such a dialogue would not come about and could hardly take place.

CHAPTER 1

Grounding Moral Worth in Suffering: A Review

One of the most basic questions in ethics is the question of what makes us have ethical concerns about some living as well as about some inaminate things while other things seem unimportant from an ethical point of view. Having asked that, one needs to ask further why it is that some things are of less and others of more ethical importance. It is the sort of question which comes up when we feel that punching a punching bag is exercise while punching a child or hitting a dog is brutality and, therefore, immoral. The difference between the punching bag and the child or dog must rest on some prior notion of what the morally relevant differences between the punching bag, the child, and the dog are. Likewise, we would consider splitting logs to be a form of exercise but would consider slashing another's tires to be immoral. Again, something makes logs of little and tires of considerable moral concern. Beyond this, however, there is the question of why, when we must choose between competing interests and values, some seem ethically less, others more, and still others critically important. Thinking about any ethical question ultimately requires us to give an answer to such questions of actual and relative moral worth.

Historically this question of moral worth is not formally or explicitly addressed until Kant.[1] Plato and Aristotle presupposed but did not argue for the status quo in their society: free male individuals were of moral concern; slaves or women existed to serve them. Being a free male is what changes one from object to subject.[2,3] For Aquinas, on the other hand, moral worth resided in an ensouled entity of the right substance. The soul is what made humans matter and what changed them from objects to subjects.[4] Kant, on the other hand, examines the problem for-

1

mally and explicitly. For him, what gives an entity moral worth and, therefore, morally speaking, standing (what differentiates those who are themselves of direct moral concern from those who are not) is the capacity to self-legislate.[1] The capacity to self-legislate was what characterized those who were of direct moral concern and what changed them from objects into subjects. Other things that were of moral concern, things like property or symbols had either affective (aesthetic) or market value: they were of moral concern because acting towards such objects would affect those who, as self-legislating entities, were owed respect. Brutality towards animals was in a somewhat different category: it was wrong to be brutal to animals not because of the impact being brutal had upon animals themselves but being brutal to animals was wrong because brutality towards animals might foster, almost in a Humean sense, a sentiment of brutality which ultimately would affect humans.[5] Early utilitarians, Mill among them, generally assume moral worth without specifically arguing for it. Maximizing happiness is the issue and all those who have the capacity to experience happiness, including animals, would count. In speaking of ethical behavior towards animals, it was Bentham who first proposed that what was morally relevant was not a being's capacity to reason but a being's capacity to suffer.[6] Human happiness, for reasons that are not made explicit, however, seems to count more than the happiness of any other creature.[7] Then and today, while not the only defenders of the rights of animals, modern utilitarians are often the staunchest defenders of the ethical status of non-humans.[8,9]

In a previous work I have argued that it is the present or future capacity to suffer which changes objects to subjects. It is this capacity to suffer which gives a prima-facie protection against being made to suffer and which confers an obligation on all of us not to cause, and where possible to alleviate, suffering. Furthermore, when we have ethical concerns relative to entities incapable of suffering we have these concerns because of the way in which our actions towards such entities would affect those who do have the capacity to suffer. This concern for the suffering of others, whatever these others might be, is what causes us to make what we, almost intuitively, consider to be ethically relevant distinctions between rocks who are not capable of suffering and sentient beings who are.[10]

When it comes to suffering, several questions come up: (1) What is suffering and what are the conditions necessary for bringing it about? (2) How does one go about judging the presence of that capacity? (3) Why should the capacity to suffer be ethically important? (4) Even if we grant the ethical importance of suffering and since we cannot conduct our lives without in some sense causing suffering, how does one deal with the obvious conflict which inevitably must arise between and among various kinds of suffering and various entities among whom one must choose? (5) Granted that suffering should matter, how can one justify making the obligation not to cause and where possible to alleviate suffering a grounding principle? In this chapter, I will try to supply some answers to the first three of these questions, begin to discuss but not develop extensively the difficult question of hierarchies, and only touch the problem of justification (which I will discuss more extensively in the third as well as in later chapters).

WHAT IS SUFFERING?

Except for the theological literature, amazingly little has been written about suffering. The philosophical as well as, surprisingly, the medical literature reveals only a very few entries under such a rubric. Fiction is, of course, full of the notion, but in fiction the evil of suffering is taken as a background evil and is rarely further developed. Suffering, however defined, has a universally negative connotation. As defined here, suffering, whatever else it is, is a disagreeable experience and one which all who have the capacity to suffer would wish to avoid.[10] Even when, as is the case in some religious views, suffering is redemptive, it is redemptive precisely because it is a negative experience and because it is an experience ordinary persons under ordinary conditions would seek to avoid. No one wishes to suffer and when they do so willingly they do so for an ultimately higher end. When sado-masochists inflict pain on themselves (pain which might in others give rise to suffering) it is a different matter: in a pathological way, sado-masochists derive enjoyment from this and cannot, therefore, be said to be truly suffering. In what is to follow and in the way that we shall use the term, the redemptive value and the other supposedly positive aspects of "suffering" will be largely ignored. Suffering, to be suffering as here defined, is suffering precisely because it has, at least in the eyes of the sufferer, few if any positive aspects.

Suffering and pain are not identical concepts.[11,12] One can have physical pain without necessarily suffering (hitting one's shin on a chair or having one's ear lobes pierced) and one can suffer and suffer intensely without having any physical pain (a mother seeing her child dying or a person seeing her work trivialized suffers without having physical pain). In the medical setting, for example, patients dying of cancer, even when kept relatively pain-free may suffer and suffer intensely. The sick suffer in ways which may be quite distinct from their pain. Suffering, as Cassell points out so well, is an existential experience, subjective and peculiar to the particular individual suffering.[12] Suffering, furthermore, happens at a given time and in a given context: a stimulus may provoke suffering at one but not at another time. We bring to our suffering a whole baggage of past experiences and integrate them into our present experience as well as into our perception of the future.[10]

Frankl has pointed out that we suffer when the experience provoking suffering has no wider meaning for us.[13] "Meaning" here can be used in a double sense. To have meaning, in the one sense, something must be remembered (however briefly), integrated and understood: without this, it remains a single, fleeting stimulus. In the other sense, meaning can be used to indicate purpose or goal: noxious stimuli which serve an understood or accepted purpose continue to be noxious but they are not necessarily or usually thought of as suffering. The first sense of "meaning" is the necessary condition of the second: unless a stimulus is recognized (almost in the Kantian sense of re-cognized: known again) as a stimulus by us, it can have no wider meaning.

According to Freud, suffering can come to us in three ways: (1) "from our own body which is doomed to decay and dissolution…;" (2) by external threats "raging against us…;" and (3) (and to Freud most importantly) "from our relations to (with) other men" (p. 24).[14] Freud feels that the suffering that is brought about by and in our relationship to others is the worst kind of suffering because it is "gratuitous" and brought about by another's volition instead of being brought about by forces beyond human control. One would presume that, in a sense, the first two ways in which suffering can come to us are due to forces of nature whereas the other, broadly speaking, are not only suffering brought about by our intimate personal relations with others but likewise suffering brought about by easily controllable but callously ignored social circumstances.

This concept of "meaning" as well as Freud's three ways in which suffering can originate are sometimes thought to apply only to human animals. Many have argued that since lower species allegedly lack a history, they can find no meaning. If, as is most likely the case, most lower species do indeed lack a history it is a lack of history in the sense of a species or clan history rather than in the sense of a personal history that is lacking. Since suffering is an existential experience peculiar to the sufferer and occurring at a given time and in a given context, it is the personal far more than the species history that matters. Anyone who has ever owned a dog, a cat or a parrot is fully aware that such animals have and are aware of having a personal history: they differentiate other animals from each other and relate to specific ones in different ways, know and relate to their owner, remember where their food bowl is, and often and obviously remember and remember well places they have visited sometimes long before. Furthermore, if it were indeed true that lower animals cannot "grasp the problem of meaning" then the pain of animals would far more easily turn into suffering than would the pain of higher forms. Pain that is not understood, events which are perceived as a threat because they lack explanation must be especially troublesome.[10] It is for this very reason that we must have special concern when dealing with the mentally retarded or impaired.[15]

Clearly, furthermore, lower species are capable of meeting Freud's three criteria. Their body is most certainly as prone to "decay and dissolution" as is the human body, and lower animals are certainly aware of that process in themselves. Lower animals are most certainly threatened by forces of the external world and are aware of these forces; animals, moreover, have relations with other animals including humans which can cause them pain, grief, and evident and undoubted suffering.[10]

The claim that animals lower on the evolutionary scale than man cannot reason and that, therefore, they cannot suffer is a secular expression of the religious argument that animals have no soul. Therefore, if one follows the argument to its inevitable conclusion, what we do to animals does not matter. The conclusion, that because one does not have a soul what happens to one is irrelevant, does not follow: the religious argument can, of course, be easily turned about. If one accepts the fact that animals have no soul (and if there is such a thing as a soul is, of course, something we can neither prove nor disprove) then their standing is indeed different: persons, who have souls, will have a brief span on earth followed by eternal life; animals have only their brief time on earth. Therefore, it would seem that what happens to human animals who will live in eternity should be of lesser importance (an argument by means of which religion over the years has helped keep the masses enslaved) than what happens to lower animals on earth since what happens on earth is the only life animals have. But while the argument that animals have no soul can be neither proven nor disproven, the argument that animals cannot reason is patently ridiculous. Anyone who has watched animals solving problems cannot seriously maintain such a position. To argue that such reasoning is, in a sense, purely algorithmic and that such algorithms are simply biological or conditioned reflexes is specious: if the reasoning of animals can be simply shrugged away by reducing reasoning to biolgical or conditioned reflex, there is no reason why the thought processes of humans should be of a different kind; if animals, furthermore, cannot reason, their capacity to solve quite new problems and individually (as distinct from species) adapt to new conditions cannot be readily explained. Furthermore, reasoning is a biological function, one which like all other biological functions evolves over time and over species rather than emerging full-blown in one species and at one time.[16] To maintain that reason sprung forth in the human species and was entirely unanticipated in lower forms is to flee into a rather crass form of creationism. Reasoning better, just like the ability to see, hear or run better, in general has survival value. And reasoning "better" must have antecedents in prior reasoning.[10]

Suffering, however, is not merely an existential experience peculiar to the one suffering, but is an existential experience occurring in, shaped by, and often even brought about by the community.[10] The nature of suffering (not only our behavior while suffering but those things which cause us to suffer) is conditioned, defined, in a sense determined, and then played out by and in community. A person suffering severely in a given time, place, and culture may not do so or may do so far less under other circumstances. The hospice movement is, among other things, based on that assumption. Furthermore, what is a stigma in one culture (and what, therefore, causes the stigmatized to suffer) may well be a positive attribute in another. Epilepsy, to take but one example, has been variously regarded as insanity, sin, or as an expression of holiness.

Hopelessness and despair are factors strongly associated with suffering.[10] It is, therefore, especially important not to dash a person's hope. In medicine this pretext has often been used as an excuse for lying to patients. I am far from suggesting that lying to patients is a proper thing to do: hope does not necessarily solely depend upon a belief in survival but may well be enlisted in other causes. Despair, in a sense, goes beyond this: it is a more global concept which makes it impossible for the sufferer to find satisfaction in anything. It is hopelessness generalized. To be hopeless is to be alienated and withdrawn, beyond protest or tears. It is, as Elizabeth Barrett Browning has pointed out, "passionless."[17] That may be the reason why in some religions despair is the most desparate sin: when one despairs, one believes in and hopes for nothing, not even in the ultimate goodness of God or in His infinite mercy.

When I have options, my suffering is greatly reduced or ameliorated. To have options means, in some sense, to have at least some control over one's own destiny. Having no options, or believing that one has no options, being impotent to do anything about one's condition, aggravates suffering and can sometimes convert otherwise endurable pain into profound suffering. My situation or my pain has lasted a long time, is interminable, and there is nothing I or anyone else can do to lessen it or to escape from it. The knowledge that some options, however dismal (even the option of suicide), exist is preferable to none. Patients riddled with cancer have been known to take comfort in having the means of suicide at hand even when, as is usually the case, they do not use them. It is a question of at least some power over one's desiny.

Fear is often part of suffering as is lack of understanding (lack of meaning in the first sense in which the term can be employed).

We often fear what we do not understand far more than we fear what we do understand. The human species' ongoing attempt to find explanations, often even explanations that are evidently false or even patently absurd, has been used throughout history as a hedge against fear.[10] Religions, especially the so-called "mystery religions," have gained influence and power in this very way.

If we are to perceive anything, a perceptive organ is necessary. This, by no means, is to reduce perception to the perceptive organ but it is to claim that the perceptive organ is a necessary condition for perception to occur. Suffering requires perception, be it the perception of an external stimulus, or the realization of an internal one. Such a stimulus, of course, need not be material but can just as well be a perceived or even an imagined event or a memory. The perceptive organ for stimuli of all kinds, globally speaking, is, of course, the central nervous system or brain. Without the central nervous system no perception of any kind as we understand it is possible. Most of our perceptions occur in specific areas of the brain and are integrated and finally brought to consciousness in others. To perceive the stimulus we call pain (whether the pain is brought to us from "our own body which is doomed to decay and dissolution" or from external forces "raging against us"), to translate it into a perception of that pain and finally to convert the pain into suffering requires a series of well-established neural structures and pathways.

Pain, the provoking stimulus for suffering we most frequently think about when the term is used, constitutes a warning. It is a biological alarm counseling us that something is wrong and that it would be to our advantage to find out and perhaps remedy the situation. When lower forms of life (be it plants exhibiting tropism or amoebae reacting to the prick of a tiny probe) move to escape a "noxious" stimulus, they do so reflexively. Reflexes, likewise, are maintained in higher organisms: a knee jerk in response to a reflex hammer is sensed by the person whose knee responds but sensing the tap is by no means necessary for the response to occur. A person whose spinal cord is severed and whose knee is tapped responds (and responds vigorously) but is entirely unaware of either stimulus or response. His higher centers are dissociated from the organ sensing (stretch receptors in the tendon) and the organ responding (the leg). Becoming aware of such a stimulus requires a functioning neocortex connected to the organs of reception by intact pathways. When either neocortex or pathways are absent, awareness cannot occur. Momentary perception is, however, not enough. To change a simple instance of sensation to pain requires, however primitively and briefly, the capacity to remember so as to connect one momentary stimulus with early and later ones.

Pain is neither a necessary nor a sufficient condition for suffering.[11,12,18] This is true anatomically as well as psychologically. For pain to be converted to suffering several psychological as well as anatomical conditions must be met. Pain, when it is the cause of suffering, must extend over time, although prolonged pain in itself does not necessarily become suffering. Anatomically, frontal lobes and elaborate connections of the frontal lobes to other centers are necessary. But even frontal lobes are not sufficient for pain to become suffering. We know that patients who undergo a frontal lobotomy (in which the frontal lobes are, as it were, diconnected) for severe pain, will continue to state that they have pain but, even though their pain caused suffering before, will now state that, while they are experiencing pain, they no longer suffer. Their pain, they will say, no longer bothers them.[19]

More than frontal lobes are involved. Suffering, in addition to pain or some other threat being perceived, has necessary emotional overtones. It has been shown that neural structures sometimes called the limbic system and consisting of a variety of structures including amygdala, thalamus, and hypothalamus are intimately involved with emotion. These diencephalic structures sit beneath the neocortex and above the brain stem. Evolution, as Darwin has shown, is as much involved in the evolution of emotions as it is in the evolution of physical traits.[20] Indeed, to make physical as well as emotional or intellectual traits possible, a physical substrate is necessary. The limbic system "sets the emotional background on which man functions intellectually."[21] Beyond these physical structures a complicated system of chemical neurotransmitters is involved in the functioning and integration of the whole. Suffering can no more be reduced to its physical or chemical substrate than walking can be reduced to legs or digestion to gut: but suffering, walking, or digestion, to be possible or even thinkable, presuppose the presence of the necessary physical apparatus and substrate.[10]

When we ask whether a creature has the capacity to suffer,

we need to examine its underlying neural structures as well as its behavior in the face of noxious stimuli. Movement, such as withdrawal, alone is not sufficient proof that suffering or even pain are present: after all, the knee of the paraplegic jerks in response to the hammer even though no sensation is present, amoeba withdraw from a sharp probe, and dead fish jump. Apparently intact neural structures, in themselves, do not allow us to conclude that suffering is present: merely that it is possible. But when the structures underwriting the capacity to suffer are present and when the behavior exhibited by an organism suggests that it is suffering, the burden of proof is on the person claiming that suffering does not occur. Those familiar with higher animals (animals which have, in whatever more primitive form, the necessary structures enabling the capacity to suffer) know that these creatures exhibit behavior associated with suffering in response to a variety of stimuli. They appear to suffer, just as do humans, in response to Freud's criteria. They suffer as a result of (1) illness coming from their own body; (2) injury from external forces; and (3) causes brought about by their relationship with others.[14] Anyone who has seen a dog in pain from either a degenerative illness or an injury or who has seen an animal mourning the death of a mate or the loss of an owner can attest to that. Furthermore, animals may often allow one to cause pain when it obviously seems to serve a purpose: dogs hold up a paw to allow their owner to remove a splinter even though this increases their momentary pain. In addition, I well remember a large old dog owned by one of my uncles who would occasionally go into pulmonary oedema and to whom my father would give an injection to relieve it. Not only did the dog hold still, he soon appeared to understand and would lick my father's hand in gratitude long before the drug could take effect. Anyone who claims that higher animals (those that have the necessary neurological substrate and exhibit appropriate behavior) do not have a memory, cannot think, or lack the capacity to suffer assumes the burden of proof.

JUDGING SUFFERING

I have suggested that the capacity to suffer is the necessary but insufficient condition for suffering. There are, as has been suggested, many factors which can cause suffering and which, under some circumstances may and under others may not, cause suffering. If we are to have an ethic based on the capacity to suffer and if that ethic would impose a prima-facie obligation not to cause and where possible to ameliorate suffering we need to have a clearer understanding of those things entailed.

All creatures have at least two types of needs: biological and, in a broad sense, social. Likewise their capacity to be hurt (using that term in its broadest sense) boils down to these two factors. We can be injured physically, can become ill, can be in pain, or can be hungry, thirsty or cold and, therefore, suffer. On the other hand, we may be deprived of opportunities, unjustly treated, thwarted in our affection, or see our work trivialized and, in consequence, suffer. The two factors, the social and the biological, are by no means entirely separable: social mistreatment can have biological results, just as biological factors can deprive one of social opportunities.

In judging what actions must be avoided if the suffering of another is not to be caused, these two factors must be considered. The evidence for judging that certain actions bring about suffering and that, therefore, such actions must be avoided is historically empirical: we judge that bringing about certain circumstances will cause another's suffering and we judge this from past experience in similar situations and with similar creatures. When it comes to ameliorating suffering, the evidence is both historical (we can anticipate that certain circumstances will elicit suffering) and directly empirical: we judge that others are actually suffering because they exhibit behavior we generally associate with suffering. There are certain commonalities in this: in many ways all higher animals display similar behavior when suffering. On the other hand, there are many individual as well as social differences among those who suffer, not only in what brings about suffering but in the way the sufferer responds or acts.

One may ask whether the ability to reason or to elaborate formal concepts is really relevant to the question of a non-human animal's moral standing.[22,23] I have claimed and will continue to claim that non-human animals most certainly can reason even if they are not capable of elaborating (or, at any rate, of verbalizing) formal concepts. That certainly makes them different from human animals. But merely being different does not in and of itself change anyone's moral stature or place. It is the particular differences examined in the relevant context which can provide a reasonable support for treating things or persons differently.[23] In his superb book on the subject, Rachels makes this point in a very simply and beautifully crafted series of analogies: one person having a broken arm and another an infection entitles the physician to "treat" the persons differently; having an infection or a broken arm (while certainly a difference) is not relevant to, say, admission to law school.

The fact that animals do have moral standing and that such standing grounds itself not on their capacity to talk or even to reason but on their capacity to suffer was already pointed out by Bentham.[6] Since suffering is an existential experience occurring in a given individual at a given time and in a given social setting, we must rely heavily on subjective factors. This makes judging difficult. Often it is the reason why some have claimed that animals do not suffer (or think). Animals cannot communicate with us verbally and, therefore, cannot "tell us about it."[24-26] Unless one speaks French, French persons (unless they also speak English) cannot directly tell an American that they are suffering when they are: when we judge that they are suffering, we base this judgment on knowing that they indeed have the necessary substrate and are exhibiting a set of behaviors we associate with suffering. We do not conclude that French persons, because we cannot personally communicate with them in words, do not suffer. Beyond this, however, many have claimed that "animals lack a language" and that, therefore, what they do when they appear to think or suffer cannot be equated with what humans experience. While a given French person cannot tell someone who does not speak French that they are suffering, a translator can be obtained (although some struggling to do so may deny it, French can be learned!). But merely because animals cannot communicate in a word language with humans does not mean that they cannot communicate. Animals communicate with their masters and with each other in many ways. They express concrete desires or emotions as well as far more abstract ideas. Language, after all, is merely the use of socially understood and accepted symbols. The concept "blue," the concept "automobile," or the more elaborate concept that I want to eat is communicated by humans in words; when words fail (as when we are stranded in a country whose language we do not understand) symbolic communication by other means (much like the symbolic communication animals may use) is used. Language is the manipulation of symbols to convey a meaning to others (and often but not necessarily to ourselves). Private language (the symbols we use consciously or subconsciously when we communicate strictly with ourselves) does not necessarily entail words and is, nevertheless, certainly and to many of us quite obviously a language. From Darwin (who saw evolutionary forces developing the emotions as well as the more obviously physical traits) on, many have argued that animals think, feel pain, and can elaborate and understand symbols and concepts.[23,27] The fact that in general a non-human animal's capacity to think, i.e., to deal with symbols or understand concepts, is less than is that ability in most humans merely points to the evolution of substrate as well as of function. As the brain evolves, so does the complexity of its function.

The subjective factors we rely upon when we judge another to be suffering are both verbal and non-verbal ones. Subjectivity here is twofold: it is the subjectivity of the one suffering as well as the subjectivity of the one observing and judging. That, of course, makes judging quite difficult. It is a common experience that persons in one social (and sometimes in one physical) situation are quite incapable (or perhaps unwilling?) to judge the emotions and feelings of others who are in a different social (or physical) situation than themselves. The statement that "one ought not to feel such and such a way" is often heard. Here the subjective situation and/or the prejudice and attitude of the judger makes it impossible to judge what does and what does not constitute suffering in another. In and of itself the statement that "one ought not to feel" certain ways or "ought not" to like or dislike certain things makes no sense. Feelings, as well as likes and dislikes, are not under our rational control even though reason may, especially over time, change the way we feel. To say that I ought not to feel sad or to say that I ought to like peanut butter (or the music of Hindemith) is to say that whoever makes such a statement thinks it appropriate for me to feel another way than the way I in fact do feel. Appropriateness, in this regard however, is appropriate to a social or physical setting. Emotions can, from the observers point of view, seem inappropriate (as if I were to express extreme grief over the loss of a glove) but being inappropriate does not make the feeling itself any more or less real. Moreover, persons may claim to feel one way when, in fact, they do not. This may occur either for self-serving reasons (I may pretend an emotion in order to get something I want, say sympathy or help) or because, although it is not really felt, it seems appropriate to the social context (my friend's loss may leave me cold but I dare not admit it). Judging suffering, therefore, is difficult. We may not understand the social or individual situation, we may be misled by our own past experience or by our present social setting, or we may be deliberately misled by the person pretending to be suffering.

Such considerations, however, while they make judging suffering more difficult do not imply that we cannot judge at all. Certain experiences are so universal (even if the way that they play themselves out may be socially and personally different) that we can assume that they entail suffering. Persons who would deny that the homeless, the hungry, those riddled with cancer, or those losing a loved one suffer would be thought callous and unfeeling rather than being felt to be making a rationally supportable argument. When neurological structures believed with good cause to be necessary exist, when stimuli universally felt to generally cause suffering are present, and when behavior generally and reasonably associated with suffering is exhibited, the burden of proof is on those who would claim that creatures so endowed and behaving in such a way are not suffering.

Suffering may be brought about by different factors in different societies: what usually causes persons in one society to suffer may do so to a greater or lesser extent or may not do so at all in another society. Nevertheless, while the causes of suffering within a given society may differ from the causes of suffering in another in certain ways, they will still be acknowledged as valid within a particular society. The neural substrate, the emotive feeling, and in many primitive ways the way in which these emotions are expressed are much the same even when the stimulus may be somewhat different.

I have claimed that the fact of the capacity to suffer or to make others who have the capacity to suffer suffer is, if not the sole at any rate one of the critical characteristics which gives an entity moral standing. Ethically the prima-facie rule to refrain from doing those things which may cause suffering is unaffected by what it is that causes such suffering; what is affected are the specifics as to what is to be refrained from. When it comes to ameliorating suffering, it is again the rule that stands even though the kind of suffering to be ameliorated may differ.

ETHICAL IMPORTANCE OF THE CAPACITY TO SUFFER

Why should the capacity to suffer be ethically important? All persons recognize that the concept of obligation exists even when, as is so often the case, they may differ as to the nature of a specific obligation or to the way such an obligation is grounded. The formal concept of obligation is not in dispute even when the content cannot be agreed upon. Social life of even the most primitive sort is not possible without a recognition that all of us are in some way and for some reasons obligated to others.

When we say that A is obligated to do or not to do b we can mean one of two things: either we may mean that under a given set of physical circumstances A can do no other than to do b or we may mean that under a given set of socially agreed upon circumstances A must do b because to do otherwise would violate such socially agreed upon cirumstances. (The very concept of agreement is, of course, itself parasitic upon a prior notion of obligation). The first meaning of the word (as when A is hanging from a window and must fall [do b] if he lets go) is ethically uninteresting; it is the second sense of obligation, a sense in which A could do (and, perhaps would like to do) otherwise which is of ethical concern. When we, therefore, say that A has an obligation to do or not to do something we are implying that making a choice is possible. This, of course, presupposes the existence of free choice at least when it comes to some, if perhaps not to other, things.[30] The proposition that free choice, at least in some areas, exists is a proposition I shall, like Kant, assume and not argue for.[1] Without such a presumption any work in ethics would be pointless.

When we further claim that something is a "prima-facie" obligation we claim that under some circumstances it would be acceptable for A to violate such an obligation. A concept of "prima facie" as contrasted to a concept of "absolute" obligation provides greater flexibility even when it fails to erase an existant obligation.[31] We are, however, not saying that even when under some circumstances not doing what one is obligated to do is acceptable, not doing what one is supposed to do is in any way meritorious. When a prima-facie obligation exists and reasons for not discharging it appear sufficient, the obligation does not as much vanish as it is suppressed by overwhelming reasons to the contrary. The obligation persists and not discharging one's obligation, albeit understandable, remains troublesome.[32,33] When we say that a person did "the right thing" (even when doing "the right thing" violates one obligation in order to meet one felt, with good reason, to be greater) we mean that the person exercised good judgment and that, therefore, their choosing is meritorious or praiseworthy; we do not imply that violating an obligation was, in itself, meritorious.

When morally overriding considerations would necessitate causing suffering, such suffering must be held to the minimal amount of suffering necessary to achieve one's purpose. Any more than that would violate the original rule: causing more than the minimal amount of suffering necessary to achieve a goal seen as being of overriding importance, produces suffering for which no adequate argument can be made. The prima-facie condition permits overriding to achieve a given goal; it does not permit one to cause suffering beyond this. Restraining or arresting a dangerous person may cause them suffering but it is a suffering one may regretfully have to cause in pursuit of a higher claim; using means in excess of those needed such as beating them remains inexcusable.

When I have an obligation to repay my friend a sum of money by a given day and when on that day I find that my family and I are penniless and hungry, the obligation remains even though it can obviously not be discharged. In that sense, the obligation, while persistent, is practically moot. If I now find a ten dollar bill on the street my obligation to give it to my friend rather than to buy my family and myself something to eat becomes real. Nevertheless, if I choose to feed my family and myself rather than to pay back my friend, my failure to discharge my obligation is morally most understandable and my act of agonizing over the moral decision to buy food for my family, even if not perhaps the decision itself, may even be praiseworthy. But my obligation to repay my friend remains in force. It is a prima-facie obligation which can (and under certain circumstance sometimes must) be overruled.

Obligations exist in a community. If there would not be a

community and, therefore, others who are affected by our actions, obligations would make little sense. Acting in a way which has no effect and no potential effect on anyone (if such an acting could even be thinkable) is without ethical significance. Ignoring the whole question of duties towards one self, actions to be ethically significant must, in some way, impinge on contemporary or future others. Actions affecting others may be of benefit to them (they satisfy one of their desires or needs) or may harm them (they cause pain); or actions even when they affect others may neither harm nor benefit them in any way. The question, as I shall develop it here, concerns those actions (1) which affect others negatively ("hurt them" in some way) and refraining from which generally is a duty similar to the Kantian "perfect" or obligatory duties; as well as those actions (2) which affect others positively (prevent or ameliorate harm or, even more strongly, bring about actual good) and which, therefore, fall into the category of beneficent acts. These latter, in general, are the Kantian "imperfect" or optional duties.[1] I shall ground both in the capacity to suffer and, as we shall see in later chapters, in the way in which infants are nurtured and communities structured.

This grounding of obligation is in many respects another way of determining which objects are and which are not worthy of moral concern. We have obligations either to objects we consider to be of moral concern or to other objects which, while we do not consider them to be of moral concern in themselves, are of moral concern because of the value which others place in them. The one question asks: What is the basis (grounding) of obligation? The other asks: What are the properties of things to which we owe such obligations? I shall claim that it is the capacity to suffer as well as the way we envision community which are the main factors invoked when we answer either of these questions.

Basing obligations on utility suffers from the many and often-made criticisms of utilitarianism. It would or could, at least formally speaking and without another prior framework of "rightness" or "wrongness," allow a number of actions we intuitively feel to be wrong. Sacrificing a very few persons for the overwhelming advantage of many others is often given as one of many examples. Respect for persons and for their "rights," on the other hand, suffers from another set of equally serious and often-cited objections. When respecting a persons "rights" has grave and perhaps devastating consequences for others or for the community, such consequences cannot be totally ignored. One can neither totally ignore consequences (they do matter and matter very much) nor can one entirely act upon what pure utility counsels. In a sense both points of view presuppose each other.[10]

We can answer both of the questions I posed ("What is the basis (grounding) of obligation?" and "What are the properties of things to which we owe such obligations?") from a utilitarian or from a "respect for persons" or Kantian perspective. Neither of the two answers will leave one satisfied. Utility would provide an answer in which a person's individual rights and standing may go begging (in which the respect we owe to persons is ignored); Kantianism may entirely sacrifice all public good to the overwhelming duty to respect individuals. An ethic based on the capacity for suffering and on a view of shared experience and community may provide a different basis and go a small way in overcoming such objections.

For Kant, respect for persons is located in their capacity for self-legislation. When one bases all individual "rights" merely on the capacity to self-legislate one leaves out entities one intuitively feels have moral standing. One would leave out infants, many of the mentally retarded or senile, many psychotics or those who have been totally brainwashed as well as (in the opinion of many who feel that animals are totally without the capacity to self-legislate) animals. But that is absurd: such beings very evidently have moral "rights," at the very least negative ones. I shall claim that the capacity of such entities to be hurt (their capacity, in other words, to suffer) is a grounding which is a far deeper and more universal one. Since individuals develop and exist in a community, one cannot simply ignore the communal implications of one's acts. Further, when one ignores the role of community in our understanding of obligation (to be discussed later on) and the role that community serves in producing, preventing, or ameliorating suffering or, beyond this, in enriching individual existence, one ends up with a necessarily narrow and distorted viewpoint of individual as well as communal obligation. Suffering, then, is central to our understanding of communal as well as of individual obligation.

The answer to the questions "what is the basis (grounding) of obligation?" and "what are the properties of things to which we owe such obligations?" has been answered by others in terms of relative power and on the obligation which our common vulnerability presents us with. By virtue of this common vulnerability, the strong are necessarily obligated to the weak by virtue of such a difference of power.[34-36] In speaking of community, I shall later use this concept of common vulnerability and differential power together with Rousseau's shared "primitive sense of pity" and link it with my notion of suffering. Suffice it to say at this time that the capacity to suffer likewise is linked with our common vulnerability and with this power differential. Basically, sufferers lose power and those with the capacity to prevent or ameliorate such suffering are in a position of strength. All who have the capacity to suffer are vulnerable and, therefore, all with that capacity share a common interest in the prevention and amelioration of suffering. Further, not only does suffering produce weakness but to be weak is, in a broad sense, to suffer. Suffering, as I have delineated it, is not merely or even mainly a function of mere pain. The vulnerability to suffering we all share together with the power differential which suffering necessarily imposes underwrites an ethic based on that capacity.

I have often been asked what impact new neurological discoveries would have on my basic theory. What if quite different neural structures were involved in the capacity to suffer, neural structures which showed that organisms heretofore thought capable of suffering could not suffer? The answer to this is that it would, of course, make no fundamental difference to the basic theory although it would have a profound impact on the way in which the theory is applied. I have argued that what gives an entity and its interests moral standing is its capacity to suffer. If it were to be shown that worms (who according to Darwin's work may have the capacity to engage in a primitive form of reasoning[37]) had that capacity, worms and their interests would have moral standing. If, on the other hand, one could convincingly demonstrate that frogs could not, their standing would be lost.

The notion of giving moral standing to entities which can suffer (rather than to entities which can self-legislate or giving it to utility) has often been accused of committing the "naturalistic fallacy" of extracting an "ought" from an "is."[38] Suffering, at least the way I have painted it, is a natural, empirically verifiable trait and cannot serve as a basis for what we ought or ought not to do. Just because something can be shown to have some particular empirical property does not permit us to extract a moral imperative from it. But if this is the case then basing moral standing on the capacity to self-legislate or on having utility commits the same fallacy: both self-legislation and utility can be shown to exist and are, therefore, at least in that sense, empirical. The notion of the "naturalistic fallacy" and of the rigid is-ought distinction rides piggyback on the alleged distinction between "facts" (supposedly empirical) and "values" (assumed to be metaphysically a priori). Such distinctions constitute a dualistic way of looking at things: "facts" can be understood only in the embrace of values and "values" are not isolated entities from the facts to which they must necessarily address themselves. Does giving moral standing to entities having the capacity to suffer "reduce philosophy to biology"? Can one, in fact, do philosophy in any meaningful sense outside the physical reality with which sooner or later even philosophy at its most abstract must deal? And above all, can humans (who are, whether we like it or not, biological beings: yes, animals) really reason outside the context of their own biology which of necessity forms that framework of reasoning? Accepting scientific findings (not "facts" in the immutable sense but "facts" which we use to manipulate our daily existence and which must, if they are to go anywhere, shape our thoughts) and acknowledging that we human animals are bound to reason within the framework set by our own biology (after all, it is our biological brain that reasons!) is hardly "reducing" our thoughts to their substrate or reducing the content to its form! It is merely to claim that biology necessarily forms the framework of our very thinking about all human endeavors (and that, therefore, it is best not to ignore its role) as well as to assert that function without substrate is an incoherent concept.

GRADATIONS OF VALUE AND SUFFERING

Even if one assumes suffering as a grounding principle, one must still deal with the obvious conflicts which inevitably arise between and among various kinds of suffering and various entities among whom one must choose. One can hardly assume that the capacity to suffer forbids another to cause or forces such another to necessarily ameliorate all possible suffering. Life cannot be lived without causing, even at times deliberately causing, suffering or harm to another.

In a previous work I have proposed that moral worth can be divided into what I call "primary" and "secondary" worth.[10] Primary worth belongs to entities which now or in the future have the capacity to suffer. It is the common property of those who in addition to being alive have a life.[39] Such entities, beyond the biological properties which determine their being alive, have features which allow us to claim that they have a history, have at however primitive a level, thoughts, hopes, and aspirations. It is this capacity which makes killing immoral.[40] The capacity to suffer is the first and most primitive step in this direction. There are many whose capacity to think, hope, and plan can be reduced to an interest in not suffering: the totally demented person whose awareness appears limited to their awareness of pain is an obvious example. No matter how primitive their capacity to suffer or how attenuated their interests and life plans may be, all beings capable of suffering enjoy primary worth. They are more than objects: they are subjects and others have a prima-facie obligation to refrain from causing, and a weaker obligation where possible to ameliorate, such suffering.

Other things may or may not also have worth, but such worth is not primary but secondary. Such objects do not have worth because they can suffer or because they can be "harmed" in any meaningful sense and are, therefore, subjects; such objects are of moral concern because of the value they have for others. Such secondary worth, furthermore, may be either material or symbolic and such worth can be positive or negative. My bank account has material value of a positive sort, my debts have negative material worth; pride in one's work, memories of loved ones, religious objects one treasures all have positive symbolic worth. Material as well as symbolic worth can be negative: a bomb about to go off, a swastika as a memory of Naziism are examples. A given object, furthermore, may be of positive value for one person or under one set of circumstances and have very negative value for another person or under another set of circumstances.

The medical context may provide a fitting example. A person delivered to the hospital after a severe accident with the possibility of recovery remains (at least tentatively) a subject: the capacity to suffer has not, at least potentially as far as one can then judge, been eliminated. The person not only is alive but has a life. Such a person continues to be of primary worth and of direct and primary concern to the health-care givers within the framework of our current understanding of such obligations. If such a person is later found to be brain-dead or permanently vegetative circumstances change. They are no longer (except in a symbolic sense) subjects but have become very much objects: things to be acted upon and of positive or negative value to others. While they are alive they are no longer, except symbolically, the subjects of that life. Such a person now has secondary worth. Such worth is material as well as symbolic: positive material as a potential donor of organs, negative material as occupying space and consuming resources perhaps much needed by others; symbolic as a loved one, as a former member of community, and as a symbol of our own past and future.

Choices, often hard choices, need to be made. Not all subjects, not all those who undeniably have primary worth, are equivalent. All have standing in court: producing or even where possible not ameliorating suffering needs to be defended. Wantonly causing harm or causing suffering so as to enjoy trivial advantage becomes indefensible. It is an act of the strong against the weak and ignores an appeal to our common vulnerability. Causing suffering unless such suffering can be carefully justified by higher considerations is an act which cannot be universalized and, therefore, an act which affronts even our most primitive sense of what the logic of morality is all about.

Such value judgments rely on a prior framework of assumptions. When we speak of "having a life" with all its thoughts, hopes, and aspirations we make such a statement because we assume that life without such thoughts, hopes, and aspirations, a life not self-realized, can have no value to such a self. When we go beyond this and claim that some thoughts, hopes, and aspirations may have more value than do others (that some subjects have greater and more enduring primary worth), we enter dangerous territory. To the life valuing—provided that it has the capacity to value—its own life is of infinite worth. Such life, however, occurs in a community which, inevitably, must confront, grapple with, and ultimately base its actions on such choices.

The choices we make depend among other things upon the

necessity of the contemplated action. This is often a function of utility. One can make an argument that killing higher animals so as to eat them is ethically difficult—or perhaps except under exceptional circumstances impossible—to defend whereas using such animals for vitally needed experiments to cure disease may be morally more defensible. Eating meat is not necessary to sustain life (at least not, under ordinary circumstances, to sustain human life) whereas carefully limited medical experiments may be. Causing suffering so as to titillate our taste buds is far different from causing suffering so as to save a large number of human as well as non-human lives. Neither, in itself, is a moral good: but on a prima-facie basis the one may and the other may not be defensible.

One could, furthermore, claim that some subjects have very little capacity of having a life: their thoughts, hopes, and aspirations are minimal in intensity, depth, or extent. Their ability to suffer is shallow, their emergence from an insentient state primitive. It is here that such notions as the capacity to self-legislate may play a role: it is a capacity which certainly denotes higher integration even though it is not invariably present in all humans and is arguably hardly limited to the human species. Self-legislation in its broadest sense denotes the capacity to deliberate about our options and then to make choices; such a capacity is not necessarily moral but may simply be a choice to eat one rather than another food. In its usual (Kantian) sense it denotes a moral capacity: the capacity to "tell right from wrong" and to make subtle discernments of this kind.

When decisions must be made (say a decision to save the life of a student rather than the life of a mouse) it is safer to make them on the basis of carefully thought out and weighed considerations rather than on a purely instinctive or intuitive basis. Such a way of choosing between entities has obvious danger: trying to judge the depth of the capacity to suffer or the intensity of our thoughts, hopes, and aspirations could easily lead to actions none of us would want to countenance. The reason we would not wish to countenance such actions is (while not entirely, at least to a large part) a function of symbolic valuing. The severely demented person who certainly has a reduced capacity to suffer and whose intensity of thoughts, hopes, and aspirations is minimal, nevertheless has great symbolic (and universally symbolic) value for all of us. When we choose among entities capable of suffering the symbolic standing of humans, rather than the sometimes greatly reduced capacity of a particular human to suffer, prompts us to attach a much higher value to human than to other life.

Judging and adjudicating between subjects, all of whom enjoy primary worth, in circumstances where such choices must be made can evidently be based on a variety of factors. Such factors are considered, developed, and ultimately carried out in community. They are not immutable. They are prone to error and misunderstanding and are subject to learning and growth. Our understanding of what are legitimate and relevant distinctions inevitably changes over time. Our sense of what is right is subject to disciplined logical examination as well as to an increasing understanding as such inquiry proceeds.[42] Such an inquiry, however, necessarily forces one to make value judgments about subjects something that, and for good reasons, one is very leary of making. I shall grapple further with some of these concepts in the third chapter.

REFERENCES

1. Kant I: *Grundlegung zur Metaphysik der Sitten*. In: *Immanuel Kant Kritik der Praktischen Vernunft, Grundlegung zur Metaphysik der Sitten*. Band VII (Wilhelm Weischedel, ed.) Frankfurt a/M, Deutschland: Suhrkamp Verlag; 1989.

2. Plato: The Republic (Peter Shorey, trans.). In: *Plato: The Collected Dialogues* (Edith Hamilton and Huntington Cairns, ed.). Princeton, NJ: Princeton University Press; 1978.

3. Aristotle: *Ethics* (J. A. K. Thomson, trans.). New York, NY: Penguin Books; 1978.

4. Copleston FC: *Aquinas*. London, England: Penguin Books; 1988.

5. Kant I: Duties towards Animals and Spirits. In: *Immanuel Kant: Lectures in Ethics* (Louis Infield, trans.). Gloucester, MA: Peter Smith; 1978.

6. Bentham J: *The Principles of Morals and Legislation*. New York, NY: Hafner; 1948.

7. Mill JS: *On Liberty*. New York, NY: W.W. Norton and Co.; 1975.

8. Singer P: *Practical Ethics*. Cambridge, England: Cambridge University Press; 1979.

9. Regan T and Singer P: *Animal Rights and Human Obligations*. Englewood Cliffs, NJ: Prentice-Hall; 1976.

10. Loewy EH: *Suffering and the Beneficent Community: Beyond Libertarianism*. Albany, NY: SUNY Press; 1991.

11. Cassell EJ: The Nature of Suffering and the Goals of Medicine. NEJM 1982; 306(11): 639–645.

12. Cassell EJ: Recognizing Suffering. Hastings Center Report 1991; 21(3): 24–31.

13. Frankl VE: *Man's Search for Meaning*. New York, NY: Simon and Schuster; 1963.

14. Freud S: *Civilization and Its Discontent* (p. 24) (James Strachey, trans.). New York, NY: W.W. Norton; 1961.

15. Loewy EH: Treatment Decisions in the Mentally Impaired: Limiting but not Abandoning Treatment. NEJM 1987; 317: 1465–1469.

16. Darwin C: *The Origin of Species* (Morse Peckham, ed.). Philadelphia, PA: University of Pennsylvania Press; 1959.

17. Browning EB: Grief. In: *The Pocket Book of Poetry* (M. E. Spear, ed.). New York, NY: Pocket Books; 1943.

18. Cassell EJ: The Relief of Suffering. Arch Int Med 1983; 143: 522–523.

19. Kosskoff YD, Dennis W, Lazovik D and Wheeler ET: Psychological Effects of Frontal Lobotomy Performed for the Alleviation of Pain. Res Publ Assoc Res Nerv Ment Dis 1948; 27: 723–752.

20. Darwin C: *The Expression of Emotions in Man and Animals*. New York, NY: D. Appleton and Co., 1873.

21. Cobb S: *Emotions and Clinical Medicine*. New York, NY: W.W. Norton and Company; 1950.

22. Singer P: All Animals are Equal. In: *Animal Rights and Human Obligations* (T. Regan and P. Singer, ed.). Englewood Cliffs, NJ: Prentice-Hall; 1976.

23. Rachels J: *Created from Animals: The Moral Implications of Darwinism*. New York, NY: Oxford University Press; 1990.

24. Descartes R: Animals are Machines. In: *Animal Rights and Human Obligations* (T. Regan and P. Singer, eds.). Englewood Cliffs, NJ: Prentice-Hall; 1976.

25. Wittgenstein L: *Philosophische Untersuchungen* 3. Auflage Frankfurt a/M, Deutschland: Suhrkamp; 1975.

26. Frey RG: Rights, Interests and Beliefs. Am Phil Quart 1979; 16: 233–239.

27. Voltair: A Reply to Descartes. In: *Animal Rights and Human Obligations* (T. Regan and P. Singer, eds.). Englewood Cliffs, NJ: Prentice-Hall; 1976.

28. Darwin C: *The Descent of Man.* New York, NY: H.M. Caldwell; 1874.

29. Rollin B: *The Unheeded Cry.* New York, NY: Oxford University Press; 1989.

30. Dennett DC: *Elbow Room: The Varieties of Free Will Worth Having.* Cambridge, MA: MIT Press; 1985

31. Ross WD: *The Right and the Good.* Oxford, England: Clarendon Press; 1938.

32. Loewy EH: *Textbook of Medical Ethics.* New York, NY: Plenum Publishers;   1989.

33. Brody B: *Life and Death Decision Making.* New York, NY: Oxford University Press; 1988.

34. Jensen UJ: *Practice and Progress: A Theory for the Modern Health-Care System.* Oxford, England: Blackwell Scientific Publications; 1987.

35. Jensen UJ: Are Selves Real? In: *Harré and His Critics* (Roy Shaskar, ed.). Oxford, England: Basic Blackwell; 1990.

36. Jonas H: *Das Prinzip Verantwortung.* Frankfurt a/M, Deutschland: Suhrkamp; 1984.

37. Darwin C: *The Formation of Vegetable Mould through the Action of Worms.* Chicago, IL: University of Chicago Press; 1965.

38. Moore GE: *Principia Ethica.* Cambridge, England: Cambridge University Press; 1903.

39. Kushner T: Having a Life versus Being Alive. J Med Ethics 1984; 1: 5–8.

40. Rachels J: *The End of Life.* New York, NY: Oxford University Press; 1986.

41. Dewey J: Logical Conditions for the Scientific Treatment of Morality. In: *John Dewey: The Middle Works, 1899–1924* Vol. 3 (Jo Ann Boydston, ed.). Carbondale, IL: Southern Illinois University Press; 1977.

CHAPTER 2

Perceiving Community and Compassion: A Summary and a Sketch of Things to Come

Communities play a central role in a morality based on the capacity to suffer. Their role in suffering is multifaceted. Suffering is an existential experience which, although it is an intimate individual experience unique to the person suffering, is inevitably defined and shaped, as well as often and unfortunately even brought about, by the community.[1] Even when individuals "suffer alone" the community has and continues to play a central role in their suffering. The nature of suffering (not only our behavior while suffering but those things which cause us to suffer) is conditioned, defined, in a sense determined, and then played out by and in community. Even when hermits suffer they must rely in the particulars of their suffering on their previous experience with and their eventual separation from community.

Obligations, as I have pointed out previously, likewise exist and are enunciated by and in community. Without community and, therefore, others who are affected by our actions, obligations would make little sense. When one ignores the role of community in our understanding of obligation or the part community plays in producing, preventing, or ameliorating suffering (or, beyond and interwoven with this, in enriching individual existence) one ends up with a necessarily narrow and distorted viewpoint of individual as well as of communal obligation. Obligation links our concept of community and of suffering: the obligations communities as well as individuals feel, accept, and in that sense indeed have towards each other, depend among other things upon a recognition of the concept of suffering. The way we suffer and the way we view suffering is, at least to a large part, determined by our understanding of and by our solidarity with community.

In a previous work, I sketched the various ways of looking at social contract as well as the types of communities which emerge from such views.[1] In this chapter I will very briefly review and summarize the work done to date, and in order to lay the groundwork for later chapters, will in addition somewhat amplify and extend these previous notions. In reviewing and summarizing such ideas, I will very briefly (1) examine the nature of social contract; (2) sketch the kind of community which emerges from such a structure; (3) show that caring for the suffering of non-human animals or of other communities than our own does not entail not caring for humans or for conditions "at home"; and finally (4) point out the difference that such viewpoints make to our perception of justice as well as to the way we view our mutual relationships and obligations.

WAYS OF LOOKING AT SOCIAL CONTRACT

One can only surmise the genesis and ontology of early association. In general, the social contract has been considered to be not as much an historical fact as an heuristic device, an heuristic device unfortunately often treated as though it denoted historical fact. Most thinkers, however, have simply accepted that social contract must have come about when free-living individuals associated and that, therefore, individuals were necessarily ontologically prior to community. In the view I shall present here the notion that individuals are and inevitably must be ontologically prior to community is held to have deformed many prior discussions.

In the way the concept is used here, "social contract" is held to consist of the tacit and unspoken agreements which allow and sustain communal existence. Social contract is a social understanding basic to communal structure and function, an understanding which, in the view presented here, is an evolving one rather than one which is frozen in time or place. As such it is exemplified by those things among people which "go without saying" and no community or even loose association can come about, exist, or endure without it. Even though some of these agreements are codified in law most breeches of such agreements are handled by social sanctions. The way we structure our communities as well as the way we think about justice is a function of such considerations and, therefore, what we consider to be just obligations, just laws, or what we take to be a just allocation of resources, is intimately associated with the way we imagine our social contract. In turn, our understanding and experience with the law may modify our understanding and evolution of social contract. Although fundamental to human life, social contract—like all else in a dynamic and living world—evolves and grows.

In order to understand the view of social contract I shall espouse, a brief examination of previous points of view is needed. Although views of social contract are implicit in most of the works of thinkers who deal with social concerns, the first relatively modern explicit exposition of the notion belongs to Hobbes.[2] Hobbes's picture, as most of the pictures presented by others, is evidently not meant as an historical one but rather is presented for its heuristic value. Like most other thinkers, Hobbes sketches his picture so as to suggest that "if one were to live like this (as isolated beings in terror of each other, in the case he presents) such and such would result." For this purpose, Hobbes posits unassociated and isolated humans as necessarily living in a miserable condition prior to social contract: their life, as he says, was (or would be) "solitary, poor, nasty, brutish and short" (p. 100).[2] Without having an agreement such persons readily killed, raped, or looted and therefore lived in a state of constant fear and terror of one another. Their ability to enjoy a meaningful existence, or to pursue their own short- or long-range plans, was therefore severely limited. To create conditions in which they could more readily develop their individual lives, such persons agreed to respect each others freedom and to refrain from doing each other active harm. Their "covenant," forged in terror, was purely one of mutual non-harm; beneficence in no way was part of such a bargain. To safeguard such an agreement a sovereign, short of killing his subjects, was given absolute power. An absolute state in which all persons were free to develop their own lives but were prohibited from actively harming their fellows was the result.

Others who used social contract to fashion their perception of justice and community looked at such an original contract in different ways. Locke, whose belief in natural law shaped the way he looked at things, thought of social contract as one of evolving trust; trust, that is, in a legal sense.[3] Natural law is "obvious," there to be discovered rather than created. Observation and common sense rather than social necessity or reason proves it to us. Persons hold the execution of the laws of nature in each others trust: executing these laws is everyone's responsibility and those who violate such laws put themselves "in a state of war" against all others. In turn, a proper sovereign holds these laws in trust from the governed and is subject to their ultimate control. The contract is between equally free persons and not between unequal ruler and ruled. To Locke the state of nature, while non-productive of social progress, was generally peaceful. Communities do not evolve out of social contract; rather, community and an economy precede any notion of such a contract. Natural law, which guarantees life, freedom, and property, necessitates such a notion. As Jefferson, in part borrowing and somewhat modifying a page from Locke, would later hold:

> ...We hold these truths to be self-evident, that all men are created equal, that they are endowed by their creator with certain inalienable rights, that among these are Life, Liberty and the Pursuit of Happiness. That to secure these rights Governments are instituted among men, deriving their just power from the consent of the governed....(p. 453)[4]

The modification is not trivial: the "pursuit of happiness," rather than property, which is hardly the same thing, is what is stressed. To Jefferson, it was "self-evident" that men were endowed with these rights by nature or by "nature's God" as he was to put it elsewhere. Governments (a governmental rather than strictly a social contract) were instituted to secure (but not, strictly speaking, to fashion) such rights. In such communities mutual obligations transcend merely the obligation of mutual non-harm. The individual, even if not morality, is seen as long preceding community.

Rousseau also did not see the "state of nature" as being a necessarily savage or brutish one. Rather, persons amorally pursued their own self-interest although, and importantly, they were endowed with "a natural sense of pity."[5] Far from "natural law" which simply is there to be discovered rather than shaped, Rousseau thought that the social contract manifest by social association first initiates a sense of morality. Morality, or at any rate the way morality is envisioned, is created by the society in which it is played out. When societies become degenerate, morality likewise degenerates. Individuals are still prior to social contract and, therefore, to community, but morality can develop only within social organization; it is social organization which first changes persons from amoral savages into communal and, in this fashion, into moral and, therefore, responsible beings.

The "sense of pity" of which Rousseau speaks is considered of major importance to an ethic of suffering and of community as developed here. This sense of pity (or compassion) he characterizes as *"la répugnance naturelle"* (a natural repugnance) to see the suffering of another. Rousseau does not always use the word *pitié* or "pity:" he speaks as readily of *"l'impulsion intérieure de la compassion"* (the internal compulsion of compassion) which, according to him, is at times overpowered only by *"la conservation de soi-même"* (self-preservation).[5,6] The German word *Mitleid* (and its Dutch counterpart *Medleiden*) gives perhaps a fuller sense of what is meant than does the word pity: it is the capacity to suffer with someone, to be touched by another's suffering and to have innate feelings of experiencing something (at least something negative) with another. The word "compassion" may be the best, even if not a perfect, translation.

If pity is to be "natural," if it is to be conceived as a capacity inherent in our biological structure, then such a trait must be understood in terms of having positive or negative survival value. If this internal impulse to compassion is what eventually moves us, as I believe it does, not only to help others but to take into account how our actions will affect others, then this impulse (or, if you will, instinctive feeling) must be examined in that light. Darwin sees our social instincts as fundamental to morality and argues that these social instincts and the actions to which they lead ultimately have survival value for such species as are endowed with them.[7] A misinterpretation of Darwin (which has at times been referred to as social Darwinism and about which I wil have more to say in later chapters) is often invoked to excuse the ethics of the American capitalist system. It has been evoked by some industrialists (Carnegie and Rockefeller, for example) to not only excuse but indeed almost to sanctify brutal forms of competition or callous dealing with individuals in poverty or need.[8] The social instincts, those things in humans and other animals which prompt individuals to seek out others and work together for the common good, include what Rousseau had called a "primitive sense of pity" and is expressed, according to Darwin, in an altruism not unqiue to human animals. Altruism results from beneficence: the desire to help others. Compassion leads to a desire to be of help and is expressed in behavior we hold to be altruistic. I shall argue and continue to argue in later chapters that such an instinct has survival value. It has survival value for the individual because individuals at some time in their lives are inevitably dependent upon the compassion of others; further, it has survival value because such an instinct helps communities to remain as cohesive units. Solidarity in communities and, therefore, as I shall argue, the ability of communities to flourish and grow, requires a sense by all that their neighbors not only will not harm them but will, as the need may arise, come to their help.

The standing of the concept of "pity" has been a source of analysis from ancient times onward.[9,10] Plato and Aristotle considered pity to be one of many irrational (i.e., not reason-bound) stirrings on par with pleasure, fear, hate, or anger. To Plato and Aristotle, pity and reason are, in a sense, opposed to each other in the same way in which other strong emotions may oppose or overwhelm reason.[9-12] In general, the stoics (among which Seneca presents an extreme but hardly an isolated example) likewise felt that pity ill became the man of cold forebearance and reason. They held that benign persons could and would accomplish, when motivated by reason, the same amount of good as they could or would motivated by the basically irrational (or prerational) "gut feeling" of pity.[9]

Kronauer, in his major review of the problem of pity, notes that one of the early church fathers (Lactantius) in the fourth century (and in contrast to the stoics) again takes up the role of pity as a positive force. Lactantius felt that it was pity which first enabled humans to join together.[9] His understanding of the role of pity in many ways foreshadowed Rousseau.

Mandeville, who denies the existence of motives other than those originating in self-interest, considers pity to be a weakness akin to anger, pride, or fear. Pity, according to Mandeville, is an extremely forceful but irrational and, therefore, destructive emotion, and it tends to get in the way of self-interest.[13] Since self-interest, according to Mandeville, is central to morality and does, according to him, tend to stabilize society, pity makes little sense. When pity prompts one to act (for example when pity motivates the establishing of schools for the poor) societal instability results.

Others have recognized this innate sense of pity or compassion but have looked upon it in a variety of ways. Such points of view have ranged from the claim that "pity" is an emotion which often is inimical to proper behavior and to justice, to making "pity" a central feature of morality. Plato, Spinoza, Mandeville, and Kant all and in various ways and to a different degree viewed pity as essentially inimical to dispassionate and cool reasoning and as, in a way, opposed to justice. Aristotle (despite his assigning a cathartic function to tragedy which stimulates fear and pity) also saw pity as a sentiment tending to interfere with the purely intellectual analysis of problems. Nietzsche (despite his disdain for cool reasoning) despised pity and saw it as interfering with the development of a strong personality. Pure reason (for all of these thinkers except for Nietzsche) will lead one to choose to do what is right; one's emotions (and an innate sense of pity is just that) will get in the way. A contemporary, careful analysis of the history and meaning of the concept concludes that this innate sense is "morally neutral."[10] To claim that "*l'impulsion intérieure de la compassion*" (the internal compulsion of compassion) is, in itself, morally praiseworthy, blameworthy, or neutral in my view evades the role which compassion, "*l'impulsion intérieure de la compassion*," or the "natural sense of pity" plays in ethics: like any other "natural impulse" (the impulse to mate, for example) it is not in itself either ethical or antithetical to ethics. Rather than being morally positive, negative, or even neutral, the innate sense of pity and compassion is the condition and not the content of morality. It is a natural impulse, a given of normal constitution as much as is the presence of testosterone in the normal male without which the impulse to mate does not occur. It is not ethical or unethical in itself: it is one of the forces (if not indeed the main force) which serves to stimulate ethical judgments and, prior to this, which allows the ethical question to present itself. Without this prod, the weal and woe (or at least the woe) of our neighbor would leave us cold and questions of ethics would, if they presented themselves at all, present themselves as sterile questions, as a puzzle or as a game of logic. Answers to such questions would be insulated from the humanity which the answers are meant to serve.

Rousseau stressed the importance of what he calls the "natural sense of pity," a primitive drive according to him already innate in pre-social beings, as well as the importance of the drive for self-preservation (as quite distinct from self-love which he holds to be a product of civilization).[5,6] This natural sense of pity is modified when persons join in a social contract. Coming together in social associations adds something else to these "natural" senses: pity as well as self-preservation now are not only natural and primitive stirrings but are modified by one's own experience and by one's social context. The natural sense of pity easily can become subverted and the sense of self-preservation can become a narcissistic sense of self-love.

A natural sense of pity unreflectively prevents one from inflicting hurt on another unless such a sense were to be forcefully overridden by the need for self-preservation. Becoming acquainted with one's own suffering prompts one, in proper circumstances, to actively help another who is suffering. Not harming another, to Rousseau, is prompted by a "natural" sense; helping another requires reflection as well as personal and, as in *Emile*, proper experience and instruction.[14] Beneficence, or at least the basic impulse to be beneficent, is social and it can be taught. True, civilization has often accomplished the opposite, making persons callous and self-loving. It has often made them not only not eager to help but actually has managed to blunt their innate natural sense, their *l'impulsion intérieure de la compassion*.[5,12] But that speaks for the particulars of civilization and not against either the natural sense of pity or the possibility of its proper development. To first develop a sense of beneficence, as I read Rousseau, community, and a properly functioning community, is essential.

The notion of an innate sense of pity and compassion is of critical importance to what is to follow. It will be further developed and frequently appealed to here as well as in future chapters. I shall argue in this work that the nurture and beneficence necessary for the survival of all infants is the foundation of community and that it underwrites the later development of obligation. While Rousseau speaks of the family as a group and of the nurture of children as an inevitable experience, he views the family unit as a (primitively) temporary association. Rousseau argues that once the mission of bringing children to relative self-sufficiency has been accomplished in primitive society, the bonds are dissolved without another thought. Neither parents or children have any long-term interests in each other and neither extracts any enduring obligations from the relationship. To Rousseau such a group is not a community and operates from instinct rather than from a more rationally established social contract.

Rousseau's natural sense of pity, something innate in all sentient forms, or at the very least innate in all higher animals, is of immense importance for a number of reasons. Since traits which establish themselves do so because, in the long run, they have survival value for the individual as well as, and perhaps more importantly, for the species, one can assume that this natural sense of pity likewise has survival value. And, indeed, it makes sense that such a primitive sense of pity does have survival value for species as well as for individuals: in many instances our personal survival depends upon such a sense of pity in others, our survival as a group or tribe depends upon the solidarity within such a collective, and our survival as a species ultimately hinges on the survival of individuals and groups within it. Like Schopenhauer, I believe this sense of pity to be the driving force (*Triebfeder* or "driving power") of ethics.[15] It is this sense of pity which prompts us to ask the question basic to all ethics: How will my action affect others? Without such a basic sense of pity, which gives rise to compassion and empathy as well as to sympathetic understanding, my concern for others is, if ever present at all, purely a self-serving one. Unless such a basic sense of pity is presupposed, we are apt not to come to each others help; without the comfort of knowing that others would come to our help, solidarity would be fragile and temporary and community could not survive and flourish. Like most higher non-human animals, man is a social animal and the species, without community, would be unlikely to sustain itself.

There is a critical difference between empathy with and sympathetic understanding for another. When I empathize, I can easily feel myself in that person's stead; when I have sympathetic understanding, I have sympathy for that person and can, at any rate intellectually, understand his/her point of view even though I cannot imagine myself in that position. I have empathy with a disadvantaged person in the ghetto; I have sympathetic understanding for a member of the Ikh tribe. I have empathy with my wife's problem writing a paper but sympathetic understanding when she has dysmenorrhoea. Sympathetic understanding, on that account, is more sophisticated and elaborate than is empathy. For all of these capacities, however, an initial sense of pity constitutes the necessary condition. Without it, empathy is impossible, compassion does not present itself, and understanding remains purely intellectual. All of these are community traits and all of them make survival of individuals as well as survival of the community more likely.

A primitive sense of pity, compassion, empathy, and sympathetic understanding, furthermore, implies that there are differences in capacity and power. This is as true of individuals as it is of communities. If we all had the same capacities and were all equally powerful, a sense of pity, compassion, or sympathetic understanding would have little cause to be invoked. Such capacities and power are, furthermore, not an all or nothing condition specific to a given individual or community. Persons as well as communities are generally more capable and powerful in one, and less capable and powerful in another, respect. Relative power and relative weaknesses interdigitate with each other and such differential capacities constitute a critical aspect and source of all relationships.[16]

All biological creatures are vulnerable when it comes to being weaker or stronger than others. All of us as individuals as well as all communities are endowed with greater or lesser capacities relative to others. Such capacities, furthermore, inevitably change over time. Inevitable common and shared vulnerabilty and compassion with others fueled by a sense of pity as well as the sheer individual and species desire for survival implies that the strong are necessarily obligated to the weak.[17-19] When in later sections and chapters I develop the concept of community further, I shall use these concepts and link them with the concept of suffering.

The view of social contract I will present as mine is one of an evolving understanding.[1] Looking at the way social contract began may, in this view, serve as an heuristic device but understanding the initial contract or its original genesis (if indeed an "original genesis" can be imagined) as more than this begs the modern question. There is no question that there are basic commonalities of "those things that go without saying": things so basic to human existence and social function in all societies that any conceivable understanding of social contract and any conceivable structure of community must include them. Such commonalities may well be conceived as an interaction between what Kant calls the "common structure of our mind" and the social conditions produced by common basic material forces.[20] Basic commonalities have remained basic because they have to date created indispensable conditions for individual and communal survival.

Like all else, however, the social contract that unites any particular group or society today is a product of a variety of interacting material forces and has moved far beyond its basic understandings. This is neither to deny such basic understandings nor to shortchange the importance of forces which cannot very well be thought of as material; rather it is to claim that even such forces and basic understandings have their original roots, even if not their current expression, in the material. The ontological question (Do individuals develop out of community or are communities merely associations of individuals?) is, in this view, an unanswerable and basically irrelevant question.[1] When one looks at the question of the "original genesis" one inevitably ends up with the cards stacked: to create something inevitably requires components and this necessarily ends up with individuals who have joined together. In that such a claim suggests de novo creation such a claim is an almost creationist one. The ontological question seen from today's point of view is largely a chicken and egg one, equally insoluble and equally irrelevant to actual praxis. What I suggest here is a slow, adaptive evolution of such a contract and consequently of the way in which communities have structured and continue to evolve and structure themselves.

The question of such original genesis is similar to another question we may ask: instead of asking of what is community composed and, inevitably being forced to answer of individuals, we could ask of what is our body composed and end up with the equally inevitable answer of organs or even of cells. But would we, therefore, conclude that cells (or organs) are prior to our body? To conclude that our cells or our organs are prior to (rather than a necessary part of) us and, therefore, of our body would, on the face of it, be nonsensical. Our cells differentiated and coalesced to finally become our body; in that sense "they pre-existed." But they did not do so as single, separate entities pursuing their "own interests" but as a harmonious and cooperative venture. At all stages of development we are of what we are composed and what we are composed of could not be without the us which it maintains and builds. Or, on the other hand, could we conclude that our body is prior to our organs (or cells)? But that would be a mystical assumption for such a body would lack substance. The existence and integrity of the individual cells or organs is as dependent upon the existence and integrity of the body as is the existence and integrity of the body on the existence and integrity of the individual cells or organs. In that sense to ask which is more important or which is prior does not make much sense. In that sense also, to look upon the relationship as a competitive instead of as an intrinsically cooperative one misses the point.

Such an "organismic" approach certainly is not new and is not in any sense meant to reduce the philosophical question to the biological (about which later: see chapter 3). Rather it is an approach (even if an approach in a somewhat different form) suggested by others in the past. The influence of Darwin, Huxley, and others from the biological sciences has been profound and has not been ignored by philosophers. It is an approach John Dewey as well as others used extensively.[21]

It seems to me that the question of the priority of organ (or cell) and body could be readily acknowledged to make little sense. The question is unanswerable, irrelevant, misleading, and flies in the face of what we know about biological ontology and evolution. Furthermore, such a question would be unserviceable: if organs (or cells) were prior to our body would that mean that the task of our organs (or cells) was to see to their own flourishing regardless of these others? Cells, organs, and bodies are interdependent and their succesful function depends upon a reflex realization of such dependency. The health of our cells (and organs) depends upon the harmonious function of all components (in a sense, about their "caring" for each other's welfare) and the health of our entire body depends upon this harmonious and smooth functioning. Cells, organs, and bodies are separable conceptually but not when it comes to their survival. This notion of inseparability and of working together for a common interest is basic to what is to follow. In a previous work I developed the notion of a dialectic relationship between the demands of the community or of social justice and the aspirations of the individual for liberty.[1] In this work I will go beyond this and suggest that a more fruitful model for or way of examining these issues may be a homeostatic relationship.

Infants at birth are incapable of differentiating themselves from their environment and, therefore, cannot distinguish self from non-self. This, interestingly enough, is true psychologically as well as immunologically. In this state, infants are entirely dependent upon the nurture of others. Without nurture, infants can never achieve a differentiation of themselves as entities, a condition which must necessarily be achieved before mutual obligations or autonomy can be thought of. Social contract, therefore, develops slowly in an inevitable setting of nurture. Whether one speaks about "original" social contract or of social contract in the sense of an evolving condition of association, our initial experience of nurture (as infants as well as to a lesser degree throughout life) forms a necessary background. All persons necessarily undergo this experience and their initial impulse to associate, therefore, does not originate in terror. Rather, their initial association is a biological fact, a necessary condition for the existence of any conceivable individual or society. Freestanding individuals without community are no more possible to think about than are communities not ultimately composed of individuals. Communities and individuals are separable conceptually but not when it comes to the survival of either. The social contract emerges from this primitive realization of dependence upon nurture and from the realization that the nurturing of others is necessary if the social contract is to endure. This concept is, of course, closely linked with the concept of differential strengths and weaknesses as well as with vulnerability.

One may concede the dependence of infants on nurture without drawing any ethical conclusions. Often the question is posed in the following manner: Since I did not ask to be born or sustained, why does the fact of my having been nurtured and sustained constitute an obligation? It is a strongly individualistic question and one which presupposes the definability of obligations entirely outside of the context of social contract, history, or community. In future chapters, and especially in chapter 3, I shall deal further with this question, essentially one of justifying obligations. I shall argue that, important and helpful as deductive reasoning is in arguing for or against obligation, it is neither the necessary nor the sufficient condition for accepting an obligation as a valid one (see chapter 3). For now, let me merely suggest that we who exist today owe an obligation to the future because others whose future we were have in the past nurtured and sustained us. It is this sustaining and nurture by others in the past which made our attaining our individuality possible. Individuals have individual lives: they have a definable beginning and a definable end. But these individuals lives occur and are enabled in the context of a community in which a myriad of individual lives overlap. In that sense, no individual can be thought of as freestanding; our individual obligations to tomorrow are rooted in this fact. When we were still unidentified, unnamed and future others, specific then-existent and identified others living in their own today created the conditions which allowed our own existence and survival in our own today. We could not have survived in the past and we cannot survive today without the empathy, sympathetic understanding, and ultimately the help of others.

Communities do not have definable beginnings and ends as do individuals. Communities, composed of a skein of individual and overlapping beginnings and ends and of a skein of obligations rooted in personal as well as communal history cannot be that easily defined. Individuals, although their personal beginning is well defined, owe their survival to the nurture of a community that stretches backwards and forwards without definable beginning or end. Individual obligations, therefore, encompass future as well as current considerations. The question of why past nurture and the action of others in a past stretching back into the shadowy past should impose an obligation on individuals who did not ask to be (but who are and who evidently, since they continue to exist, are quite willing to be) part of the present is, therefore, not a really coherent one. We know our present because others, whose future our present was, secured it.

WAYS OF STRUCTURING COMMUNITY

Community, except apparently for Locke, is preceded by some notion of social contract. Although it is difficult to accept a Lockian notion which sees social contract as emerging from community, it is quite possible to see the relationship as a dynamic one. The way social contract is envisioned influences the way in which community is structured; in turn, the way community is structured and our social experiences within such a structure shape the way in which we envision social contract. In such a view the reciprocal relation is dynamic and growing, subject to growth, learning and evolutionary forces. That which serves survival best and in its broadest sense is the direction in which evolution will inevitably be forced to proceed.

A community which sees social contract as forged in mutual terror and, therefore, conceives of the relationship between persons as being one in which they have merely promised not to harm but have given no promise to help each other is one often called "minimalist."[22] In such a community freedom and a respect for autonomy have overwhelming force. Advocates of libertarianism exemplified by Nozick and stimulated by the social contract theory of Hobbes, see community as constituted not just mainly but, in fact, as constituted solely to vouchsafe individual freedom.[23] Freedom, as Nozick would have it, acts as a "side-constraint" of the moral life: that is, respect for individual freedom and protecting such freedom constrains all else. Freedom, in such a philosophy becomes (as Larry Churchill remarked) a paramount value and, therefore, one which has veto power. Communities are established to allow their individual members maximal freedom consistent with equal freedom for all others. All members of the community must have equal access to the opportunities such communities may offer; but having access is defined as not being interfered with, not as being facilitated. Insofar as our misfortune is a product of the "natural lottery" over which no one has any control and not due to the active doing of another, no responsibility to ameliorate misfortune is entailed.[24,25] Solidarity in such communities is brought about because each individual within it realizes that the community will safeguard the right of each individual to exercise his/her individual autonomy short of violating the autonomy of others. Individuals, therefore, feel that they can pursue their own life plans more freely than they could without such a contract. In that way maximal liberty is, at least theoretically, assured. To ameliorate one's neighbor's misfortune may be a "nice" thing to do; but such "niceness," just like other beneficent acts, has no moral force. Beneficence becomes either the peculiar concern of particular moral enclaves within the greater community (moral enclaves which perhaps require this as a condition of membership) or it becomes a matter of personal taste and volition. In shedding its moral force beneficence acquires an almost aesthetic quality. It may be nice to be beneficent but such "niceness" is not a moral but, rather, is an aesthetic "niceness." A community solely shaped on such a model has two obligations: to assure maximal individual freedom for all and to enforce freely entered contractual arrrangements. Persons relate to each other as free agents. The market place in which all can freely choose is the proper arbiter of public morality: when persons can select freely, the best conditions for all will be ensured. Adam Smith's "hidden hand" (at least the way Smith—who Larry Churchill points out started with a social philosophy—is popularly interpreted) sees to it that justice prevails.[26] Such a world-view, of course, entails not only capitalism but capitalism in its crassest forms. It is a world-view in which cells or organs are far more important than the body which they compose.

The antithesis of such an individualistic libertarian community is a community in which individual interests are completely submerged by those of the community. What has been called "Marxist Communism" has often been pointed out as an example. Anyone who, beyond its admittedly often annoying polemics, even superficially understands Marx and Marxism with its insistence on democracy and its purpose of fostering the basis of individual existence knows this to be untrue.[27,28] Stalinism or Bolshevism, despite its claims, is not representative of what Marx and his vision of communism had in mind. Stalinism, however, comes as close to an example of allegedly serving solely communal interests and disregarding the individual as can be imagined. All personal labor, personal destiny, or even personal innocence or guilt is offered up to a vision of community which becomes the sole goal of individual existence.[29] It is a world-view in which the body has no regard for its own individual organs or cells.

In libertarian communities, individuals count for everything and the community, beyond assuring the liberty or private fetishes of its members, for nothing. Solidarity in such communities comes about because the individual members can count on being left alone to pursue their life plans: if they fail, even if they fail miserably and through no fault of their own, their failing may be unfortunate but it surely is not the community's responsibility to come to their aid; if they succeed, so much the better. In

Bolshevik-type communities, solidarity comes about because members are, at least in theory, assured of the basic necessities of life. Beneficence, albeit distorted, will provide this to them. Solidarity rests on this realization. When persons are hungry, cold or homeless, when persons lack medical care or clothing, the state (at least in theory) will provide. Beneficence (at least as it played itself out in Bolshevik countries) becomes crass paternalism: unless supporting the flowering of individual hopes and aspirations is seen as necessary for the community's own narrowly perceived goals, the community feels no obligation to support individual aspirations.

In reality, no community pursues either an entirely libertarian or a crassly communitarian philosophy. Communities can structure themselves on a model in which individual rights and individual interests are far more important than communal ones: such communities emphasize obligations of respect for freedom and autonomy and will be ready to sacrifice beneficent obligations in order to safeguard individual rights. Other communities may give more importance to communal needs and obligations: such communities will emphasize beneficent obligations and in order to do this will be more ready to limit individual autonomy and freedom. No society totally limits one in pursuit of the other. Even in the Soviet Union under Stalin some individual choices were encouraged and some individual talent found its expression. Even in the most crassly capitalist state, a minimal safety net is grudgingly provided.

The relationship between the desire for autonomy or individual rights and the communal urge for beneficence or social justice has been painted as a dialectic. I have argued in the past that the communal ethos of a particular community at a particular time emerges from the working out of these two tensions—a working out much dependent upon the way that initial and evolving social contract is perceived and accepted.[1] When predominant communal values strongly favor autonomy, one is apt to end up with a nation in which social justice is largely ignored in order to maintain a narrowly defined respect for individual "rights"; when values favor beneficence, a nation in which such "rights" are easily sacrificed for the sake of narrowly defined social justice is apt to result. In what is to follow, I shall go beyond the dialectic relationship and argue that these two values are inseparable, that one entails the other and that the relationship between them is, rather than a dialectic, a homeostatic one serving the common goal of individual and communal survival and growth.

HOMEOSTASIS

It is necessary to take a closer look at what is meant by the term "homeostatic." *Webster's New World Dictionary* gives three overlapping definitions: (1) a tendency towards maintainance of a relatively stable internal environment in higher animals through a series of interacting physiological processes; (2) a tendency towards maintainance of a relatively stable psychological condition of individuals with respect to contending drives, motivations, and other psychodynamic forces; and (3) a tendency towards maintainance of relatively stable social conditions among groups with respect to various factors (as food supply and population among animals) and to competing tendencies and powers in the body politic to society or culture among men. These senses give an initial notion of what I have in mind in the use of the term. One should stress that homeostasis is not merely a physiological property peculiar to higher animals but is one manifest throughout nature. It is fundamental to individual, to species, and, indeed, to ecosystem survival. As such it constitutes part of the evolutionary process and, therefore, the stress on relative stability rather than on stability alone. Homeostasis as well as evolution form part of the necessary framework for our unconscious as well as for our conscious thoughts and actions.

The essence of these definitions lies in the notions of "balance" and "equilibrium" between disparate forces tending towards the "stability" of an entity, be that entity a cell, an organism, a society or, casting our net more widely, an ecosystem. Homeostatic relationships consist of a balance between two or (and in fact) usually more forces which serve the teleological goal of individual, species, or other natural survival. One can, therefore, with equal force speak of homeostatic relationships in nature which serve to return nature to a viable state of affairs. A lake, all life seemingly extinguished by pollution, can yet "right itself" and in some years regain its previous vigor. In a species there is a balance between forces acting to promote its proliferation and those opposing growth so that a balance can be maintained. When such balances are removed (as when natural enemies disappear) growth gains the upper hand, and an explosion of individuals who often are destined to starve occurs. If the species is to survive, a new equilibirum with a new set of reference points emerges and homeostasis now oscillates about these points. New organic life is maintained by a myriad of forces in balance with each other to serve the common end of survival. When homeostasis is successful, life continues; when it fails death is unavoidable.

Homeostasis denotes a dynamic equilibrium with continual change: adjustments are made for the common goal of survival. What appears to be a steady state is really a complex series of adjustments between external forces and internal controls. An organism (be that organism a cell, a plant, an animal, a species or a culture) responds so as to maintain an equilibirum and attain a balance which oscillates about a preset range of values. When such values are exceeded, corrective forces come into play so that what appears from afar and from the outside like a "steady state" again ensues. All such natural systems are "open," that is they are prone to a myriad of diverse outside influences and not closed as they would be in a balanced aquarium or a test tube. When changes are great, when natural enemies die or profound environmental conditions impinge, a new steady state will have to be created and the homeostatic plateau or range will have to be adjusted. If it is not, survival is not possible.

It is readily apparent that evolutionary change necessitates both the maintainance of a relatively steady state for a time and the ability to adapt to forces by resetting the limits within which homeostatic balance is maintained. Species that can do this, species which are flexible and can adjust and, therefore, adapt, are the species which ultimately survive. Those too rigid to adjust die. The same is true of societies: those which can adapt to changes in circumstances and evolve new methods of adaptation are prone to survive; other societies perish. Those which can maintain relative stability within a framework of values and usages while dynamically adjusting as well as re-examining, those which are able to experiment and to learn from such ventures, are those liable to endure.

Homeostasis does not imply conflict in the sense of one force vanquishing another. When that happens, the victory as often as not turns out to be pyrrhic. One cannot reasonably speak of insulin "vanquishing" a high glucose level but of helping to adjust it so that balance can be maintained. Not even physicians, if they are at all sophisticated about physiological process and even though they are often prone to use (and in my view overuse) the military metaphor, speak of homeostatic forces in this way. A species lives in balance with another: it does not ordinarily "vanquish" it. When it does vanquish, balance is upset and the "victor species" without a counterbalance may now find that its unchecked expansion leads to its own destruction. Rather than competition in its crudest sense, dynamic cooperation for a common goal is apt to serve all interests most effectively. The example of HIV comes (thanks to John Moreno who suggested it!) to mind: until recently the HIV virus or its closely structured precursors peacefully existed in nature; having either altered slightly or having found a receptive population group it became the threat that it is. If, however, infection with the virus universally leads to AIDS and if AIDS universally leads to death the virus has written its own inevitable demise into its "success." Unchecked by homeostatic forces, it will destroy itself in the process of destroying its host population. Either homeostatic mechanisms ("natural" or in the form of effective treatment) will develop or the organism together with its host will die.

Balance and equilibrium denote something rather different than merely dialectic tension. The two limbs of a dialectic (thesis and antithesis) are in opposition to each other with each devoted to its own goal. Such tension must ultimately be resolved by a new state of affairs which now becomes one new limb of the dialectic (a new thesis) serving its own end and opposed by yet another new antithesis which again will be solved in a new way. Inherent in a dialectic is the notion not merely of starkly dualistic opposition but of hostility and struggle. The ends served are quite different and their reconciliation is not so much a compromise as an armed truth. Balance, in the sense of homeostatic balance or equilibrium, on the other hand, carries the notion of a mean, the notion not only of a "middle road" but of a middle road whose telos is the common good. It is a much richer and more complicated concept than the fundamentally dualistic concept of hostility or struggle between opposing forces each seeking its own end; it carries within itself the idea of resolution and striving: a resolution sought and found so that the common end of survival and development can be met.

The notion of stability within any of these systems needs scrutiny. In the way that I shall use homeostasis and in the way in which, I believe, most biologists perceive it, homeostasis is not meant to imply an absolutely steady state. Such a state, in individuals, species, or ecosystems, would be a steady state leading to extinction: persons do not stand still. Survival necessitates adaptation to the environment, cautious experimentation and learning. Homeostatic forces in infants do not oppose development, growth, or the evolution of the new from the old. Evolution does not proceed despite but in large measure because of homeostasis. Without homeostasis serving the common good of all the forces involved, the wheel of progress, learning, and growth would constantly stall as one force mindless of all else "vanquished" the other. Homeostatic forces here merely channel development so that excesses are dampened and steady progress towards the goal of survival can be realized. When stability becomes dead uniformity it soon dies whether it is uniformity in individual behavior, thought, or action, whether it is uniformity in social life or uniformity in nature. What appears "stable" when examined under low power is seen to be quite dynamic when examined with a more powerful lens.

One can think of a number of social examples. Shopkeepers and their employees have to work for the common good even though they also have individual interests. Destroying their employer is not in the interest of the employee and creating conditions in which persons refuse to or only grudgingly work is not in the interest of the shopkeeper. Private interests are played out within the framework of the common good: when they are not, mutual destruction follows. Likewise, the shop exists within the framework of a larger community and while the shop's individual interests may differ they have to be played out within the framework of the larger community. And this interrelationship, as I will try to show later, holds in a similar fashion when a far more complicated skein of worldwide interactions occurs.

COMPASSION, NON-HUMANS, AND STRANGERS

It is popular to accuse persons who have a high regard for animal rights of not caring for those of humans. In a similar vein it is popular to respond to those who concern themselves about the misery of persons living in the underdeveloped world by claiming that they somehow put the interests of "foreigners" ahead of the interests of their own peoples. Before proceeding further I want to examine some of the several fallacies in this way of reasoning.

Persons who are concerned about the suffering of animals are hardly the ones most callous to the suffering of humans. Often (if not invariably) the opposite is true. Those like James Rachels, Peter Singer, or Tom Regan, most concerned to prevent the mistreatment of non-human animals, are at least equally concerned about the mistreatment of humans. A theory of suffering which grounds moral worth in an entity's capacity to suffer and which carefully tries to define ways of creating hierarchies of such worth lends itself to such considerations. Such a theory accepts the fact that suffering is inevitable and that causing some suffering to others likewise is at times unavoidable. But such a theory demands that before suffering is caused (or before attempts to alleviate suffering are not made) good reasons for doing or not doing so are available.

In claiming that (most) humans have a more pronounced capacity to suffer than do (most) non-human animals, a certain amount of protection is given to (most) humans. Such a claim, however, resting as it does on the capacity to suffer rather than on the genetic fact of humanhood, does not protect humans qua humans but protects humans only qua those generally most capable of the greatest suffering. A theory of this sort most certainly would favor the intelligent chimpanzee over the severely mentally defective human. A theory of this sort does not favor chimpanzees over humans or humans over chimpanzees but claims that causing wanton suffering is, in either case, not admissible. When a choice must be made, it favors those who would suffer most over those who would suffer least. Such a theory allows reason rather than the largely irrelevant fact of belonging or not belonging to a given species to decide what category a particular instance belongs to.[8]

Persons who concern themselves about the misery, exploitation, and consequent suffering rampant throughout the underdeveloped world are not (or at least ought not to be) less concerned about the misery, suffering, or exploitation evident "at home." Often (albeit not invariably) those most concerned about one are also those most concerned about the other. The claim that being concerned about misery elsewhere implies a relative unconcern about local misery is often an excuse for ignoring both and going on about one's uncaring way: a way often enabled by and enabling exploitation at home as well as abroad. Persons who argue this way are not necessarily active exploiters: rather they are generally those who (whether they do or do not disclaim any desire to do so) passively profit from such exploitation. Concern about persons outside one's immediate surrounding does not imply unconcern about persons within one's immediate surroundings. One's obligations to persons within one's circle of friends or acquaintances or within one's wider local community, may be stronger by virtue of closer relationships; but that does not imply that one has no obligations to these others. My obligations to my friend may be closer than my obligations are to a stranger: but that hardly argues against my obligations to the stranger.

The question of obligations cannot be settled this generically. My obligation to take my wife to the theater because I had promised to do so may be overruled by my neighbor's suffering a severe injury and needing my help. Obligations are rarely equivalent to each other: context, circumstances, relationships, and capacities modify almost all. This is not only true of positive obligations, obligations which counsel one "to do something"; it is also true, though perhaps to a lesser degree, of obligations which counsel one to "refrain." My obligations to help my neighbor start his car by taking time to give him a jump start may have lesser power than my obligation not to murder him: I can always refrain from doing the one but cannot always do the other. But my obligation to take my critically injured neighbor to the emergency room may outweigh my obligation not to insult my wife. The obligation to provide food to a starving person may, under some circumstances, arguably be greater than the obligation not to take another's property without their specific consent. To argue that our obligations to what is polemically called "our own people" (as though other peoples were not also a part of that "our!") always and under all circumstances outweighs our obligations to others is a shoddy way of reasoning.

There are other reasons why caring about the misery of humans in foreign lands is critical if one is to seriously propose a system based on at least a minimal appreciation of ethics. When we deny the very obvious contemporary fact that all of us in this world are ultimately interconnected and that "our" individual (or corporate communal) prosperity is enmeshed with that of all others we are likely to invite disaster. Persons denied just access to basic needs when such fair access could be provided, or associations of people denied their rightful place in the sun will, when peaceful resolution is deemed impossible, disturb and ultimately destroy the tenuous peace of their community. Desperate, given no satisfactory ways of redress or recourse, they are liable to take to more violent and more destructive ways of seeking recourse and redress.

A primitive sense of pity, which the suffering of non-human animals or of persons not in our immediate circle arouses and which prompts one to consider ethically acceptable behavior towards these others is the same sense of compassion aroused by any suffering. Such a primitive sense of pity is apt to be blunted when non-humans are treated callously; even Kant who was hardly an advocate of "animal rights" admits as much and counsels non-cruelty much for that reason.[30] Rousseau, for similar reasons, although he is perhaps more apt to regard animals as fellow sufferers, similarly emphasizes the importance of training: sentiments of compassion can be strengthened or weakened by the education afforded.[14] In a similar vein, our callousness towards those not in our immediate circle is apt to increase our tolerance towards the suffering of our neighbor. Suffering, be it that of non-human animals, that of strangers we do not personally know, or of persons outside our particular community is suffering: learning to be callous towards one is hardly apt to increase one's sensitivity to another.

JUSTICE AND MUTUAL OBLIGATIONS

Our concept of justice is central to the way we relate to and deal with others be they others who are non-human, others who are strangers, or others who are friends. Justice, if one is to abide by the traditional Aristotelian definition, means assuring that everyone receive that which is their due. As definitions go, this definition is helpful as a starting point but is quite moot when it comes to its particulars. Particulars must be provided by our values and by our understanding of community and obligation. To Kant, justice (*das Recht* in the sense of "the right principle for law") "supplies the a priori principle of possible legislation" (p. xviii).[31] In such a relationship actual law (*das Gesetz*) emerges from one's conception of justice (*das Recht*). To Kant, the principles of what is and what is not just (what "das Recht" is) are a priori and not the product of different possible conceptions of justice. While I do not take issue with the validity of such a framework (here is not the place to do this), I shall argue that the way we perceive the particulars of what justice may require is critically dependent upon our perception of community and of the relationship of individuals to their communities. (In a later section I shall try to draw an analogy between the relationship of individuals to their community and the relationship of small communities to the larger ones in which they are imbedded.)

A story may help to illustrate the point that *das Recht* (justice) leading to "das Gesetz" (the law) is intimately associated with the way we view community. Coming from a lecture and carrying a bookbag on a busy street in one of the "better" areas of Chicago, I stumbled over an unevenness in the sidewalk, crashed to the ground, broke my glasses, partly dislocated my shoulder, and struck my head. While, like a slightly blinded and stunned crab, I was trying to find my glasses and get up three persons walked around me without even attempting to help. Had a policeman seen this scene, such persons would have been held blameless: after all, a minimalist community would argue, they did not cause my accident and, therefore, had no obligation to come to my aid. In some parts of the world, such persons would have been punished for failing to assist someone in distress: after all, such a community would argue, when it is easy to help another in distress we have a moral obligation to do so. Justice (*das Recht,* or basically what is the right-making thing to do) in each situation is viewed quite differently. Ultimately the law as well as the ethics of our interpersonal relations conforms to the way in which we conceive communal structure.

In a minimalist community one's due is to be left strictly alone to pursue one's own interests provided the development of these interests does not infringe the equivalent right of others within the community. One can expect to exercise one's freedoms, one can be expected to be allowed to develop one's talents and interests, but one cannot legitimately expect to receive communal or individual help no matter how disadvantaged by fate one might be.

As long as the community or others have not had a direct causal part in causing one's personal disadvantage, such a disadvantage may be unfortunate but is not unjust.[25] Not helping, therefore, may likewise be unkind but it is not unjust. Providing help is strictly a supererogatory matter. Justice, therefore, is entirely negative: it sees to it that no one infringes another's rights. Right-making laws (*gerechte Gesetze*) are those which infringe on individual liberties only to the extent of affording protection from infringement by others. In a minimalist ethics communities cannot infringe the liberty of one to benefit another: to tax the wealthy for the benefit of the poor (or to enforce giving help to another in distress) would unduly limit freedom.

When communities move away from the minimalist model and embrace at least some beneficent obligations justice is envisioned quite differently. Beneficence is assumed to have moral force: the amount of such force varies from community to community and from time to time. In practice, no societies are or ever have been either entirely minimalist nor entirely communal. Even the most libertarian will (however grudgingly) feel compelled to some beneficence and, therefore, will collect taxes and pass legislation accordingly; even the most communitarian model makes room for some personal choices. The question is one of balance.

In what is to follow, I shall try to discuss this relationship and rely on my sketch of community for justification of such obligations. The capacity to suffer as well as our innate sense of pity at the suffering of others will be a central and at times a tacit backdrop to this discussion. I shall argue for a vision of *das Recht* which relies in part on deductive reason, in part on biological survival, and in part on a sketch of communal and personal obligation as inevitably related to the infants necessarily experiencing nurture and beneficence prior to attaining any notion of being a self. I shall argue that such a particular notion of justice (*das Recht*) entails individual and communal obligations not merely to refrain from causing suffering but, when possible, likewise entails obligations to prevent and ameliorate the suffering of its members.

REFERENCES

1. Loewy EH: *Suffering and the Beneficent Community: Beyond Libertarianism*. Albany, NY: SUNY Press; 1991.

2. Hobbes T: *Leviathan*. New York, NY: Collier; 1962.

3. Locke J: *Second Treatise on Government* (C. E. Macpherson, ed.). Indianapolis, IN: Hackett Publishing; 1980.

4. Jefferson T: The Declaration of Independence. In: Beard CA and Beard MR: *The Beard's Basic History of the United States* (p. 433). New York, NY: Doubleday, Doran and Co.; 1944.

5. Rousseau JJ: *Du Contrat Social* (R. Grimsley, ed.). Oxford, England: Oxford University Press; 1972.

6. Rousseau JJ: *Discours sur l'Origine et les Fondements de l'Inégalité parmi les Hommes*. Paris, France: Gallimard; 1965.

7. Darwin C: *The Descent of Man and Selection in Relation to Sex*. Princeton, NJ: Princeton University Press, 1981.

8. Rachels J: *Created from Animals: The Moral Implications of Darwinism*. New York, NY: Oxford University Press; 1990.

9. Kronauer U: *Vom Nutzen und Nachteil des Mitleids*. Frankfurt a/M: Keip Verlag; 1990.

10. Hamburger K: *Das Mitleid*. Stuttgart, Deutschland: Klett-Cotta; 1985.

11. Plato: Republic. (Peter Shorey, trans.) In: *Plato, the Collected Dialogues* (p. 31) (E. Hamilton and C. Huntington, eds.). Princeton, NJ: Princeton University Press; 1961.

12. Aristotle: *Nicomacchean Ethics* (M. Ostwald, trans.). Indianapolis, IN: Bobbs-Merrill Publishers; 1962.

13. Mandeville B: *The Fable of the Bees*. Harmondsworth, England: Penguin Books, 1970.

14. Rousseau JJ: *Emile: ou, De l'Education*. Paris, France: Garnier Freres; 1957.

15. Schopenhauer A: *Preisschrift u"ber die Grundlage der Moral*. In: *Arthur Schopenhauer, Sämtliche Werke, Band III*. Frankfurt a/M: Suhrkamp; 1986

16. Springer-Loewy RA: An Alternative to Traditional Models of Human Relationships. Cambridge Quarterly; 1993 [in press].

17. Jensen UJ: *Practice and Progress: A Theory for the Modern Health-Care System*. Oxford, England: Blackwell Scientific Publications; 1987.

18. Jensen UJ: Are Selves Real? In: *Harré and His Critics* (Roy Shaskar, ed.). Oxford, England: Basic Blackwell; 1990.

19. Jonas H: *Das Prinzip Verantwortung*. Frankfurt a/M, Deutschland: Suhrkamp; 1984.

20. Kant I: *Kritik der Reinen Vernunft*. Frankfurt a/M, Deutschland: Suhrkamp; 1988.

21. Dewey J: The Influence of Darwinism on Philosophy. In: *The Middle Works of John Dewey* (JoAnn Boydston, ed.). Carbondale, IL: Southern Illinois University Press; 1977.

22. Callahan D: Minimalist Ethics. Hastings Center Report 1981; 11(6): 19-25.

23. Nozick R: *Anarchy, State and Utopia*. New York, NY: Basic Books; 1974.

24. Engelhardt HT: *The Foundations of Bioethics*. New York, NY: Oxford University Press; 1986.

25. Engelhardt HT: Health Care Allocations: Response to the Unjust, the Unfortunate and the Undesirable. In: *Justice and Health Care* (E. E. Shelp, ed.). Dordrecht, The Netherlands: D. Reidel; 1981, pp. 121-138.

26. Smith A: *An Inquiry into the Nature and Causes of the Wealth of Nations*. In: *Adam Smith's Moral and Political Philosophy* (H. W. Schneider, ed.). New York, NY: Hafner Publishing Co.; 1948.

27. Hook S: *Toward the Understanding of Karl Marx*. New York, NY: Oxford; 1933.

28. Meynell HA: *Freud, Marx and Morals*. New York, NY: Barnes and Noble Books; 1981.

29. Koestler A: *Darkness at Noon*. New York, NY: Macmillan; 1941.

30. Kant I: Duties towards Animals and Spirits. In: *Immanuel Kant: Lectures in Ethics*. (Louis Infield, trans.). Gloucester, MA: Peter Smith; 1978.

31. Ladd J: Translator's Introduction. In: Kant I: *The Metaphysical Elements of Justice* (p. xviii) (John Ladd, trans.). New York, NY: Collier Macmillan Publishers; 1965.

CHAPTER 3

Suffering and Community

So far I have tried to sketch an ethic based on the universal capacity to suffer and a view of community based on a person's initial and continuing experience of nurture. I have intertwined these ideas with Rousseau's notion of an innate "sense of pity" or compassion common to all sentient beings, suggested that such a "sense of pity" is built into the common structure of our mind, and have gone somewhat beyond this in developing the basic idea. Further, I have suggested that these notions confer individual and communal obligations which transcend the minimalist obligations of refraining from harm. In such a concept beneficent obligations are seen as deeply rooted in our common heritage and experience.

In this chapter I will:

1. Grapple with the question of how one can derive an ethic from such considerations: in other words, how can the capacity to suffer and the vision of a communal life as I have sketched it become a principle upon which an ethic can be grounded?
2. Argue that communities are causally involved in the suffering of their members and that this imposes further obligations to, where possible, ameliorate and prevent suffering.
3. Since it is not always possible either to refrain from causing or to ameliorate suffering, I will continue with my attempt to develop and sketch some tentative hierarchies.
4. Lastly I will discuss the moral standing of community itself and continue to develop the notion that just communities which envision justice as more than merely maximizing freedom and preventing individuals from doing each other harm must grapple with the limits of individual freedom and action and must juxtapose and balance the individual's yearning for freedom with and to beneficent obligations.

DERIVING AN ETHIC FROM
SUFFERING AND COMMUNITY

One may acknowledge the universal capacity to suffer, recognize that individual and communal experience necessarily starts with the nurture of infants by their community, and concede that a "natural sense of pity" is built into the common structure of all normal sentient beings, and yet deny that such facts impose any obligations. I am reminded of an experience I had during a question period following one of my lectures. A theologian in the audience drew a not-at-all improper analogy between what I had said and the biblical obligation stressed again and again in the Old Testament to be kind to strangers. In the Old Testament this obligation is based on the fact that the children of Israel "were strangers in the land of Egypt." My questioner said that the causal relationship between the experience of being a stranger and the consequent obligation to understand the stranger's lot and, therefore, to be kind to him/her was never clear to him. How and why, he asked, does my experience impose an obligation? The same question can, of course, be asked about the capacity for suffering or the inevitable experience of children with nurture. How, in other words, can one establish, justify, or in some sense "prove" the existence of an obligation?

The problem of justification, the problem with justifying any given proposition, bedevils all human endeavors including ethics. Most skeptics when they question our assertions will, and rightly so, rely on questioning our justification. Yet in order to grapple with everyday problems, to move ahead in science, medicine or engineering, to make laws we consider to be just, or to talk intelligently about virtually anything including about ethics, we need to accept at least some canons of proof. Or, at the very least, we must be clear in our own minds what the concept "proof" means. For those who purport to find their propositions supported by the word of God or evident (to them) as "natural law" the problem of proof is reduced to one of proper authority. Once proper authority (whether the revealed word of God or the perceived law of nature) is accepted what that authority says proves the validity of the proposition. The problem is that such an authority (whether the authority is the presence of a given natural law or of a rule specifically said to have come down from God) is not an acceptably convincing authority to all or even most persons. To rely on authority for proof, furthermore, is eminently circular: a proposition is proven by authority and the fact that it is authority is proven by the fact that it is seen as supplying the rules to be followed. The reason for accepting such a proposition is deductive: the proposition can be deduced from the rules supplied by authority which serves as a reference point for itself.

It is, of course, true that accepting reasoning likewise is a form of accepting authority: the authority of reasoning. Reasoning, however, is an ongoing process of logical as well as empirical examination. It is an ongoing process of posing and testing hypotheses, not one of accepting a static "reality" as immutable.

What is evident to virtually all intelligent beings are certain rules of logic: for example, propositions which hold that a something cannot be "p" and "non-p" at the same time, statements that two and two are four, or claims that two objects cannot occupy the same space at the same time. These are evident by a deductive type of reasoning in which the claim of the proposition is already included in its own terms. It is analytic proof. Such claims are universally accepted because the common structure of our mind necessitates our seeing our environment in one and not in another way. If such perception actually corresponds in a one-to-one way to "reality" is a different question, a question impossible to answer without first defining what reality is. It is an answer inevitably determined by and within the given structure of our mind. What one can claim, however, is that our perception is sufficiently close to actuality so that we can deal with whatever our perceptions represent and what we then call reality "successfully:" i.e., "successfully" in the sense that we can get on with our daily lives and are capable with such perceptions to manipulate our environment. If the correspondence between our perception and "what is" were grossly out of joint, our daily lives would constantly and erratically collide with what we fail to see and our attempts at manipulation would fail. Such a procedure, however, does not constitute absolute deductive proof; rather such a procedure produces an inference and is perhaps the best explanation available to us. While not perfect, it is good enough for getting on with our daily lives.

We hold certain propositions of logic to be true and derive other propositions from them. Such a method of justification is helpful but such a method does not exhaust the justifications we must have to adequately get on with living and shaping our lives. In ethics certain propositions (Kant's Categorical Imperative, for example) come close to being deductively evident: the principle of universality appears a logically necessary conclusion. Nevertheless, while such propositions can and often must form the framework of our deliberations, they leave a large amount of play room for developing and grappling with actual problems. In this vast arena "the best possible explanation" helps us to get on with our tasks and itself helps us to examine methods of justification yet further.[1] Such an explanation is not and is not held to be immutably true for all time. But it is good enough and will serve our purposes (including the purpose of broadening further inquiry) now.

If we settle for more than a merely deductive method and hold that the best working inference can for our purposes be held to justify propositions not eternally but at least for the time being, we: (a) may get on with the task at hand and (b) may, by refining and re-examining our method, continue to grope for better ways of justification, so that we can begin to use a rich combination of evidence in fashioning our insights into the ways sentient beings interrelate on an ethical plane, how obligations arise, and communities interrelate. If we look for absolute and ultimate proof, on the other hand, we will be (a) hamstrung in getting on with the task at hand and will be (b) unable to refine and re-examine our method which, when we search for an absolute, is identical with the absolute itself. Rather than expect to find an eternally true answer to a problem, we will have to be satisfied to move it along a bit: to, as John Dewey suggests, move problems from a less to a more determinate status, rather than expect absolute solutions.[2,3] In that view, justification is part of an ongoing process of learning and growth and it becomes a necessary part of individual and communal survival.

I have claimed that the capacity to suffer is one of the characteristics that makes of a mere object an object of moral concern, that it changes objects to be freely acted upon to subjects with whom we act, and that this capacity to suffer and the universal desire of all who can suffer not to do so, imposes a moral obligation to not cause avoidable suffering.[4] Such a universal capacity to suffer imposes, I have claimed, a universal prima-facie obligation not to cause it, prima facie because it is not an absolute duty but rather is weighty enough to be only overruled by sufficient reasons to the contrary.

When one has been a stranger (or when one has suffered) a "primitive sense of pity" turns into empathy rather than merely into sympathetic understanding. As mentioned in the last chapter, sympathetic understanding is possible when I can feel myself in the place of another. This ability to feel myself in the place of another is, of course, conditioned by my prior experience. Another experience does not have to be exactly the same as the experience I actually have, but if it is similar enough to what I actually have had (or have witnessed) it will enhance my ability to see myself in the other's shoes. The more remote another's experience is from my own past exposure to a similar problem, the more difficult it is to feel true empathy. However, even when one cannot feel empathy because another's experience is too remote for one to imagine for oneself, a primitive sense of pity will motivate sympathetic understanding. It is sympathetic understanding for a universal emotion one can imagine oneself as having rather than empathy with a situation one can imagine experiencing.

When another being suffers, even if we could not imagine ourselves in that being's shoes, our common experience of suffering prompted by our sense of pity elicits compassion in the normal person: either the more remote compassion of sympathetic understanding or the warmer and more personal compassion of empathy. In either case an impetus for acting to help, if possible, even if not as yet an outright obligation to act, would be a normal response. The empirical observation that, at times, humans feel no such urge but watch another's misery with a shrug of the shoulders or even with enjoyment, does not argue against such a conclusion. It merely suggests either that such feelings have, in the course of improper education, been blunted or "educated out" of the person (just as such feelings by proper education can be strengthened),[5] or that the person was born with a defect akin to being born blind, deaf, or without some other natural sense. An absence of such a sense in any particular individual at any one time does not argue against the presence of that sense in most persons considered to be endowed with normal and normally developed faculties. Being a "normal faculty," however, in and of itself confers no obligations: the capacity to see, hear, or taste says nothing particular about my obligations.

It is easier to argue for the injunction against causing others to suffer (or not to force others into the position of being slaves or strangers), which is a largely negative injunction (an obligation to refrain from doing something rather than an obligation to do something), than it is to argue for more positive obligations. A negative injunction of this sort essentially conforms to a version of Kant's Categorical Imperative, but in my schema "respect" is evoked by the capacity to suffer rather than being evoked by the capacity to self-legislate.[6] True, such an injunction is not and practically cannot be absolute. What such an injunction can be made to do is to allow entities with the capacity to suffer their day in court and, when such suffering can be justified, to keep suffering to the minimum necessary to achieve what is held to be the overriding goal.

It is logically possible to propose a world without beneficent obligations.[6] Whereas it is not logically possible for me to will a world in which stealing or murder would be a "universal law of nature," I could state without violating logic that I do not feel bound, in the same sense, by obligations of beneficence and do not expect beneficence from others: it is logically possible for me to do so. I have claimed that communal as well as personal obligations of beneficence are grounded, among other reasons, in the fact that all infants are born helpless, unaware of their own selfness, and consequently that they are critically dependent upon nurture by others. The fact that we sit here writing or arguing about obligations inevitably means that others have nurtured us and allowed us to come to the place we are. The fact that we have individual needs, desires and talents, the fact that we strive to satisfy our own needs and seek to pursue our own interests and to develop our own talents inevitably is possible only because we have been nurtured and benefited long enough so that our sense of selfness and, ultimately our autonomy, could develop. Our autonomy, as I have stated before, inevitably develops in the embrace of nurture and beneficence. Ontologically autonomy cannot exist without nurture and beneficence. But, some will say, that is well and good; I may, perhaps, owe a little gratitude to those who nurtured me but how does that impose general obligations of beneficence rather than merely and at best imposing some expressions of specific gratitude?

There are, of course, several answers to such a question. The first is to admit that such beneficent obligations are, in fact, not quite as strictly or as logically deducible as are obligations of respect. Negative obligations, obligations of refraining, are easier to justify on a deductively logical basis. Kant himself, however, hardly evaded beneficent obligations (placing them among what he termed "imperfect duties") nor did Kant fail to emphasize that men are social animals for whom community is a necessary condition for thought and existence.[6,7] For Kant such positive obligations were weighty not because they shared strict logical necessity with negative duties, not because it was not, strictly speaking, logically possible to will a world without them, but because willing such a world would "force the will to conflict with itself" (Denn ein Wille der Dieses beschlösse, würde sich selbst wiederstreiten, p. 54)[6] or, perhaps better put, because willing such a world would force volition to conflict with itself. Kant does not ground such a conflict of the will merely in self-interest. He goes on to say that since one must always treat others (human others) as ends in themselves instead of merely using human others to facilitate one's own purposes (in other words, since human others are owed respect), one must likewise try to facilitate the ends of others in one's actions. Being human (acting as one would expect a human to act, being what in Yiddish one would call a *Mensch*) becomes one of the ends which humans must pursue. When Kant uses the term "*Menschheit*" (translatable as "mankind"), as Friedrich Heubel pointed out to me, he means rather "*Menschsein*" (difficult to translate but denoting "being a real person"—the Yiddish term "*Mensch*"). It is what in the *Magic Flute* Mozart means when the voice of Sarastro sings, "*Wen solche Lehren nicht erfreun, verdiehnt es nicht ein Mensch zu sein*" (He who does not take pleasure from such teachings does not deserve to be a human being). One should not further the ends of others, Kant says, merely because of an interest in one's own existence but just because maxims which do not include such ends cannot be understood (comprehended) as universal law.[8] ("...*Weil die Maxime die sie ausschlieszt nicht in einem und demselben Wollen als allgemeines Gesetz begriffen werden kann*" or "...Because the maxim which excludes it from my duty cannot be comprehended as a universal law in one and the same volition."[8])

Despite and consistent with his philosophy of denying all validity to self-serving motives or even to motives of self-interest, Kant also does say that since at one time or another we are desperately in need of each other's help (and, as I have argued, when we are infants and to a somewhat lesser extent afterwards our survival is entirely dependent on such help) we cannot, for this reason truly will a world in which beneficence played no role. Willing a world without beneficence would, in a sense, will our own non-existence. By its very nature, however, beneficence has to be selective and, therefore, the obligation is "imperfect" and our discharging it is, in each case, "optional."[6] As individuals we may choose to contribute to one charity and not to another; as communities we may choose to fund public roads or public hospitals but not to fund colleges or support the arts. To make contributions to every charity an obligation or the funding of all communal works compulsory would destroy the individual and the community. But as individuals or communities, we cannot refrain from beneficence altogether; we cannot, and claim to lead "the good life," turn an entirely deaf ear to the suffering of our neighbor. (See also chapter 6.)

Simply because things are not logically or mathematically deducible does not mean that they, therefore, do not exist, are not provable, or that they do not count as, or as an integral part of, justifications. The appreciation of music or poetry, love or friendship, hope or despair are none clearly logically or mathematically deducible; and yet they very much exist and some of them (like love or friendship) can and are in turn even regularly used to deduce specific obligations. The capacity to love or to have friendships is a universal human capacity and we readily acknowledge certain obligations towards those we love or towards those we claim as our friends. Being loved, loving, or having friends is, in part, definable by the obligations being loved, loving, or having friends entails. A primitive sense of pity, like love, friendship, or other feelings, has similar standing.

Deductive reasoning and the classical forms of deductive logic, in their traditional mathematical sense, are often applied outside the context of the problem they are meant to "solve." This process is an important but incomplete part of proof or justification: it is an often crucial part but it is usually only a part and not necessarily or generally the sole condition of proof. Proof, in traditional theories "(1) harkens back to more certain forms of knowledge; (2) has little place for creativity or genuine novelty; and (3) is dogmatic in what is said to be immediately known in contrast with the experimentally tested character of the object known in consequence of reflection" (p. 146).[2] Such reflection must conform to a logic which is not purely deductive. According to Dewey the scope of logic may be described in a general sense as the articulation and explicit formulation of the controlling instrumentalities and operations that function when problems are being inquired into and warranted solutions are arrived at.[3] Experience and nature are the parents of inquiry and the deciding factors in what is or what is not assumed to be warranted.

Truth is not fixed and immutable. The truth of a proposition is tested in experience and praxis. Such a point of view, as Dewey says, "puts a heavy burden of responsibility upon us for search, unremitting observation, scrupulous development of hypotheses and thoroughgoing testing."[10] Truth, then, at least truth as we can know it (whether such "truth" be truth in a physical sciences sort of sense or truth in any other sense) is fashioned and ultimately tested by us. Testing involves both an application of logical principles (principles which are universally acknowledged as principles by virtue of our common mental structure) and a testing of the proposition in everyday life. Propositions which work to move problems from the less to the more determinate are propositions which for today's usage are "true:" not immutably and unalterably true but true enough so that they can serve not only as tools of daily living but also as tools for further inquiry and growth.

Logic, as Dewey sees it, consists of far more than merely deduction.[2,3,9] Logic is a dynamic striving towards warranted "solutions": solutions not in the sense of final answers but in the sense of tentative hypotheses which carry inquiry from an indeterminate to a more determinate (or at least to a somewhat less indeterminate) situation. Such situations are more determinate because they work better in the context in which they are used, not because they are irrefutably or eternally true. A justified proposition does not become an absolute, analytically unchallengeable and immutable one; rather it is a proposition or theory which works better in dealing with the situation at hand. And "working better" denotes that it can be used to further inquiry and to stimulate growth. A theory of ethics based on suffering or a theory of community and beneficence based on the early nurture of infants is a theory which, all things considered, may "work better." This is true not only in the sense of helping to deal with more problems, and not only in the sense of fostering individual and species happiness, but also in the sense of stimulating further inquiry. In turn it may ultimately stimulate our personal, communal, and species ability to adapt and grow and, therefore, may serve to promote individual, communal, and species survival.

Beneficent duties can be argued for in several ways. First of all, there are several historical arguments at least in Western civilization going back at least to Plato, Aristotle, the Talmud, and the early church fathers, and most clearly in its more modern form to arguments enunciated by Kant. As I have already mentioned, Kant asserted that while one might logically will a world without beneficence such a wish would, since we all were and are critically dependent upon the beneficence of others, cause the will (or volition) to conflict with itself.[6] But I shall argue further that certain bio-psycho-social facts of our existence impose such obligations. Infants, as I have mentioned, are totally dependent on a community of others if they are to survive long enough to become aware of themselves and of their autonomy.[4] Even later, they continue to be in critical need of help and guidance: help and guidance which is aimed at making them sturdy and self-reliant enough to be set free to pursue their own peculiar aims, goals, and destinies. And even when they have reached their adulthood, have achieved their identity, have begun to see their possibilities and are pursuing their goals, they continue to be critically dependent on their community to enunciate, shape, and enable their identity, possibilities and goals. Individuals never are and never can be entirely "free"; indeed, it is the very framework which nature and community sets which allows freedom to be meaningful. Freedom without such a framework is no more imaginable or useful than is unlimited and undemarcated space.[10] Freedom plays itself out amidst a variety of natural forces and, like everything else, is prone to the dynamic interplay of homeostasis.

Achieving goals then, whatever these goals might be, depends upon initial and continued community support. Infants, far from first experiencing terror, first experience at least a minimal beneficence and love. Trust inevitably grows from this.[4] An infant groping for the nipple does not expect to find a snake or a hot iron instead. It is only later disappointments which engender fear, a fear which originates in disappointed trust. The initial experience of nurture remains as the inevitable and universal first datum in all of our personal diaries no matter what later experiences occur. No matter how profound our disappointments, no matter how terrible our experiences or our suffering, that initial nurture and its consequent feeling of natural trust is inevitably deeply ingrained within us. Our life experiences (as Hampshire has pointed out) are not an aggregate like a heap of stones but rather are like a compost heap: they do not stand alone but interpenetrate one another forming a mix in which the single components have interacted to produce a new whole.[12] But the original components cannot be expelled or denied. Trust may be penetrated by experience to produce doubt, blind trust may become cautious confidence or even skeptical distrust; but trust is the original and foundational condition.

This development imposes, in its turn, a compost heap of obligations. Separating the components strictly into positive and negative obligations is analytically useful but functionally sterile. Our positive as well as our negative obligations are not merely logically deducible (albeit that logical deducibility strengthens and affirms their power) but have an historical as well as an inevitable bio-psycho-social dimension. Thinking of our negative obligations already entails at the very least an awareness of the existence of positive opportunities. On the one hand, the prohibition against theft or murder is grounded on the realization that theft or murder are possible; on the other such an injunction at least raises the possibility of positive action: theft or murder may be thwarted and another helped.

If I should refrain from causing suffering (because I do not want to be made to suffer) should I not also try, at least when doing so is very easy, to prevent or ameliorate another's suffering (because I would not only hope but would indeed expect another to do this for me)? The reasons are parallel; the difference lies, among others, in the notion of "when it is very easy." If, for example, it were possible but very risky for me not to shoot someone trying to kill me, would *not* killing such an assailant be a more binding duty than stopping a man who could easily be stopped from doing serious mischief to another by tripping him with my foot? The one—not killing the assailant—is indeed possible, though risky; the other—stopping another from being killed—under the conditions set forth would be very easy and probably not at all risky. Which of the two obligations would be judged to be greater? Under these circumstances, would I be more blameworthy for killing my assailant or more blameworthy for not interfering with the murder of another? If refraining from causing minimal suffering would be very hazardous or costly and ameliorating severe suffering would be an easy and not costly thing to do, where would my more convincing duty lie? Positive and negative obligations, rooted in our shared capacity to suffer and grounded in our necessary experience of nurture, complement and necessarily interpenetrate one another. Being kind to strangers because all of us were strangers in the land of Egypt (or anywhere on this earth), refraining from causing suffering and accepting obligations of beneficence are interwoven in our common human language whatever its particulars, in our shared vulnerabilities and in our inevitable human experiences.

Species survival depends upon acquiring characteristics which allow adaptation. Survival is the first drive and, in a biological sense, the first obligation for any species. The question "why should one's species strive to survive" is, with that in mind, not a question for which a purely rational answer can be supplied. In a biological sense such a question in itself is an irrational one and, indeed, incoherent. I will, therefore, not attempt an answer but will take species survival and evolution as the biological raison d'être of a species, fully aware that such an argument cannot escape a certain circularity. I will, in other words, simply accept and not argue for it.

Ethics and the obligations ethics entails as envisioned here has, among other things, long-range adaptive survival value. Species at war with themselves, especially species with the devilish ability to construct devices for self-destruction, will not survive. This modern capacity, the capacity to destroy not only oneself and one's small polis but the capacity to destroy life itself, has changed our notion of ethics and imposed a quite different and far broader set of obligations.[13] This relatively new fact, then, has transcended the basically individualistic concern of traditional ethics which asks: What is my duty to you and what is yours to me? The new fact necessitates much more than merely a minimalist conception of community.

Although he does not state it in so many words, Hobbes's

initial contract forged in terror to prevent "the war of all against all"[14] did more than merely allow individuals to get on with their lives: it had adaptive species value. Nevertheless, a contract of refraining from doing harm to each other without any correlative beneficent obligations provided only the most minimal conditions for survival or morality, as well as providing only the most minimal conditions for communal solidarity. Knowing—or, at least, being reasonably sure—that my neighbor feels obligated not to attack me will make me feel a bit more secure, a bit less hostile towards a neighbor who is a non-enemy and at least minimally bound to a community which assures such conditions. I cannot logically wish to destroy the community to which I look for protection against the neighbor I fear. But that is far from being cohesive and far from firm or staunch solidarity. Undoubtedly such a state of affairs has greater survival value than one in which my neighbor was entirely unrestrained and in which my life was consequently "solitary, poor, nasty, brutish and short." Such a state of affairs is certainly an improvement, even if it is hardly a great comfort.

Communities bound firmly by solidarity can meet the challenges of their environment more successfully than can communities in which solidarity is more tenuous. Persons, at least persons who reflect at all upon their condition, are aware of their ever-present vulnerabilities.[15] Human relationships, perhaps all relationships, intimately depend upon factors linked with relative weaknesses and complementary strengths.[13,16] Knowing that others and their community feel and accept an obligation to prevent and ameliorate suffering rather than accepting only an obligation not to inflict harm, provides a sense of security. Knowing—or, at least, being reasonably sure—that my neighbor will, if possible, feel obligated to come to my aid, makes me feel more secure in my vulnerability, friendlier to my neighbor (who is now not merely a non-enemy but has become at least somewhat closer to being a friend), and tightly and more warmly tied to a community interested in my weal and woe. Logically I will be more tightly bound to and feel more a part of such a community, and solidarity in and with such a community will be at least less tenuous if not indeed far firmer. Such a state of affairs, a state of affairs in which I feel secure not only in my personal safety but also secure to develop my individual capacities and talents, is a community which can more easily thrive, grow, and develop as can the individuals within it. Such a community, by virtue of its greater solidarity and capacity to adapt, has a far greater survival value.

Arguments for positive obligations, then, can and do have several roots. Some of these are logical even if they are not as deductively simple as are arguments for negative ones. Others depend on bio-psycho-social factors. All these arguments interpenetrate, support and confirm each other. The task before us is not only to justify obligations (be they positive or negative), by only one strictly logical and deductive type of justification, helpful as such justifications may be and in fact are. Justifications, even of a strictly logical kind, are still dependent upon bio-psycho-social factors, anthropological factors, if you will. They are dependent upon, even if certainly not reducible to, such factors. Bio-psycho-social factors are critical if only because humans of necessity are bio-psycho-social creatures whose logical possibilities and whose logical framework determines the range of their options. We cannot exceed that framework nor do we need to fear its limits: humans have only gone a small way in realizing its opportunities and possibilities. The task before us is to give reasonable explanations and reasonable justifications for negative and positive obligations and then to get on with delineating and defining their range and their peculiarities. As this activity of delineating and defining their range proceeds, we may see that our previously conceived framework likewise has changed. Form and content inevitably affect each other. With that in mind, our task is to create a community in which individuals can thrive, grow, and evolve so that community itself can likewise survive, grow, evolve, and thrive.

COMMUNITIES AND THE CAUSES OF SUFFERING

Communities are intimately and very frequently causally related to and with the suffering of their members. In part because of this connection between communities and their members, communities in the ethical relationships I have proposed and shall continue to explicate, must ethically have a distinct role in ameliorating suffering. Often communities, even though they may not have direct causal responsibility for the existence of suffering, form an important part of the causal chain which initiates such suffering or which allows suffering to continue. Communities, therefore, have distinct obligations which transcend not causing and include preventing and ameliorating suffering. In turn, individuals have obligations to their communities which transcend their individual interests and desires; these obligations, as I have and shall continue to argue in this book, go far beyond merely refraining from doing each other or the community harm. Such an argument, I shall maintain in a later section, holds not only for the ethics of the relationship between individuals and the community to which they may belong: it can, with equal force, be argued to hold for the ethics of the relationship between smaller and larger communities. Larger or more powerful communities can be and frequently are causally implicated in the suffering of their smaller or weaker neighbors. Examples in the relationship between the more developed powerful industrial nations and their less developed and less powerful neighbors in what is euphemistically and arrogantly called "the third world" abound.

Communities can cause the suffering of their members in many ways. Sending persons to war, executing or imprisoning them, unreasonably restricting their personal liberties, and sitting idly by while segments within the population are economically or culturally deprived are but a few. These examples are not equivalent: the role of community in executing persons or in restricting their personal liberty is often a more direct one in the causal chain than is the community's role in economic or cultural deprivation. But while the causal chain may be longer or more complex and while many more factors enter in, the community not only is the stage on which these other forces act but itself continues to form a critical link in the causal chain. I shall claim that communities have an obligation to intervene, where possible, in the suffering of their members for three reasons: (1) by the way communities have structured themselves and continue to allow themselves to be structured, communities have a causal relationship in most of what befalls their members; the causal chain may be longer or shorter but somewhere along the length of that causal chain communal structure and action is involved. (2) Communities inevitably are the setting permitting these other factors latitude of action. And (3) Communities even when their involvement may be remote or minimal, have beneficent obligations towards their members. Such beneficent obligations as I have argued have several roots. The realization that our communities at some point have such obligations plays a major role in our solidarity with it.

Communities necessarily structure themselves so that some will suffer: coal miners, despite all precautions, will have a higher rate of silicosis, members of the police will risk being shot and crippled, and members of the fire department will risk being burned or overcome by smoke and severely injured to a greater extent than will those in other occupations. Causation of this sort is not frequently entirely or even partially preventable: communal survival and well-being depends on miners, police officers, and fire fighters, among others; but, at the very least, causal responsibility can be acknowledged and partly compensated for in other ways. Here causal responsibility is more direct: the causal chain between harm done and responsibility in a coal miner's having silicosis, a police officer being shot, or a fire fighter being burned is far less complex and, therefore, shorter than is the causal chain when it comes to poverty or lack of opportunity for education or health care.

Communities are causally implicated in far more subtle ways. The way in which poverty, lack of education, or social or racial disadvantage exists or plays itself out depends upon the way communities are structured. Given similar economic conditions, communities which accept the obligation to prevent hunger or homelessness and which accept obligations to invest their resources in trying to accomplish these aims have made a decision to structure themselves in a quite different way than have communities which allow hunger or homelessness to continue. They may, for example, have decided to tax their wealthier members more heavily (thereby limiting the liberties of the wealthier somewhat) and/or they may have decided to invest their resources in eliminating poverty and hunger rather than in building a powerful armed force.

The way communities structure themselves inevitably distributes the advantaging or disadvantaging of its members in different ways. Communities, for example, which keep slaves have decided to disadvantage a certain segment of their population as a trade-off for advantaging others. Defining slaves as not being members of the community does not define the problem out of existence for it flies in the face of fact, reason, and experience. It is intelligent members of the community who must be involved in doing much of the community's work and slaves most certainly cannot be denied either such involvement or, and therefore, such intelligence. Likewise, when communities economically disadvantage a segment of their population (women, blacks, or the marginally paid "working poor" in the United States are some obvious examples), others within that community are in turn advantaged. The disadvantaged suffer at the hands of the advantaged. In the sense that those advantaged may not wish to be benefited at the expense of another's suffering and may even strongly oppose it, the "lucky" one's are not "at fault": they are not, as it were, culpable. But in the sense that (want it or not) they gain an advantage at the expense of those less lucky and lead, as it were, better lives as a result, they are responsible for seeing to it that such conditions are ameliorated and eventually entirely changed. Depending on circumstance and context, responsibility and culpability are not equivalent concepts.

The poor, the racially or socially disadvantaged as well as persons who have little or no access to medical care suffer greatly. Persons who must watch while their perhaps more talented children or their children in need cannot avail themselves of educational and other opportunities which others less talented or less in need are afforded, suffer. When persons are unable to develop their individual talents or are frustrated in pursuing their interests and talents, suffering ensues. Such suffering is not individual suffering alone: communities suffer, and in today's world communities will ultimately perish if they fail to develop or greatly waste the talents and capabilities of their members. When more black males are allowed to languish in jail than are afforded a fair opportunity to go to college (as is the case in the United States today) not only do those jailed suffer: the community which is deprived of a pool of talented and potentially productive people whose talents are now wasted and whose potential remains unrealized, suffers. Such communities, compared to others in which such wastage does not occur, enjoy little solidarity, fail to develop as they otherwise could, and ultimately must perish.

Communities structured on a minimalist model inevitably will tend to have vast and often frozen class differences. Such communities, contrary to what they claim, do not in fact support individual liberties if by that is understood, among other things, the individual's capacity to flourish and to develop his/her talents. They may provide maximal opportunities of this sort to those who are well- or at least tolerably well-off. Minimalist communities have a good deal more poverty, hunger, and lack of at least higher educational opportunities than do communities which take their beneficent obligations more seriously. By not making the necessities of biological existence available to all, such communities fail to assure the most primitive conditions needed for the exercise of individual rights: knowing that we can freely speak or assemble is of little comfort when we are hungry or cold. By not making those things needed to avail oneself of reasonable opportunities freely available to all (things like higher education or good health care), such communities fail to assure the further conditions needed for individuals to flourish: intelligent and talented persons who have been prevented by economic conditions from developing their talents are not comforted by knowing that they would have been free to write and publish a masterpiece if only they could have learned how.

Communities constitute the setting in which class differences do or do not emerge and are or are not perpetuated. Provided they had the necessary resources to do so they could, had they so wished, structured themselves differently. They are, therefore, causally implicated. Those fortunate enough to have been born to wealthy parents will have opportunities to develop their talents; equivalent opportunities are denied those born to poorer parents. In turn, the offspring of the wealthy are likely to have the same chance as their parents. A frozen class structure is quite apt to result. Such a frozen structure not only brings about more suffering but likewise, by depriving such communities of the development of all its talents, prevents or at least slows down the progress communities can make. In turn this aggravates the original problem.

Minimalist communities are, therefore, on the horns of a dilemma. While such communities do not readily concede that beneficent obligations have moral force, they will concede that those who have caused direct harm to another have legitimate obligation to that person. Even the most libertarian community will hold the driver of a car that caused another's damage liable for the damages. When it can be demonstrated, therefore, that minimalist policies result in harm to their members, such communities will be hard pressed to deny redress.

Minimalist communities, unfortunately, readily find a way out of such a dilemma. Their answer is, of course, a totally individualistic one. In the minimalist view, communities came together primarily to vouchsafe individual liberty. This was and remains their single and overriding concern. Autonomy is far more than merely a very highly held value: it is the sole condition of morality itself. Unless that condition is satisfied as completely as possible, ethical action cannot occur; to the extent that the condition is not satisfied, to the extent that personal liberty except to vouchsafe everyone else's liberty is impinged upon, actions are not ethically permissible. Liberty, as Nozick puts it, is the "side-constraint" of morality: it is the condition which constrains all other possible rules.[17]

When individuals in minimalist communities cause damage by their immediate action, they may be liable. However, when the nature of the compact itself causes such harm, individuals cannot either be held liable (individuals did not cause specific harm by specific personal behavior) or, therefore, be expected to contribute to that which they themselves have not caused. Persons came together to prevent personal harm to each other so as to be better able to get on with their lives. If now their liberty would be infringed so as to help another who they themselves did not harm, the entire basis of the contract would be abrogated.

From a minimalist's perspective, the poor, the socially disadvantaged, or the sick are in an admittedly undesirable position; they are unfortunate and to be pitied; but they have been neither unfairly nor unjustly treated and they therefore have no morally valid claim against specific individuals or against society at large.[18] Homeostatic forces in minimalist communities oscillate about a very narrow range of individualistic values. This limits their ability to respond to outside or inside forces. Unless the range is reset and dynamic possibilities are restored, such societies have little flexibility to evolve, change, or adapt. Survival itself is put in jeopardy.

I do not claim that individuals are not implicated in many of the problems that befall them. Alcoholics who develop cirrhosis, smokers who come down with lung cancer, addicts who share needles and acquire AIDS, the person who has an opportunity to work but doesn't and therefore remains poor: all these are certainly implicated in their own fate. Such implication, however, is not by any means the only factor involved. Decisions to do or not to do certain things are heavily conditioned by the culture and community in which they are played out. Factors which the community could control (by, for example, controlling advertising or making greater efforts at education), social settings which are the result of the way in which the community has seen fit to structure itself, or which it has failed to pay attention to (by allowing the persistence of poverty areas in which hopelessness abounds so that opportunities are not even recognized) all play their part and cannot be dissociated from the "personal" or "individual" decision. That does not absolve individuals from responsibility for their fate; but it does denote that, depending on circumstances and conditions, culpability for one's fate is variable and that it is, in fact, never absolute. It is extremely difficult if not impossible to tease out the place where personal culpability begins and ends.

A case can certainly be made that under the right set of circumstances persons may be held virtually entirely responsible for what befalls them. Persons who go skydiving or motorcar racing generally know what they are doing and persons who rob banks not in order to survive but to enrich themselves have, without a doubt, made a largely (even if I do not grant it to be an entirely) deliberate choice. Some community participation cannot be argued away in either case: in the former case and at the very least communities permit and by their values and mores promote activities like skydiving or carracing. Communities constitute the setting which has allowed (or in some cases even fostered) the development of the criminal. But even when communal participation is tenuous or weak, communal responsibility to help those who come to harm does not end. Would one wash one's hand of the uninsured badly injured racing car driver or allow the robber, shot in the course of a holdup, to bleed to death? Beneficent communal obligations, even when the causal culpability of the community is minimal, necessitate coming to the aid of another.

The rhetoric of self-causation which would hold persons entirely responsible for their actions does, on further reflection, fail to make a plausible case. Individuals are necessarily far too intertwined with their communities to support a notion of stark individual responsibility. This does not mean that persons are not to be held accountable for their actions or, that they are not on the one hand blameworthy for their misdoings and on the other hand praiseworthy for acting well. But it does imply that such praiseworthiness or blameworthiness exists in a communal matrix which to some extent conditioned behavior if only by instituting explicit or tacit rewards or punishments. Such tacit rewards and punishments might include official praise or blame, might be seen to lead to altered insurance premiums (or in cases in which the state assumes responsibility might include involuntary higher taxation for health matters) but hardly in a community which considers itself both just and compassionate could, when callamity—even callamity brought on as a result of one's actions—be allowed to lead to social abandonment.

Moreover, I have and shall argue that: (1) communities have beneficent obligations regardless of individual merit towards all members of the community; (2) more powerful, larger, or more encompassing communities have beneficent obligations towards their constituent communities; and (3) individuals in community in turn are obligated to their community. Such obligations are intermeshing, interpenetrating, and not static. They are played out in a dynamic homeostatic relationship which simultaneously acts to promote stability within a framework of values and possibilities while allowing that interplay to gradually alter the frame itself so that evolution, growth, and, ultimately, survival can occur.

ESTABLISHING HIERARCHIES

It is not possible to either prevent or ameliorate all suffering. Inevitably at least some if not indeed most of our actions are prone to cause suffering to another. Trade-offs, as it were, have to be made and ways of making such choices in a just and equitable manner must be conceptualized and established. The capacity to suffer, which is what I claim gives an entity "primary worth," is a minimal condition: it gives moral standing to an entity and makes a mere object (which cannot suffer) into a subject (which can). Such a minimal condition makes the subject worthy of our serious attention. Likewise, the value invested by one who can suffer in objects which themselves would otherwise have no moral standing, lends such objects moral value "by reflection." Such objects, which I have called objects of "secondary worth," have such worth precisely because what happens to them is of interest to others for whom we have legitimate moral concern. I have further divided such secondary worth into "material" and "symbolic" worth and have claimed that, while primary worth is always positive, secondary worth can be either positive or negative. In the first chapter I gave a rather simple example from medical practice.

Having "moral worth" (whether that worth is primary or secondary) implies having "standing in court": not, of course or of necessity, a court of law but the "court" of judgment which must decide what is and what is not ethically allowable action. One could, of course, argue that in a day and age when our actions not only affect our immediate surrounding (our own polis, as it were) and our immediate time but have a greater or lesser ripple effect for far-flung others and for a distant future, all objects have some "moral worth" or moral standing.[13] Such a claim is, I believe, valid. The unowned and as yet undiscovered mine or oil well (or the owned forest) have distinct moral standing since any action which involves them may have protean implications. While this does not give them immunity, it does mean that we have to carefully evaluate what at first may seem simple usage either of our own or of no one's property. In a libertarian framework and with a minimalist ethic it would be hard to argue in this fashion: restricting our liberty to fashion whatever we will out of our own property whatever the consequences (unless such action immediately impinges on the freedom of equal others) would be unthinkable.

Our knowledge of nature and our ability to manipulate it for our ends inevitably has the potential of affecting the future well-being of others positively or, at times, devastatingly and irremediably. Therefore, our accumulation of knowledge which can have these consequences itself as well as our decisions of what we ought and what we ought not put at risk takes on a new moral dimension.[13] Our right to undisturbedly engage in this sort of Vabanque game with the future of others and the future of our earth itself is arguably limited. Considerations of care and responsibility are invoked, even if they are not invoked explicitly, when environmentalists afraid of seeing a species endangered or extinguished argue passionately for care in using nature. Destroying or seriously interfering with the working of nature may destroy or seriously damage our very future itself.

Having moral standing has several implications. At least, it: (1) gives a subject (or object) its "day in court" so that acting upon it is not a morally neutral thing; (2) implies that when an object has significant moral worth actions which are potentially harmful must be kept to a minimum (suffering must be minimized) in pursuit of a legitimate goal; and 3) counsels extreme care in all of our dealings not only with objects which are of immediate concern today but also in our dealings with abstract and concrete things which could significantly affect the future itself. Having moral standing, then, implies nothing absolute or guaranteeable besides having such standing. It is not absolute because, when all is said and done, such standing must be seen in relation to other individual and communal needs.

Moral worth, then, produces a formal condition whose particular application must be worked out. By itself having moral worth does not resolve the problem of moral standing. Primary moral worth (based on having the capacity to suffer) in that sense is somewhat akin to the "respect" which Kant's Categorical Imperative asserts all those capable of self-legislation deserve. Persons worthy of respect cannot be used merely as a means but become "ends in themselves." They have "dignity" or "worthiness": their intrinsic moral standing is absolute and, therefore, as Kant puts it, "beyond price." Objects of what I am calling "secondary worth," however, are, in the Kantian system, not those worthy of respect. They have "value": i.e., their value is not "beyond price," not absolute. At least in theory a price can be assigned to them. In the Kantian system, such value can be either "material" ("*Marktpreis*") or aesthetic ("*Affektionspreis*").[6] This category is reminiscent of secondary worth in its material and symbolic representation.

The system I propose owes much to Kant but has some essential differences. It differs in at least two rather fundamental respects: (1) Moral standing is derived from the capacity to suffer (a much more fundamental capacity) instead of being derived from the capacity to self-legislate (a much higher capacity); and (2) moral standing, even primary worth, is not like the respect owed to self-legislating beings: it is not absolute but can be overridden by weighty considerations. A third point of difference is less fundamental: variable moral standing is also given to objects which, while they lack intrinsic worth, have moral worth because of their value for those who themselves have intrinsic value. In the system I propose knowledge itself has moral worth: it must itself be considered as having moral, and potentially morally devastating, effects for the future existence of those who have primary worth. Some time ago, in a system suggested by Hans Jonas, the very future itself was given moral standing.[13] Since entities of primary as well as secondary worth are not absolute, trade-offs between them are, at least conceptually, possible to make. In today's world with the capacities we have today, it is difficult to imagine very many significant objects entirely devoid of moral standing. Obviously, if such a system is to be useful at all, some hierarchies of value, some method of valuing, and some procedural avenues of approach to delineating such hierarchies needs to be established.

Determining hierarchies of value so that individual as well as communal choices between different things, all of which have some sort of value, can be made, requires a framework of decision making. Such a framework can be viewed, just as truth, either as "discoverable" or as "structurable": either we attempt to discover some unchanging principle or value of God or nature according to which such decisions can be made or we attempt to fashion guidelines in full realization that they are neither enduring nor immutable. The underlying premise throughout has been that "truths" are human constructs rather than being discoverable. Such a thesis, of course, cannot be proven: we cannot know that tomorrow someone will not come up with an entirely convincing proof of such a discovery. All we can say is that this has never happened and that the likelihood of it happening is small. On the other hand, we can show that humans have been evermore successful (sometimes devastatingly so) in fashioning their truths, at structuring their systems, and at manipulating their environment. Certainly this has hardly been an entirely upward progression in the moral and social sphere; we have slipped back, at times disastrously so. But when one takes a long historical view, slow progress (if this is measured in terms of our ability to affect nature, of human happiness and of human possibilities) has occurred. In the real world, we must act and cannot wait for the discovery of truth itself: we are left with fashioning our truths and structuring our systems as best we can.

If we acknowledge that fallible humans will have to shape

their hierarchies and produce their guidelines, one can leave such decisions to one all-powerful and all-wise individual (a sort of "philosopher king" as it were), can leave it to a set of somehow determined "experts," or one can rely on communal process to achieve such an end. Philosopher kings are not easy to come by and when they are supposedly "found" they have universally proven to be a disappointment if not indeed a disaster. Like discoverable truths they may be appealing in theory but wanting in practice. Leaving such decisions purely to the "experts" (as contrasted to using such carefully fashioned "experts" as advisors), is likewise a dangerous thing. It threatens to allow technically rather than broadly trained individuals to make decisions which ultimately and inevitably affect all of us without leaving us recourse or redress. Such "experts," when left to their own devices and given sufficient power, tend to become autocrats whose chief occupations is self-perpetuation. Neither the "philosopher king" nor a resort to a series of "experts" has worked. Communities, properly fashioned and carefully structured, are, I believe, the proper instrumentalities for such choices: they are not ideal but they are far better than other available alternatives. The way I envision hierarchies as being constructed will give primacy to the community in making such choices. Lest I be accused of vagueness, I do not propose a vague notion of community which by some mysterious process and in some uncertain way comes up with such choices. Rousseau's expression of the " volente general" (the "common will") is not some mystic evolution of spiritual forces in the way I conceive it. I propose a fundamental notion of community in which (1) an initial communal dialogue about issues takes place; (2) "experts" serve as trusted and as trustworthy advisors when communal decisions must be taken; and (3) an eventual and fair legislative process affirms such communal decisions in its laws.

Of course, such a process (1) requires a framework for holding such a dialogue; (2) necessitates developing "experts" in ways which includes not only their technical expertise but also their moral development in and by their community; and (3) and above all, and so as to make the whole workable, presupposes an educated, alert, and interested electorate (something which in today's America is hardly present).

Such presuppositions constitute an essential reason for structuring communities so that persons not only are assured of equal access to those things necessary to sustain life itself but also are given a fair and equal opportunity to develop their talents and fulfill their possibilities. Communities which do not provide such opportunities, communities in which poverty oppresses many and a lack of opportunity for some talented segments of the population is wanting, are not communities which can fruitfully engage in such a dialogue, develop morally sensitive and technically well trained "experts," or have a fair and representative legislative process. The presupposition for proper communal action is a fair and just community itself. This may at first glance appear circular: to make good decisions, decisions which are just, equitable, and which promote community cohesion, solidarity, and survival, a fair and just community which can make such decisions is needed in the first place. Further reflection, however, will show that unless such a community can be achieved little progress can be made. Our first task, then, is to fashion a workable and working community. It is not a hopeless task and is done, like all else, in an ongoing manner which includes trial and error, success and failure.

Our starting point, then, in delineating hierarchies is to look at our particular society. Where it is found wanting, we must begin to devise remedies and affect changes. This is an ongoing process; as collectives becomes firmer, juster, and as individuals develop the sense that what they are about improves their condition and their lives, trust and then solidarity and cohesion will grow. When this occurs the ability of community to engage in constructive dialogue, to create trusted and trustworthy "experts," and to develop fair legislative process will likewise be enhanced. Fundamental to this vision of communal process then, is not only access to those things needed to sustain life itself but likewise to those things promoting a "fair opportunity range" for all.[19] Not only is justice served: providing a "fair opportunity range" enhances communal evolution and survival itself.

As a point of departure one may profitably look at America and its market-oriented system today. Abject poverty is hardly rare and lack of equal educational opportunity forces many in the poorer classes to go with their talents and abilities under- or entirely un-developed. American poverty areas are breeding grounds of hopelessness, crime, and violence. The quality of even primary and secondary education is unequal for the wealthy and the poor. Higher educational opportunities are only grudgingly, sporadically, and often capriciously given to some among the poor. Worse, most who grow up in traditional poverty areas where poverty is the main article inherited from their parents and grandparents, cannot even imagine such opportunities or conceive of what to do with them even if they know of their presence. Their future is foreclosed by their milieu and by other social forces long before they are of an age at which such choices can be made. Even the very notion of hope has often been crushed. True poverty cannot be measured in terms of income or possession; true poverty consists of a tradition of hopelessness and despair. The fact that many in such conditions turn to drugs and to crime is not only understandable but is, indeed, predictable.

The well-acknowledged fact that the sense of community in today's America is sorely wanting cannot come as a surprise. It is difficult when one lacks the basic necessities of life and lives surrounded by drugs and crime in a society in which violence is the daily fare of the main available source of amusement, to envision educational opportunities or to develop more than a very self-serving idea of obligation. Educational opportunities, furthermore, even when a person has survived his/her tradition of hopelessness and by dint of luck or superhuman effort on their or their parent's part has become aware of achievable goals and available opportunities, are sparse. They are largely available only to those who have incredible talents or/and to those willing to accept a crushing load of loans or stipulations which already foreclose a future most cannot even imagine. It is not surprising that in America today there are more young Afro-American males in jail than there are in colleges, that drug usage, AIDS, and crime are rampant in our ghettos and that violence, drugs, and crime infiltrate the wealthier areas no matter how such areas try to insulate themselves from reality.

A favorite charge leveled by the middle and wealthier classes in America today against the traditional poor, is that "they" are lazy and anxious only to stay "on welfare" (the implication is that this is somehow a genetic trait which has largely spared those who are better off, especially if those who are better off are white and preferably native-born Americans). Either such persons are what they are, so the argument goes, because they are genetically inferior (this, in polite society is not discussed but is, nevertheless, often assumed to be the case) or such persons are blamed for bringing on their problems themselves. Such persons are then held responsible for their own disadvantaging. After all, it is argued, the "opportunities are there." And at once classified newspaper ads listing jobs are produced and a few token persons who have managed to escape from their abysmal situation are pointed to. The fact that most jobs are either in areas to which those needing them most have no access or that those who have managed to escape have done so by dint of peculiarly fortunate and often unique combinations of personal luck and personal skill is not mentioned.

At times, population groups that worked themselves out of supposedly similar poverty are held up as examples which could allegedly be easily followed. Such population groups (say, Jewish immigrants on the East Side of New York or other poor immigrants in the more recent or more distant past) are contrasted to the traditionally poor: especially, of course, to Blacks. It is assumed that the traditionally poor "could, if they would," that they need only "pull themselves up by the bootstraps," and that it is either their genetic predisposition or their lack of personal gumption which prevents them from achieving all the wonderful things America has to offer.

These assumptions rest on critical errors. They ignore both psychology and history. There are indeed population groups many of whose members have worked themselves out of similar material conditions. But such population groups enjoyed a rather different history and they were, for historical reasons, not as readily saddled with a psychology of hopelessness and despair. In general, such population groups came from a background in which a strong family structure and respect for education was traditional. Often they had a tradition of "self-help" and institutions to implement such help. They may have been materially poor, even crushingly poor, at times: but they were not in poverty in the same sense as are some of these others. Lack of opportunity had not become institutionalized and hopelessness had not been handed down from their ancestors. Education traditionally had been productive for these groups: Education, instead of being punished and having negative survival value, was rewarded in some tangible and intangible ways. The comparison between such population groups and others lacks force: most population groups, so to speak, at least had boots whose straps could be pulled!

The population groups in the United States most generally thought of when one thinks of the traditionally poor are either Afro-American or what has been referred to as "white trash" (implying, of course, that whites are different from non-whites; whites are generally not thought of when one thinks so charitably of "trash": the assumption is that whites are not generally "trash" to begin with!). As every child knows (or, with a decent, thoughtful, and truthful educational system would know) Afro-Americans have had a rather different history. Not only were they slaves whose families were frequently and callously crushed and who were discouraged and frequently cruelly punished for even the most primitive attempts at getting an education less than one hundred and fifty years ago, their emergence from slavery was arranged so as to inevitably return blacks to a different and in many respects more vicious form of slavery. When slavery ended and blacks began to make astounding progress, when blacks began to educate themselves successfully and even began, in some places, to make common cause with poor southern whites, Washington's initial help and protection was abruptly withdrawn and the very same elements responsible for slavery were allowed to re-assert themselves. When blacks came North, they found not only hostility but a system in which employers saw them as a God-sent supply of cheap labor. They were easily exploitable and in the industrialized world exploitation in a form other than physical slavery had become more profitable.

Blacks found that in order to survive, they had to accept a minimal wage and live in separate areas. Their wage barely supplied life's necessities. Rents were high and overcrowding resulted. Poor whites, even the few who were inclined to make common cause with their poor black neighbors, were manipulated into seeing their black neighbors as competitors for the little there was and to hate and despise them. When tentative coalitions were attempted the Klan rode, killed, and burned. And the law winked or gave the Klan explicit or at least tacit approval. Any possible coalition with poor whites was smashed. The system, down to today, provided either no education or education which was largely inferior. There was little incentive to avail oneself of the educational opportunities, bad as they were. Family structure was never able to become secure: in former days, the father was apt to be in fact "sold down the river"; in modern times the same results were achieved by creating a welfare structure which discouraged and continues to discourage family unity and cohesion. It is often more profitable—indeed it is sometimes the only way in which children can survive—for fathers to leave the family and allow the mother to fend for herself. It is not rare that husbands will secretly visit their wives because living together openly would jeopardize their family's survival.

Until communities see themselves as units and not as fragmented and basically hostile groups, any notion of peaceful communal action remains moot. In later chapters I will sketch the interrelationship between diverse communities, a relationship which is as critical for survival of the larger and ultimately the world community as is the relationships between individuals and their communities. None of us, whether individual or community, exists out of context with their neighbor. Racism, based on the implicit assumption that the stranger is an enemy,[20] makes a sham out of any notion of community. Nationalism based not on a notion of national difference but on the notion of implicit national superiority likewise makes a wider notion of community impossible. In fashioning workable and meaningful hierarchies, then, I place primacy on structuring community as the necessary condition of further development. In the view I have espoused, a sense of obligation develops in individuals in the embrace of community. Without community and its nurturing, individuals could not endure long enough to become first aware of their selfness; without community and its nurturing, selves could not become aware first of the notion of obligations and, later, of the specific nature of their obligations. Moral development is necessarily given its early impetus in the embrace of beneficence and nurture. These are the early conditions during which selfhood, compassion, and a notion of obligation first necessarily develop.

Later experience and education mold and shape our specific ideas of specific obligations. The type of community we experience early in life and the kind of education afforded us modify, but cannot entirely eliminate, all of these early experiences and their inevitable etching. When experiences and education are conducive to developing a generous personality, such a personality is more apt to develop; when later experiences show the developing individual that opportunities are arbitrarily closed to them and when education stresses and often glorifies ruthless competition with others, an individualistic notion of obligations ripens.

As it stands today, the American community assigns an extremely high value to individualism and personal freedom while slightly ameliorating devastating social conditions by grudgingly supplying minimal necessities to those who are in the most abject poverty. The American ideal is personal success of the most crassly materialistic kind, resulting in immense personal wealth and in an oppulent lifestyle. A generally unwarranted belief that one can personally achieve such success (and a feeling that we owe others very little except to leave them alone) makes many persons blind or callous to the actual conditions about them. The American educational system does much to perpetuate the myth that all can achieve whatever they want if they would only truly try. Reform of the social system, structuring community, and ultimately making peaceful communal choices is possible only if an educational system favorable to such a venture can be constructed. As a more cohesive community takes shape it will have to grapple with enunciating and shaping its values. This activity is one which, if we are to succeed, must be promptly started. Unless values are tentatively determined, tried, found useful or wanting and then adapted in an ongoing manner, community itself cannot reconstruct itself and endure.

In setting hierarchies we cannot allow ourselves to be paralyzed. However shoddy our community, however deplorable our conditions, the work of shaping our values and determining our hierarchies must go forth. Only in such an ongoing way can community itself evolve. And while I have largely spoken of America, conditions in the rest of the world are likewise far from ideal. On the one hand, the former Bolshevik system was, even if in a different way, just as destructive to human survival, dignity, and, ultimately, community as is American capitalism. The underdeveloped, or so called "third world," has in many respects held the same position vis-à-vis the industrialized nations as Afro-Americans have held within American society: they were and are seen as eminently exploitable and, therefore, are exploited. Areas in which far better conditions pertain, much of the European community and in particular the Scandinavian countries, likewise continue to have some problems, problems which some want to "solve" by introducing a more dominant market system, a solution which others (including myself) think would severely compound rather than solve these problems. Basic to all such solutions is a grappling with values and a setting of priorities and hierarchies accordingly.

When it comes to grappling with values and delineating obligations, obligations of not causing needless suffering to others will be accepted by most. At any rate, at least lip service will be paid to such obligations. Obligations of ameliorating suffering are more apt to grow out of nurturing communities: communities in which the necessities of life are assured and in which opportunities to unfold one's personality and develop one's talents are not arbitrarily foreclosed, are apt to develop a broader sense of obligation in their members than are communities in which the necessities of life are tenuously provided and opportunities to unfold one's personality and develop one's talents are arbitrarily available to some and not given to others. When I speak of hierarchies as inevitably set by and in communities, such considerations play a significant role.

In Kant's system, being deserving of respect—being able to self-legislate—gives one absolute value and allows of no compromise. Using the language of "moral worth" or moral standing, the capacity to self-legislate is what gives primary worth. In the Kantian system, once an entity has primary worth, hierarchies cannot be carved out. If one answers the question of moral standing by claiming that the capacity to suffer is what gives one primary worth, one can either "hook into" or not "hook into" the Kantian system. One can leave Kant's edifice largely intact by superimposing it on the new: one can say that while the capacity to suffer gives one moral standing such standing becomes absolute only once the capacity to self-legislate is present. Such a system would, for example, give relative moral standing to all those capable of suffering until creatures with the capacity to self-legislate were to be reached: at that point standing becomes absolute. Or one can consider that all forms, be they self-legislating or not, have, in the final analysis, only relative standing. In a system in which those with the capacity to self-legislate are given absolute standing one would be unable to make choices between or among people when it comes to allocating limited resources:

habitual ax murderers whose delight it is to cause suffering to others would have the same moral standing as would those who had spent their lives caring for and helping others at great personal sacrifice. Both would have to have equal standing when it comes to receiving a heart transplant and a lottery might be the only way left to choose. In a more flexible system, while the capacity to self-legislate might have considerable weight in the adjudication, it would still have only relative value.

Realistically, it is difficult to "hook into" the Kantian system. Doing so would force us into a position in which one could not choose between entities all of whom required (absolute) respect. The choice between the ax murderer and the philanthropist could not be made and would, at best, be left to a lottery. The Kantian system as it stands has other problems. If we are to assign absolute value to persons with the capacity to self-legislate, then no choice, under any circumstances, between such a person and an entity also of primary worth or one of secondary worth could ever be conceivably made. But this also fails to be convincing. Choosing between the habitual ax murderer and a loyal dog (who, at least according to Kant—although I would dispute this—cannot self-legislate), we would have to choose the ax murderer. This too leaves at least many of us unconvinced.

Furthermore, one does not have to think of situations which are quite as extreme as the ax murderer and the altruist. We must choose between persons when allocating organs or when devising systems of rationing. Rationing of health care, for example, inevitably means that we will have to make choices in which certain persons or certain persons with certain conditions are sacrificed. Even though many in America today cling to the belief that rationing of such resources as health-care or education does not take place, rationing is, indeed, the order of the day. Whenever something that humans want is limited some form of rationing is inevitable. Rationing, as it plays itself out in America today, is done by the market: those who can afford (by insurance or otherwise) health care and those who can afford (themselves, through their parents, or by scholarships or loans) higher education will get it; others will not. In such a system the choices are clear: some persons of primary worth will receive and others will not receive services which ultimately spell life and death, comfort or despair, opportunity or lack thereof. To say that we do not make such choices is to compound injustice with hypocrisy.

Moreover, at times communities make quite deliberate choices in which they show a preference for articles of secondary worth over beings of primary worth, even over beings who certainly have the capacity to self-legislate. Sometimes such choices are indefensible: one can get along without some extremely dangerous undertakings. But sometimes societies could not go about their business without such decisions. When coal is mined, skyscrapers are built, police or fire brigades are constituted, or speed limits are set for a given speed, we know that a certain number of persons who can self-legislate will inevitably be killed. True, they themselves have chosen to mine coal, build sky scrapers, stop crime, extinguish fires, or drive at certain speeds: but they have been provided at least with this opportunity by a society which would find it impossible to get along without these activities. (I will leave undiscussed the question of voluntariness in many of these circumstances. When persons take on extremely dangerous jobs in our particular society it may be and often is a free choice in form only: when no other jobs are available and the livelihood of one's family is at stake the voluntariness of such choices may legitimately be questioned.) It may be nice to buy into the Kantian system of absolute standing (and, as I shall argue, at some point we may indeed have to) but if communities are to get on with their work, they will be hard pressed to do so.

Certain choices, however, become so dangerous and may set such a socially destructive precedent that they are felt to be impermissible. This is a variation of the slippery slope argument which says that when we do certain things we inevitably open the door to others. If we are to overtly ration health care or if we are to choose between persons who are to receive a desperately needed organ, some have argued, we are opening the door to a disrespect which, ultimately, may lead to Auschwitz. Arguments of the slippery slope kind are not in themselves persuasive: many if not most human activities can be looked upon as slippery slopes. Having a good dinner or a glass of wine with dinner may lead to gluttony or drunkenness. Giving an injection of morphine to a patient may start an addiction. The possibility, no matter how remote, exists. The fat may, indeed, be in the fire. But that does not stop us from eating dinner, drinking wine, or giving injections of morphine. We calculate the risk, take appropriate precautions and then get on with what we feel needs to be done. Slippery slopes, in real life, should encourage one to be cautious and, where necessary, "to put down sand"; slippery slopes should not stop driving altogether. True, some slopes are so slippery, some actions set such a dangerous precedent or open up such terrible and immediate possibilities that prudence would incline one not to pursue them.[21] Sand, we feel, no longer suffices: barriers, at times arbitrary in that they are erected in one rather than in an earlier or later place, must be erected. Distinguishing between degrees of slipperiness, deciding when to put down sand and when to erect barriers rather than resorting to the argument that "something is a slippery slope and, therefore, is not to be done" is the better part of wisdom. It requires discernment and judgment, and is an activity communities and their expert advisors properly engage in in an ongoing fashion.

In that sense we can decide at some point to arbitrarily hook into the Kantian system of absolute worth, deciding that not to grant such standing is apt to be socially destructive. A particular point at which "absolute worth" is granted for here and now may have to be decided. But the conception of what is and what is not deemed to be of such "absolute worth" is liable to change with circumstance and experience. During times of relative plenty, one may decide that judgments about whom to operate on after an injury and whom to allow to die must not be made; during times of extreme scarcity (be it a scarcity of resources or of time) such choices regrettably become necessary. Triage, be it triage on the battlefield or in the emergency room, is at times unavoidable. As humans we have the choice of making such triage decisions on the spur of the moment, leaving them to the individual caprice of the person deemed to be in charge, or we have the choice of sorting and sifting as much as is possible beforehand by at least setting up certain categories and establishing certain hierarchies in a more reasonable, equitable, and productive way. The place we can afford to hook into the Kantian system depends upon the situation we actually face as well as upon the kind of community we actually conceive ourselves to be.

I would suggest that in general and for the most part entities of "primary worth" (entities which have the capacity to suffer) have a higher hierarchical standing than do objects of "secondary worth." But even this is not absolute. When a choice between the existence of Notre Dame cathedral and, for example, a mouse has to be made such a statement loses some of its initial intuitive appeal. Likewise, when an arsonist is about to destroy the cathedral or when Hitler decides to try to burn Paris and when perhaps the only way to stop either is to shoot the arsonist or to destroy Hitler, those of primary worth may, ultimately and some would argue justifiably, lose out. Not even here can an absolute be defended on a pragmatic basis. My argument is that a Kantian system in which somewhere an entity is given absolute standing is a system which societies must resort to when they erect barriers and say, "so far and no further." It is a system which has much merit in a given context but it is not a system which established for one situation or context necessarily will be found adaptable to another.

As society with its needs and resources is constituted today, we can afford to set an arbitrary line and to give at least almost absolute, and under most circumstances unquestioned absolute standing to all humans who have the capacity to suffer. I do not suggest that merely being human is what gives one such standing. Rather, I am suggesting that humans who do not have the capacity to suffer have a far different standing, a standing which, under some circumstances, may be less than that of non-humans who can suffer. Beyond the capacity to suffer, I suggest that the degree of capacity for formulating hopes, aspirations, and life plans plays a part in setting such hierarchies. In such a system an intelligent monkey may have far higher standing than a barely conscious demented person and certainly far more than an anencephalic infant. By virtue of a deeper capacity for suffering, a deeper capacity for sentience, and, therefore, perhaps a more profound capacity to suffer, an intelligent monkey would have higher standing than would a pigeon.

As some see it, this type of approach runs the danger of allowing us to do what we must not do: differentiate not only between non-humans and humans but also among humans depending upon their capacity for formulating hopes, life plans, and aspirations. Such fears are often expressed and are not unwarranted. The fact that we now differentiate between humans in making critical choices immediately affecting their chance for living and their lives and that, at least in America, we generally base such choices on their ability or inability to pay is not an acceptable excuse for allowing us to make such choices in the first place: it merely establishes a perhaps regrettable empirical fact but does not speak to the permissibility of making such choices. While some may think it proper to make choices of this kind in some way and may, indeed, argue as I do that making such choices is inevitable, making such choices merely on the capacity to formulate hopes, life plans and aspirations may, indeed, be dangerous. Among other things, using such a criterion, aside from the difficulty of determining what shall count as "better" or more worthwhile hopes, plans and aspirations, may well be the very point at which a slippery slope becomes so slippery that barriers need to be erected. We cannot as a community afford to make such differentials not only because judging whose life plans, hopes and aspirations are more worthy is difficult if not indeed impossible, but because it is not necessarily a foregone conclusion that the ability to do this denotes a higher capacity to suffer. Those who are mentally impaired (the senile, the mentally retarded, the simple) have a particularly poignant relationship to their environment and to others. When their experiences have allowed it, they easily develop a sense of trust in the nurturing and loving nature of those around them. Since they often cannot understand elaborate plans and goals, they often cannot comprehend that disagreeable or painful procedures are "done for their good" as can normal persons. Therefore, when medical treatment, for example, is necessary there is the great danger of disrupting their prior trust and making their life worse rather than better. They suffer in a different way.[22] Making a choice between a human being who cannot suffer at all and another human or non-human being who can suffer is a far different thing than making a choice between two humans on the basis of their degree of sentience. A choice between a human who has lost the capacity to suffer (who is permanently vegetative, permanently in coma, brain dead or anencephalic) and another creature who can suffer is not as difficult as choosing between humans who, to a different extent, can. (Many of us would give precedence to a creature with the capacity to suffer over a creature without that capacity.) The argument here is not that making such a choice is inherently and by some ethical (and not by some religious) principle "wrong," but rather that doing so runs a great danger of leading to an uncontrollable slide. It is at this point that communities may be well advised not only to put down sand but to erect barriers.

When all is said and done, communities, no matter how defective they may currently be, will have to start grappling with such choices and setting such hierarchies. In turn, the process of grappling with such choices may foster the building of juster, healthier, and more enduring community.

COMMUNITY AND ITS MORAL STANDING

If what I have said so far about suffering, communities, and the role communities play in human lives seems reasonable, community as a concept and communities as particular realities themselves must have some moral standing. While it can be argued that communities can and do suffer, and that, therefore, they have primary worth, such suffering is too abstract, mysterious, and almost mythical a notion to be translatable into concrete action. One can base one's argument for the moral standing of community on two notions: (1) One may argue that community, since it is properly and at least to some extent valued by all of its members, has secondary worth. Such worth then would be material in affording protection to its members as well as creating those conditions of life conducive to personal survival and flourishing; symbolic in that it stands for an idea and an ideal as well as being a particular, concrete entity. Desirable communities, furthermore, could be seen to have positive worth while largely undesirable communities could be seen as having largely negative worth. Or (2) one may argue that communities have neither primary nor secondary worth but are the necessary condition for any valuing to take place. Their moral value, therefore, would be a prior one. Communities could be seen as having "prior worth." In that sense one could analogize having community to being alive: both being alive and having community are the necessary but insufficient conditions of experience. These aguments are not mutually exclusive but rather, as I shall show, are mutually reinforcing.

Life, in the way we commonly use the term, includes elements of what the Greeks differentiate as *zoe* and *bios*: the one biological existence and the other life as it is lived with its hopes, aspirations, and life plans.[23] The difference between these two is the difference between "being alive" and "having a life." Since "being alive" is the necessary condition for "having a life," killing is held by many to be wrong not so much because killing a person extinguishes biological existence but because killing a person eliminates the necessary condition for having (or leading) a life.[24] Being alive is the form, having a life is the content.

I shall argue that there is an analogy between the broad notion of life and the broad notion of community. Both these notions, depending on their usage, may refer to two different things: to a necessary condition or to the way it is then fleshed out. In that view community is both a necessary condition of valuing (and, therefore, has "prior worth") and beyond this and depending on the way it is then constructed, community is of secondary worth. In that sense it constitutes both necessary form and content. The idea of community is form in a symbolic sense, the way it is fleshed out gives material expression to this symbolic idea. The reality of community constructs the symbol and the way we see the symbol in turn inevitably shapes reality.

Community as having secondary worth can be conceived both positively and negatively depending upon the way the symbol of community has been translated into the reality of daily life. When communities have strong positive worth (when persons within them are not made to suffer arbitrarily, when their inevitable suffering is, to the extent possible ameliorated, when persons are fairly treated, reasonably prosperous and capable of pursuing their life plans) acting so as to disrupt such communities is arguably a destructive act; when communities have strongly negative attributes (when persons within them suffer arbitrarily, when suffering which could easily be ameliorated is allowed to continue, when persons are inequitably treated, are in poverty, or are deprived of equal opportunity) disrupting and even destroying such communities can sometimes be justified. Destroying, rather than working peacefully to reshape, a specific particular community, however, is acceptable only as a last and desperate measure when all other attempts to restructure community fail. Inevitably, destruction of a particular community leaves behind a conceptual and actual void.

Community as a necessary condition, the idea of community or its symbolic representation, is a critically important concept. Destroying the concept itself is quite another matter than destroying a specific vision of the concept. Destroying a specific vision, when it must be done, is morally only thinkable when the vision of community itself is maintained. If that is not the case, when the idea of community itself is lost, anarchy results. Specific communities may be destructive of the idea of community itself and disruptive to its solidarity. When that is the case, when communities lack solidarity and stability and for essential purposes fall apart, there may be nothing in their place and anarchy once again is the outcome. Man cannot endure and prosper, evolve or survive without community.

Under most circumstances, it is preferable to slowly alter a system than to break it. Even when one has a different thing to put in its place, a slower changeover is likely to be less painful and more productive: it is likely to be associated with less suffering. This, however, is not always possible. As a last resort, before a community is allowed to destroy itself leaving no vision of any community in its place, forceful action underpinned by a definite plan and idea may become necessary. When this is the case, homeostatic mechanisms have failed. In what is to come I shall examine some of these mechanisms as they apply not only to a balance between individuals and their community but also as they pertain to an interrelationship among communities themselves.

REFERENCES

1. Lipton P: *Inference to the Best Explanation*. London, England: Routledge; 1991.

2. Dewey J: *The Quest for Certainty*. In: Boydston JA: *The Later Works of John Dewey, Vol. 4*. Carbondale, IL: Southern Illinois University Press; 1988.

3. Dewey J: *Logic, the Theory of Inquiry*. In: Boydston JA: *The Later Works of John Dewey, Vol. 12*. Carbondale, IL: Southern Illinois University Press; 1991.

4. Loewy EH: *Suffering and the Beneficent Community: Beyond Libertarianism*. Albany, NY: SUNY Press; 1991.

5. Rousseau JJ: *Emile: ou, de l'Education* . Paris, France: Garnier Freres; 1957.

6. Kant I: *Grundlegung zur Metaphysik der Sitten*. In: *Immanuel Kant Kritik der Praktischen Vernunft, Grundlegung zur Metaphysik der Sitten*. Band VII (Wilhelm Weischedel, ed.). Frankfurt a/M, Deutschland: Suhrkamp Verlag; 1989.

7. Arendt H: *Lectures on Kant's Political Philosophy.* Chicago, IL: University of Chicago Press; 1982.

8. Heubel F: Misunderstanding Kant. Paper given at meeting of the European Society for the Philosophy of Medicine and Health Care, Oxford, UK; July 1991.

9. Kant I: Foundations of the Metaphysics of Morals (L. W. Beck, trans.). New York, NY: Macmillan Publishing Co.; 1986.

10. Dewey J: *Reconstruction in Philosophy.* In: *John Dewey: The Middle Works.* Vol XII (J. A. Boydston and B. A. Walsh, eds.). Carbondale, IL: Southern Illinois University Press 1988.

11. Dennet DC: *Elbow Room: The Varieties of Free Will Worth Having.* Cambridge, MA: MIT Press; 1985.

12. Hampshire S: *Innocence and Experience.* Cambridge, MA: Harvard University Press; 1989.

13. Jonas H: *Das Prinzip Verantwortung.* Frankfurt a/M, Deutschland: Suhrkamp; 1984.

14. Hobbes T: *Leviathan.* New York, NY: Collier; 1962.

15. Jensen UJ: Are Selves Real? In: *Harré and His Critics* (Roy Shaskar, ed.). Oxford, England: Basic Blackwell; 1990.

16. Springer-Loewy RA: An Alternative to Traditional Models of Human Relationships. Cambridge Quarterly; 1993 (in press).

17. Nozick R: *Anarchy, State and Utopia.* New York, NY: Basic Books; 1974.

18. Engelhardt HT: Health Care Allocation: Response to the Unjust, the Unfortunate and the Undesirable. In: *Justice and Health Care* (E. E. Shelp, ed.). Dordrecht, The Netherlands: D. Reidel; 1981.

19. Daniels N: *Just Health Care.* New York, NY: Cambridge University Press; 1985.

21. Levi P: *Survival in Auschwitz: The Nazi Assault on Humanity* (Stuart Woolf, trans.). New York, NY: Collier Macmillan Publishers; 1986.

22. Loewy EH: Drunks, Livers and Values: Should Social Value Judgments Enter into Transplant Decisions? J Clinical Gastroenterology 1987; 9(4): 436-441.

23. Loewy EH: Treatment Decisions in the Mentally Impaired: Limiting but not Abandoning Treatment. NEJM 1987; 317: 1465-1469.

24. Kushner T: Having a Life versus Being Alive. J Med Ethics 1984; 1: 5-8.

25. Rachels J: *The End of Life.* New York, NY: Oxford University Press; 1986.

CHAPTER 4

The Homeostatic Balance between Freedom and Community

In prior chapters, I have argued for an ethic which gives moral standing to (1) entities because of their capacity to suffer, and I've called such entities entities of primary worth; (2) other things because of their present or potential value for those of primary worth and I've termed this secondary worth; as well as (3) the future itself and to those things that affect it. I have then gone on to (1) sketch methods of delineating hierarchies of worth within and among such categories; (2) discuss a communally based ethic which is based on the inevitable beneficence and nurture experienced by all infants prior to the emergence of their autonomy; and (3) derived from this a viewpoint of community in which neither individual nor community interests predominate but in which both serve the common goal of survival, growth, and learning. In addition, I have sketched (1) a method of justification beyond that of pure deductive reasoning and (2) connected the notion of suffering as a grounding condition for ethics with the idea and value of community. This has led to giving moral standing to community itself, first because it is the necessary condition of valuing (and therefore of "prior worth") and beyond this, and depending on the way community is then constructed, have given moral value to community because of the role it plays in the lives of its members. So far we have alluded to the relationship between the needs of the individual for self-realization and free expression and the requirement of the community for incorporating such yearnings into a structure which strives for the common good.

In this work I have argued and shall continue to argue that one needs to go far beyond previous attempts to see a dialectic relationship between communal interests in the welfare of all its members and its consequent obligations (beneficence) on the one hand and the striving of individuals for autonomy (freedom or individual rights) on the other hand. I have begun to develop a notion in which the ends and means of both community and individual interact to produce a homeostatic balance. I will pursue this task by (1) looking somewhat more closely at the interrelationship between nurture, individuality and community; (2) examining the concept of homeostasis more carefully and showing how the balancing of individual interests with the interests of community relates to such a concept; and (3) concluding that a healthy balance of this sort is conducive to communal solidarity, evolution, growth, and survival.

INTERRELATING NURTURE, INDIVIDUALITY, AND COMMUNITY

In the past the relationship between individual and communal interests has generally been pictured as a competitive one, a dialectic whose tension develops out of the clash between autonomy (or individual rights) and beneficence (or social justice).[1] In a previous chapter, I have suggested that the relationship can be more fruitfully perceived as a homeostatic balance in which supposedly conflicting elements in seeking a resolution envision the same goals. Individual survival is so enmeshed with the well-being and survival of the community and every other being within it, and the community is so dependent upon the flourishing of its individual members, that seeing this balance as a struggle may well be the wrong picture.

A model of competition and struggle fits well into a Capitalist vision of humanity. The misinterpretation of Darwin and of the evolutionary idea which he developed takes its origin largely from such a concept. What is today called (and I believe wrongly called) social Darwinism sees such a struggle as ultimately beneficial in eliminating "weaker" and, by implication, less desirable members of the community. Extending this view logically leads to the proposition that interfering with such a process is mischievous and ultimately harmful to society. Supporting our poor (at least our "undeserving" poor: there must be those since one always speaks of the "deserving" ones!) or helping out those who have failed (materially failed, at any rate) in the race is ultimately socially destructive. It is socially destructive because according to such a view of Darwin's works doing so must result in breeding more and more of the "unfit" who will procreate, weigh down, and ultimately destroy society.

The theory of natural selection (or Darwinism as it is sometimes called) states that there are individual differences within a species and that some of these occur by chance. Some of these differences, furthermore, are heritable. Such differences may confer advantages or disadvantages on the individual when it comes to personal survival or when it comes to reproduction. Those who fare best will be able to leave more of their own genes behind. Such advantages or disadvantages when heritable give an advantage or disadvantage for survival to this particular type of animal or species. Disadvantages tend to extinguish themselves while advantages tend to establish themselves and to become the characteristics of a species. Species with more advantages will tend to survive, those with fewer advantages or with disadvantages will tend to die out.

According to Darwin's theory of natural selection individuals within a given species vary from one another in a variety of ways. Some of these ways are immaterial for survival (that is, they neither enhance nor impair an individual's ability to cope with its environment or to reproduce); others confer strengths or benefit on such an individual; and still others are detrimental. Darwin's studies and studies since that time have shown that most of these variations are due to the particular recombination of genetic possibilities while others are either produced or enhanced by the environment. Occasionally some variations may be due to slight spontaneous alterations in genetic information and are then heritable. At times, such changes confer an advantage or a disadvantage in terms of coping with the environment or in reproducing. When the trait is one which confers an advantage, it will tend to establish itself and eventually it will become a trait characteristic of a given species at a given time. Such a species is now more fit and, all things being equal, will have a better chance at survival. Traits which confer a disadvantage will tend to die out and if they establish themselves in a species will inevitably weaken such a species. Survival of the fittest allows the best-equipped individuals to establish their gene pool throughout the species and allows the fittest species a leg up in survival.

Positive traits, however, are not necessarily "physical" traits.

The human species, a puny species compared to many others when it comes to physical strength, has survived largely because of its more highly developed capacity to reason, think, and learn, and, therefore, because of its superior capacity to manipulate its environment. The physically strongest members of the human species would be hard pressed in purely physical combat to prevail over a moderately strong and angry wildcat. Humans prevail because their better reasoning capacity allows them to develop instruments and strategies with which to deal with the physically much stronger members of other species. The basis of this superior mental strength is, of course and at least in part, due to the greater development of the central nervous system.

Vital as the central nervous sytem is as a substrate, the full development of this substrate's potential depends on social factors. The possibility for the development of these social factors, the in-built social nature of the animal, perhaps even what Rousseau calls its "primitive sense of pity," has a genetic substrate but requires for its fulfillment the very social forces which it enables without specifically prescribing. I mean by this that while the social drive pre-exists and is perhaps, in that sense, determined, the shape the drive (and consequently the social forces) will take depends upon the way our volition works itself out within that framework. To a large extent, humans structure the kind of society they wish to have; but they do so within a biological framework which permits them the necessary "elbow room" of freedom.[2]

The human animal, furthermore, appears to be the only species which is aware of its own history, can transmit its own history, and, therefore, could (all evidence to the contrary) at least potentially learn from its history. Transmitting knowledge from generation to generation allows a steady expansion of knowledge and facilitates successful manipulation of the environment. Today is or can be built on yesterday and tomorrow can glean the fruits of today's transmitted experience. Transmitting an oral or written history (or caring about it) requires a far more sophisticated society than non-human society. It requires the development of the social so that the physical can flourish. Separating one from the other may be conceptually useful but, like a Venn diagram, overlaps in reality.

The fact that human beings are social animals with the capacity and indeed the drive to band together, to transmit their history, and to learn from their experience has further increased the importance of the intellectual for survival. Intelligence is, of course, basically a physical trait no less than is eyesight, hearing, or the capacity to appose the thumb. But intelligence, while it requires a physical substrate, cannot be reduced to the substrate and is much more than the sum of its parts. Intelligence is conditioned, modified, and shaped by the social milieu. The physical substrate forms the condition for the social development of intelligence. It is, as it were, the limiting factor. When social conditions are not conducive to intellectual development, development is stunted and potential remains unfulfilled. If intelligence has survival value for the individual and ultimately for the species and if intellectual potential remains largely unfulfilled without the social conditions necessary for its development, developing social conditions conducive to intellectual development is vital for species survival.

Man is a social animal. Persons can realize their individual and species potential only within the framework of a supportive community. What Norm Daniels calls "normal species specific function"[3] is only in part an expression of physical possibility; physical possibility can only be realized within the embrace of a supportive social setting which, as much as possible, enhances the physical possibility and allows it to flourish. An individual then needs the community to support its physical being (to provide access to what I have termed "first order necessities") as well as requiring the community's help in realizing such physical potential: i.e., to have true access to the "fair opportunity range"[3] of a given society. Communities which fail to provide either when it is within their range of legitimate possibilities (i.e., when the resources are there but are simply badly distributed) fail not only their members but themselves.

The way the term "social Darwinism" is used today implies that society will be somehow strengthened by regarding its losers in what is seen as "the battle for survival" not as objects worthy of compassion or worthy and deserving of help, but as hemshoes on society's progress and, therefore, as persons owed no help. Beyond this, the argument goes, society may be harming itself by providing help to such persons: helping may be soft-hearted but, according to such thinking, it is not only soft-hearted but is in fact soft-headed and ultimately wrong-headed and destructive to society. If one believes that success in the economic and physical sphere is a marker of genetic superiority and failure a marker of inferiority, then societies are ill-advised to provide a safety net to the losers so that they can survive, breed, perpetuate more of their "inferior" genes, and inevitably produce more losers. The sentiment of compassion with those who lose in this trial defeats the very meaning of the trial itself. Losers, so the argument goes, are personally perhaps unfortunate but societies which provide persons who lose in this contest the means of living and inevitably propagating are weakening and ultimately destroying themselves. A sense of compassion, in such a point of view, is destructive to societal evolution and growth. Communal destruction follows when the genetic pool is sufficiently weakened. The rule of "tooth and claw," so the argument goes, holds for humans no less than it does for Bengal tigers. Such an argument is reminiscent of Mandeville's argument against pity, an emotion he regards to be a form of weakness.[4]

Applying Darwin's work in this way is, in my view, grossly misreading Darwin. Darwin does recognize compassion and he recognizes compassion as a trait which can foster survival in important ways.[5] Just as Darwin speaks about the evolution of emotions and of the role this development plays in fostering survival, he briefly examines compassion and finds it to have survival value. A tribe, in Darwin's view, is made more cohesive when members know that they will receive mutual help, will come to each other's aid, and will consider the interest of others as well as their own interest when it comes to making decisions. Such tribes carry on their daily lives in a more successful fashion than would tribes in which the members knew that they could depend only on themselves. This cohesiveness which allows survival to the individual, to the tribe, and ultimately to the species is quite close to the way in which I use the concept of solidarity in this work.

The species and the individual in Darwinian and biological terms are intimately interrelated. Species spawn individuals but they do so for their own survival not in order to assure individual survival. When the lion or the individual swallow is injured, the pride or flock will not usually stop its activities to help. When it comes to the young of a species, things often are different: the young are nurtured as a necessary insurance policy for the species survival. The individual is seen as the necessary condition for the survival of the species and survival of the species is an unexamined end in itself. Most, but not by any means all, non-human animals clearly are programmed to put the survival of the community above that of the individual. Having only personal but no species history, they are usually unable to engage in transgenerational learning (recent studies with certain species seem to show that this is not always the case: food washing among certain Japanese monkeys is a learned activity passed on from generation to generation).

Historically human animals have placed a much greater but by no means universal emphasis on the individual. This emphasis on individual autonomy and on the overriding importance of respect for the individual has been slowly emerging over the centuries. The emergence of the individual, so pronounced in the eleventh century, gave impetus to the rise of Protestantism with its emphasis on individual salvation. Capitalism is underwritten by an emphasis on the individual and has developed readily in the same atmosphere which gave its initial thrust to Protestantism.[6-8] In recent years this rise of individualism has inverted the previous pyramid: individuals and not the community are now what counts. From at least Hobbes onward this emphasis has given rise to a minimalist ethic in which the community's role has become purely one of ensuring personal liberty.[9] Such a point of view is evident in Nozick's notion of "freedom as a side constraint" and Engelhardt's insistence that entrepreneurialism provides a proper foundation for medical morality.[10,11] Individuals are strictly obliged to respect each other's autonomy and to adhere to freely entered contracts. If peace is to be maintained, insisting on obligations beyond those of utter respect for freedom is not possible. Beneficence loses moral force.

Such a philosophy must either deny Rousseau's "primitive sense of pity" or "l'impulsion intérieure de la compassion" or relegate it to the same order of thing as the sex drive: a natural impulse, perhaps, but one which seeks merely its own satisfaction for inner, selfish purposes. I have not claimed that Rousseau's "primitive sense of pity" in and of itself is "moral"; by virtue of being an inborn drive over which we have little initial control, it cannot itself be moral. My claim is that it is not only, in Schopenhauer's words, the *"Triebfeder"* for ethics but that this drive initiates the ethical question itself. It prompts us to have concern for others and enables us to develop fellow feeling and to put ourselves in another's place. Other drives, such as the sex drive, do not do this. A totally individualist philosophy in which respect for freedom would be the sole driving force of ethics, relegates compassion and benevolence (which is its result) to the realm of aesthetics.

Darwin places a great deal of emphasis on the social instinct.[5] Rousseau's primitive sense of pity (or internal impulse to compassion) fuels our sense of beneficent obligation. In some individual cases one may argue that such a drive places the individual at a distinct disadvantage. The act of pulling a child from in front of a speeding car may end up with the would-be rescuer dead, and giving a great deal of money to charity may reduce the lifestyle of the giver. Benevolent persons who act out their benevolence in beneficent action may not be persons who will endure best or reproduce most or longest; indeed, they may be the very ones to die early and who fail to reproduce. But having a social instinct and consequently a sense of beneficent obligation ultimately helps one's community. When individuals in such communities feel surrounded by others with a similar social sense they will, as Darwin clearly saw, be far more cohesive. Communities which balance their sense of community with a high value for individual expression, indeed which see one of the purposes of community as fostering such expression, will be communities in which solidarity is firmly established. Such communities will be communities that can best adapt, flourish, evolve, and survive. Others that lack such solidarity are ones far more apt to perish. As Darwin saw it, our moral sentiments, sentiments which help us form communities that survive, must eventually "expand to include all mankind regardless of nation, race, social status, handicap and finally the lower animals themselves."[12]

A false interpretation of social Darwinism (as the expression is ordinarily and I believe naively understood) can be used as a handy justification (or, as some would say, as a handy excuse) for ignoring the poor and unfortunate. Indeed, when followed to its logical conclusion, such a point of view makes a virtue out of ignoring the poor and the unfortunate. After all, if society is to grow and flourish, weighing itself down with the ever-increasing ballast which the unfortunate and the poor represent must be counterproductive. Aside from its callous inhumanity, Social Darwinism rests, among other things, on three misconceptions: (1) those individuals or societies most successful in an economic or material sense are justifiably the most admired and emulated; (2) economic competition selects out the fittest in a society: those members best able to help societies evolve and survive (and, therefore, the most admired and renumerated); and (3) societies (analogous to species) evolve best in a competitive struggle with one another.

The idea that those most successful in an economic sense are also the most admired and emulated is, empirically and in American society today, to a large extent even if not entirely, true. Justifying this state of affairs is, however, another matter. Some will argue that I have it backwards: instead of society admiring its economically successful most, economic success is merely a product of the way society admires certain persons or occupations. Even in America today, where the notion of economic reward is deeply rooted, one cannot show that those most admired are necessarily those most rewarded. While many occupations which are the most admired are also richly rewarded, it is clear that the most economically rewarded in American society are not necessarily the most admired. Often those most rewarded fall into one of several other groups. Among such groups are those who are rewarded because: (1) only they are privy to a skill considered critical for survival (surgeons or attorneys) or to a skill by means of which others can earn large amounts of money (baseball players); (2) they have by skill, luck, or hard work attained a position of power enabling them to "name their figure" (captains of industry, bankers); and more and more frequently the case (3) they have inherited or otherwise become the possessors of a self-perpetuating form of vast wealth. Since we live in a society which places an exaggerated value on economic assets, such persons are often feared and because of this fear are then grudgingly and half-heartedly admired. Being admired, however, does not in itself justify admiration.

The notion that those most successful in the economic competition (those who by dint of skill, hard work, or, sometimes, luck win out) are necessarily or even usually the most important members of a society's stability and ability to gradually evolve is not supportable by observation or reason. Societies, just like individuals, are an assortment of skills and liabilities. The composite of such skills and liabilities constitute a society's (or an individual's) particular features. When we say that something was "just like Mabel" (or "just like Italy") we mean to denote that Mabel (or Italy) has certain characteristics which make them recognizable and, in a sense, predictable. It may be "just like Mabel" (or "just like Italy") to strike a clever and successful business deal, or the opposite may be the case; on the other hand it may be just like Mabel (or Italy) to be or not to be particularly sensitive in an artistic sense.

Persons and cultures generally have characteristics which are a composite of strengths and weaknesses: few persons or cultures are composed only of strengths or limited only to weaknesses. Persons (and cultures) are recognizable and often are to a large extent predictable because of their particular composite of strengths and weaknesses: it is this composite of strengths or weaknesses which gives them their peculiar character and makes them recognizable as Mabel or Italy. Relationships between and among persons (and societies or cultures) are often predicated on such a fit: the weakness of one is shored up by the strength of another.[13] A society or a person composed of these varying attributes stands in critical need of support from another whose strengths are capable of minimizing their weakness. Not only are they in need of having their areas of weakness underpinned by another's strength but they may likewise profit by being taught by the stronger to remedy their own weakness. This dependence upon another for help, if it is to be workable, must be matched by a willingness to share their own strengths with their neighbor's weakness and where possible and appropriate to help the neighbor remedy weaknesses.

In each society as in each individual it is this shaping of strengths and liabilities which makes it the unique person or society it is. Individuals and societies will not necessarily profit most by using their energies to remedy their weaknesses; often it is the case that weaknesses will be most profitably left to be made up by another while one's energy is used in pursuing one's strengths. Persons who are particularly gifted musically but have little manual skill do not usually profit if they expend their energy in developing their weak side and consequently (since time is not infinite) must neglect the development of their strongest points. Nations who are particularly gifted (be it by the resources of nature or by the way in which cultural development occurred) in one sense may do well to allow others to make up their weaknesses while concentrating on their strengths. This is obvious in a material sense: a nation with beautiful forests but almost no reserves of oil will be far better off utilizing its forests rather than trying to squeeze what is not to be squeezed out of the ground. It is, however, no less true in a sense of national talents: nations whose history and tradition makes them especially skilled in one and unskilled in another way may do best in optimizing their strengths rather than in shoring up their weaknesses at the expense of the strengths. It is this necessary interdependency which cements, reaffirms, and necessitates all relationships, be they relationships between or among humans or between and among societies and cultures.

Strengths and weaknesses moreover are not necessarily static: persons may have no artistic talent so that attempting to develop such a talent turns out to be a hopeless venture. All that a stronger one can do is compensate for the weakness of the other. But most weaknesses are relative: relative to the person's or the culture's strength or relative to others. When such persons or cultures team up with others who are strong where they are weak or weak where they are strong, learning can and often does occur so that the weakness of one can be strengthened (not only compensated for) by the other. Optimally and in a sense to some extent almost inevitably, education forms a powerful bond in such a relationship. The teacher in one area is the learner in another.

Economic health or even modest prosperity are indisputably important to an individual's or to a society's ultimate growth and eventual survival. Economic failure certainly is inconsistent with long-term growth or survival. This is clearly shown by the problem of America's poverty areas: without economic investment no conceivable progress is possible. But economic success does not, therefore, translate into long-term survival or growth. America's poverty areas clearly cannot be helped by economic intercession alone, as necessary a condition as economic intercession may be to such advancement. Survival and growth necessitate a multiplicity of factors. Likewise, cultures and societies need a variety of skills and capacities, of which economic skill is only one. A society which fails to develop its intellectual and artistic talent will ultimately fail since it is these very talents which are then utilized in developing economic ones. Unless a society develops new intellectual and artistic insights to underpin its technology, it will not have products to sell so that it may succeed in the economic sphere. To claim that it is technical or economic skill which is the be all and end all of societal worth is a dangerous assumption and, if followed to its logical conclusion, leads to societal stagnation, decline, and ultimately failure. To claim that economic competition selects out those members best able to help societies evolve and survive simply is not true.

There are, however, members of society who seem to combine a number of weaknesses with few if any strengths. They are drifters, ne'er-do-wells or even criminals. Such persons, we feel, have few if any redeeming features and act as hemshoes on any culture or society. If social Darwinism, in the form in which this term is usually applied, is to select out cultures for survival and doom others to destruction, surely having none or only a very few persons of this sort would be beneficial. And yet, I shall argue that all societies have their weak, their misfits, and those we call drifters or dreamers. Overtly, they seem to contribute little to progress. Nevertheless, such persons are human beings and members of the community and as such they also have their role, even if that role is often mainly negative, to play. How we as a society treat such persons says more about us as societies and individuals than it does about the problem itself. What we call "the failures" are persons who were reared and their personality and attributes shaped by the society in which they find themselves. If they are deprived of their standing, treated as nonmembers in community and, therefore, stripped of their privileges to basic necessities or to access to a reasonable opportunity range (even if they refuse to avail themselves of it), not only they but also their community would ultimately be the losers. Such persons, more than others, are in need of compassion. While such persons may not be seen to serve an immediate practical purpose, communities nevertheless cannot simply ignore them and cast them out. Failing to show compassion to the weak, allowing a community to be callous to the fate of any member, dilutes not only our impulse of compassion and our sense of pity but the solidarity that a community needs to survive. The way communities treat their weakest members in many respects is the measure of a community's moral standing.

In the Soviet Union all were allegedly (even if in fact this was not the case) assured the necessities of life. The weakest members in an economic sense or the weakest members as those who could not compete because of physical or mental deficiencies were taken care of. In fact, however, not only were the physically or mentally weakest not truly taken care of, a whole new class of weak were created. Being politically weak (criticizing or being in opposition to the regime) earned one severe sanctions which often deprived one of the most basic rights. The weak, in Soviet society, often were not well treated. Soviet society was hardly a community with high moral standing. In America, the weakest are apt not to receive basic necessities (hunger and homelessness are frequent and medical care for the needy—or even for those not needy but uninsured—is deficient) and a whole underclass of weak and exploitable persons has been created. The United States as it has become today is no more a community of high moral standing than was the Soviet Union.

It may well be the case that considerations such as these argue against the current interpretation of social Darwinism but fail to argue against social Darwinism itself. If by social Darwinism one means that those societies "fittest" in a wider sense are apt to endure in the long run while those "unfit" in such a wider sense will eventually not endure, it is difficult to argue against it. But such a statement is more of a tautological commonplace than a theory: it seems obvious that societies which lack features giving them internal strength and allowing them to survive will lack internal strengths and will fail to survive. It is exactly the reason why I have placed such a stress on solidarity. It is one of the chief internal strengths and one of the most critical conditions for survival a society can have, and it is predicated on a multiplicity of factors.

I have claimed that true solidarity in a community depends upon more than merely the realization that we will be left alone. Solidarity, to be firm, is inevitably bound together with the notion that my community cares for me. The fact that this caring must be reciprocal, the fact that to be community (a *Gemeinschaft* in the sense in which I shall use this word) means that all see the maintenance of community itself as a prime goal is what lends solidarity. Solidarity is not possible when individuals know that their community will not be disposed to come to their help, will not help them in their poverty, hunger or homelessness, and will have no interest in their capacity to flourish and to develop their individual talents. When such help is but grudgingly given and when only wealthy individuals can flourish and develop their talents solidarity is at best weak. Solidarity in communities has positive survival value. If social Darwinism is to offer us any insights, this insight rather than the belief that the weak, the unfortunate, and the losers in the natural lottery are hemshoes and are best disposed of, seems more appropriate.

The way we view our community and ourselves in relation to community has important ramifications not only for our personal but for our community's survival. I have argued that communities which have a less minimalist and more generous ethic have greater solidarity. Communities in which the needs of all (for those things needed to sustain life) are assured and which also try to provide all with equal access to the opportunities such societies may have to offer (while respecting personal tastes and allowing personal flourishing), will be communities in which solidarity is strongest. Communities which lack solidarity are communities which ultimately cannot evolve and survive.

The claim that societies (analogous to species) evolve not only best but only in a necessarily competitive struggle with one another is questionable. Species evolve in a seemingly competitive struggle because such a struggle is apt to select out the best genetic traits in a species—"best" in the sense of allowing survival and growth. Selection for survival is not, however, necessarily best or only modeled by "struggle." Species which develop features allowing them to cooperate or even making them reliant on cooperation rather than on stark competition may well be and often are very well suited to survive. Symbiotic forms or forms throughout nature which have learned to cooperate with one another have helped species survival and growth: a judicious mixture between competitive and cooperative capabilities may well favor a species' ultimate evolutionary survival. Always picturing survival as a zero-sum game in which only one can win and the other must lose sells the rich tapestry of evolution short.

Individual survival has undoubtedly always been enmeshed with the community and the health of the community has undoubtedly always depended upon the well-being of those within it. The model of "struggle" between them, while it has conceptual merit, seems always to have been an oversimplification. Such an oversimplified concept, however, has become less and less tenable. As humans have developed ever-greater capacities for manipulating their environment and affecting their destinies for good or ill and as the sophistication of technology has progressively grown, our notion of needs has likewise expanded. (For a discussion of needs see Chapter 6.) In the early days of tribal life, meeting the basic biological needs of existence and supplying all with those things necessary for being able to realize the range of opportunities a given society had to offer[3] was comparatively simpler. The amount of education which one might need to avail oneself of a modest array of opportunities was easily provided; health care likewise was relatively primitive and the combination of the priestly with the medical function made it readily accessible to all. As societies became more sophisticated, needs escalated. While basic biological needs remained virtually the same, their means of fulfillment and, therefore, their availability changed drastically. To avail oneself of the opportunities a given society had to offer required ever more and more sophisticated education. Health care, necessary not only to sustain biological well-being but likewise playing its role in a person's ability to reach his/her goals, likewise changed its complexion and today has taken over a larger and larger percentage of the gross national product. When segments of a population are denied equal opportunities, class differences grow and become solidified. The health, solidarity, and survival of communities in which such differences were allowed to become stark was and continues to be severely threatened.

Nurture and the kind of nurture experienced has a strong influence on the emerging personality of the individual. In part the kind of nurture experienced is a function of prevailing material conditions and the way communities use these material conditions to shape their society. I have suggested that the way communities structure themselves is a function of their perception of mutual obligation and that in turn our perception of mutual obligations has a lot to do with the kinds of communities in which we grow up and which we ultimately help to shape. Such a cycle sounds hopelessly circular: communities shape the individual in certain ways and individuals in turn shape the community. Such a state of events is, however, by no means circular. It is an expression of a dynamic homeostatic balance which, while it favors stability, permits growth, evolution, and the slow emergence of new reference points. A community, like an individual or a species, is subject to a myriad of changing external and internal forces which, in order to assure survival, must be balanced. Such a balance, however, if it is not to lead to stagnation, must be dynamic and ongoing, ever exploring for and experimenting with new reference points about which life oscillates. If it fails to do this evolution cannot occur and, ultimately, as external and internal conditions continue to change and adaptation fails to occur, survival becomes impossible.

I have claimed that our sense of community and the role it plays in our lives is intimately associated with our initial experience of nurture. No infant can survive without nurture. Nurturing, however, does not cease once a notion of selfhood has emerged; if our lives are to be even moderately satisfactory, nurturing (both being nurtured and nurturing others) must continue throughout our lives. The infant, beginning to assert him/herself does so in the embrace of beneficence; young infants cannot make the judgments or decisions and cannot themselves carry out the acts necessary for survival without some help and guidance.

Helping and guiding is a form of beneficence no matter how grudgingly given. Children may grow up under terrible physical as well as under deprived emotional conditions; indeed, in America, where one of three children (and one of two black children) go to bed hungry and where families and the security such structures may bring are often disrupted, this is hardly rare. But to grow up at all children must be the recipients at least of ongoing minimal beneficence from and minimal caring by someone. The conditions of their growing up will modify their initial sense of trust and often may severely attenuate their natural sense of pity and their compassion for others.[14] Such a pathological state, however, cannot in itself be used to argue against the fact that developing beings, by virtue of having been and continuing to be recipients of necessary beneficence, take on obligations of beneficence themselves. Pathological states counsel one to eradicate the disease causing the pathology not to use the state itself as a point of reference for normal existence.

The kind of nurture which infants experience critically influences the kind of persons they will be. In turn, the kinds of persons which ultimately make up community, their attitudes, values and priorities, determine the shape their community will take. In a sense the experience of nurture and the lessons drawn from this experience, will help shape the kind of community which results. Economic forces (those under and those not under direct human control) likewise act in shaping community; and to the extent that they are under human control they are subject to similar influences. When we draw a lesson of obligation towards others from our nurture and shape our society accordingly, we can form a far more lasting and enduring unit than if we fail to heed this lesson. Such a beneficent society will go far towards nurturing a primitive sense of pity and fostering a sense of moral sensitivity and mutual obligation.

I do not wish to reduce personality to nurture: persons may be nurtured in very similar ways with totally different results. Undoubtedly genetic as well as a multitude of other factors play a role. In general and for the most part, however, persons growing up in beneficent and loving environments will be substantially different from those whose experience with nurture and beneficence has been far more meager. Nurture and the experience of nurture guarantees little without proper education so that lessons ultimately beneficial to community survival can be drawn.[14] When children, instead of being nurtured are pampered, and not only allowed but educated and encouraged to go a completely self-serving road, the result is as inimical to communal growth and survival as is the failure to nurture. I shall argue that nurture does not imply pampering or permissiveness but rather that nurture implies teaching the emerging individual lessons of responsibility for others and for their community. The goal of nurture is the survival of the individual as a well-functioning and well-integrated entity so that not only he/she alone but he/she and with him/her the community can flourish and survive.

In America today we have fallen short on both accounts: in the poverty areas nurture is often minimal and beneficence largely wanting. Hopelessness, crime, and lack of concern with a community seen as hostile and inimical to personal survival stalk the streets. The notion that such areas are enclosed communities successfully sealed off from "the better areas" is a chimeric dream. They are neither true communities nor are they sealed off from the outside. In an attempt to survive as individuals in what persons from such an environment see as an almost hopeless situation, they will kill and rob each other: their community is not even one of an initial Hobbesian contract. Rather it is one of a Hobbesian pre-social war of all against all. And it is a war which inevitably spreads. In justified bitterness and in understandable hatred persons forced by circumstances over which they have little if any control to live in such areas often will attempt to rob and kill outside their particular enclave spreading fear, hatred, and crime in their wake.

In the wealthier areas children tend to be sheltered and encouraged to grow up with a sense of individualism which excludes the notion of community or even of more than minimal obligation. Often they are materially pampered and emotionally deprived: the teenager may have his/her own car, movies are a daily event, and luxuries are ever handy, but nurture in the sense of building a sense of purpose and of self is neglected in school and home. Children often grow up with an exaggerated sense of shallow self-worth and with a set of values which allows them to place immediate personal gratification far above other concerns. Often tacit and sometimes explicit mistrust of others not just like themselves and even overt racism is part of the atmosphere in which they are raised. The results are largely the same as they are in the poverty regions: persons who are out only or at least largely for themselves mindless of the fact that "being for one-self" outside of the community and its needs ultimately destroys the very self one seeks to create. A perhaps more genteel war of all against all, but a war of all against all nonetheless, results.

Beneficence, if it is to be beneficence, must have a decent respect for individual tastes, desires, and strivings. One cannot very well be beneficent and deny others their rightful place in the sun of their own choosing.[1,15] Individual tastes, desires and strivings, however, develop and are shaped in the embrace of a community. They are in part not only the result of innate talents and skills but are critically dependent upon nurture. It is here that education assumes its rightful and necessary place in nurture. Properly, education has to be aimed towards the goal of self and communal fulfillment not only in its immediate material sense but also in the sense of permitting further evolution and growth.

Nurturing infants has three goals: (1) to enable infants to remain alive so that they can (2) develop their awareness of self and their autonomy, and so that (3) eventually they can develop their talents and flourish and function both as individuals and as members of their community. These goals are reflected in community which likewise has three goals: (1) to nurture its members so that community itself can survive (so that community itself becomes one of the goals of community); (2) to foster individual autonomy so that (3) its members can flourish as individuals and eventually so that they can contribute to community. Communities and the individuals within them are not separate or in fact separable entities: they are a part of the same structure which enables the species, the communities, and the individuals within it to survive. The goals of individual and community likewise are not separate, separable or mutually exclusive. Rather they are properly seen as mutually interdependent, mutually reinforcing, and mutually sustaining. Only in this way can personal and communal evolution, growth, and survival occur.

BALANCING INTERESTS

The mutuality and interdependence of individual and communal goals may be well and good; but when it comes to practical everyday issues an apparent clash between communal and personal interests nevertheless and almost inevitably seems to persist. Taking care of one's neighbor's basic needs or allowing one's neighbor's fair access to the opportunities offered by society regardless of one's neighbor's ability to pay inevitably (and it would seem almost necessarily) conflicts with the private interests of individuals who earn more and who feel that their efforts (alone) have made it possible for them to achieve what they have. It is, such persons will argue, patently unfair to take hard-earned money from them in order to remedy social conditions.

On the other hand, those in communities that do take care of the basic needs of their citizens, that enable their citizens to develop their talents, and that do provide access to a fair opportunity range[3] often feel entitled to define needs and to determine what talents had best be developed and what talents had best be supressed or channeled otherwise. Ultimately they often feel that they can and perhaps even must control the lives of those whom their beneficence benefits. After all, the state is providing monies for the welfare of its citizens and the least the state should be able to ask in return is a large measure of control over the opportunities those they pay for will develop or over the particular talents they will be allowed to develop. Such actions of controlling individual flourishing and determining individual ways of life are often couched in language suggesting that what is done is really done for the good of the individual who is being controlled or channeled. And, at times, it is quite unclear if such a claim is simply disingenuous or if those in control truly feel the good of all to be their motive. Acts of this sort, done under the pretext of beneficence are, when they become crassly paternalistic, a caricature of beneficence.

Beneficent acts may or may not be paternalistic (or what is today, with little improvement in understanding the concept, called "parentalistic"). Beneficent acts may but do not have to be paternalistic ones. Dworkin's well accepted definition of paternalism states paternalism is "interference with a person's liberty of action justified by reasons referring exclusively to the welfare, good, happiness, needs, interests or values of the person coerced."[16] While, in a sense, the motive of all paternalism is, or at least is generally alleged to be, beneficence (doing something for the good of another) such beneficence is not always or (as the term is used necessarily) specifically directed at the subject of beneficent action. It can be more complicated: a society in acting beneficently is acting for the corporate good of the community but in so doing may not be directly benefiting the individual good, or at least the immediate good, of all of its members; it may, in fact, bring some immediate harm to some of them. When taxes are levied so that some needs of the poor can be met, it is done because doing so is felt to be for a community's general good even when, as is undoubtedly the case, the persons taxed hardly feel themselves to be the beneficiaries of such an action. It is, however, done in the belief that ultimately benefiting the community will benefit all those in it. This is the reason why when societies have a sense of community the wealthy may grumble, but as long as they agree to the basic fairness of the process will not greatly object.

Paternalism is generally definable as a species of beneficence. It is a form of coercion in which persons are forced or enticed to act or not to act in a way which is not of their own choosing and perhaps is even the opposite of what they would, if left to themselves, do or choose to do. In general, but perhaps not invariably, a paternalistic act is done for the subjects "own good" because subjects either (1) are unable to judge the consequences of their act properly or (2) although quite aware of the consequences are, in the opinion of the paternalist, acting against what the paternalist defines as "their best interest."[17] The former (called soft or weak paternalism) is what occurs when children are sent to school against their will, when adults are rescued from an onrushing automobile they did not see, or when mentally confused persons, believing themselves capable of flying, are prevented from trying to jump out of the window. This is basically an ethically uninteresting specimen of paternalism against which even the most autonomy-based ethic would find it hard to argue. The second version of paternalism (hard or "crass" paternalism) is one in which persons fully aware of the consequences of their act are restrained from such acts or in which they are forced to act against their wishes. Examples of this are the forcible transfusions of adult Jehovah's Witnesses or the act of interfering with a well thought out suicide attempt. Although not usually mentioned, there are gradations between these two extremes: fourteen year olds who are forced to continue dialysis against their will, extremely fearful patients whose mind may be more or less affected by their fear treated in an emergency against their expressed momentary will, and many more. Depending on circumstances, forcing a street person to seek shelter in winter may be "soft," "hard," or in between. As is often the case, it is these intermediate cases which form the material of much discussion.

Coercing one for the good of yet another is sometimes but improperly called paternalism. Restraining a person who is quite aware of what they are doing and who is plotting to kill another or taxing the wealthy to benefit the poor are examples. One might say that restraining or taxing another for the good of a third is paternalism in the sense that doing so is aimed at bringing about the good of another who does not directly ask for it and who, in fact, may not or may never explicitly know about it. Further, it could be argued that restraining the assailant or taxing the wealthy is, in the final analysis, not only done to help a third party but is also done to protect the assailant or to safeguard the wealthy person: the one from committing a crime and eventually from legal prosecution and the other from the rage of those who feel themselves disadvantaged and disenfranchised. Such an argument may hold, and hold with some force, in the case of the assailant who, some might feel, could if he were competent not make such a decision. Such an argument, questionable as it may be, is even more difficult to sustain in the case of taxing the wealthy—all of whom can hardly be felt to be incompetent. Even if one is to call such acts paternalistic ones, it is a different sort of paternalism than is the act done only to benefit the person him/herself. Such actions are, perhaps, best viewed as a species of indirectly paternalistic beneficence.

Beneficence hardly has to be paternalistic. Doing another their good (rather than doing them our own) is more frequently what we think about when we speak of beneficence. Giving sustenance, shelter, or medical care to the poor is certainly a way of acting beneficently; but in that it may be exactly what the poor themselves want, it cannot be conceived to be paternalistic. It is only when we do others our and not their good that paternalism can really be spoken of. Beneficent acts, then, can be either paternalistic or non-paternalistic.

There are overlaps: acts may be partly beneficent and partly non-beneficent. The poor or the mentally disturbed may want help but the help considered best for them may not be of the kind they themselves would choose to receive. Beneficent acts can, in fact, be consistent with autonomous decisions: I may decide to take a hungry person to dinner (a beneficent act) which may be exactly what the person wants. I act from beneficent impulse but in so doing I may (or at times may not) respect an autonomous wish. The act, Kant might say, is motivated purely by beneficence and accords to the injunction to respect persons (and their autonomy) almost accidentally. If the hungry man really wants a drink of whiskey rather than food and I grant him his wish by buying the drink, it is still a beneficent act but it is an act done in part because of respect for his autonomous choice: I say to myself that although I do not believe that this is serving his good he thinks otherwise and I, therefore and because of this, proceed to channel beneficence in accordance with autonomy. My first impulse, the impulse to help a fellow creature in distress, was beneficent: it is my primitive sense of pity which raised the issue to begin with, it is my sense of respect for individual choice (or perhaps my sense that one cannot be truly beneficent without respecting individual choice) which led to my particular act. If, on the other hand, I decide not to allow him a drink but insist that I am unwilling to cater to his desire for a drink although I am quite willing to cater to his hunger, my act becomes, at least in part, a quite paternalistic one. It is, however, still an act motivated by my initial sense of pity and it may even be that it is this sense which motivated my refusal to allow him to have a drink. After all, I might argue, if I truly believed that having alcohol was against the person's best interests (interests I either felt he was incapable of understanding or interests I chose to define) catering to his desire is not ultimately done from beneficent motives. It is arguable which of these actions was more beneficent but one is beneficent and paternalistic while the other is solely beneficent.

Even though actions done from beneficence or those done from respect for autonomy may coincide, beneficence and autonomy are classically seen as conflicting notions. In everyday life this interplay of apparently conflicting interests can be seen in many ways: societies whose predominant values favor one of these are constituted in a radically different way than are those which favor another. These values (or the principles emerging from such values) have classically been seen to be in conflict. Such a conflict is often seen as a dialetic one in which the thesis of beneficence (or yearning for social justice) is juxtaposed to the antithesis of respect for autonomy (or interest in a striving for self-expression and autonomy). It is, in other words, a struggle between two values and a struggle in which a particular viewpoint emerges (the synthesis). This synthesis which exemplifies the mores or ethics of a particular society then becomes another thesis against which another counterweight is poised and with which it must struggle. Development of communities, then, proceeds in this competition between two values. It is a dynamic concept but one in which each of these values pursues its own particular goal and in which resolution inevitably but only temporarily emerges from the ongoing struggle.

In the second chapter I suggested that a much more fruitful and realistic model may be one of homeostasis. I stressed that the concept of homeostasis is not one which merely applies to biological or physiological forces but that it is a concept which can easily be seen to operate throughout nature. I do not limit the concept of nature to physical, chemical, or biological life processes but rather use it in a far more inclusive manner. Anything which concerns itself with processes in which living organisms participate or are engaged is, in that sense, natural. Ecological, psychological, or sociological forces, reasoning whether it be reasoning about daily problems, scientific matters or ethics itself is, in that analysis, a "natural activity"—not, I hasten to add, an activity which is in any sense reducible to nature but an activity which inevitably must take place in the framework which nature and biology supply. To argue otherwise is to flee into the mystic. Nature and biology provide the necessary framework and substrate without which no sociological, psychological, ecological, or ultimately ethical process or discussion could take place. To argue whether nature and biology play a role in our rational deliberations (the argument as to whether mind can somehow be envisioned as separate from nature) is—inevitably and with logical necessity—done in a framework provided by biology and nature.

The dynamic equilibrium called homeostasis is not a modern concept. Its roots go well back into ancient times and certainly the notion, even if not explicitly expressed, is there in Plato's dialogues or in Aristotle's notion of the "mean": a balancing of forces between two opposites seeking, according to the context in which they are to be used, appropriate resolution. By virtue of being two juxtaposed and opposite things such a balancing of forces is seen as a tension between opposites and is, perhaps, closer to being what later is spoken of as a dialectic. Looking at a relationship as a dialectic tension has analytic usefulness: it allows us to examine two factors separated from others and, therefore, allows us to conduct a "thought" or actual experiment outside the context of other complicating factors. In that it allows us a more critical and undisturbed examination, separating our specific concerns has merit; but it is these complex and complicating factors which make up the problem and which ultimately participate in shaping the solution. And here the model of conflict breaks down. When I speak of a homeostatic relationship, therefore, I include the notion of dialectic but it is a dialectic which fits into the wholeness of the problem and which must adjust its working out mindful of the myriad of other forces operating in the same context.

In a sense such a relationship may well be seen as composed of many forces working to balance each other, but such a balance must serve not merely the goals of both members of the particular relationship but rather the goals of the entire complex entity in which a particular balance plays itself out. When insulin balances blood sugar or when one species balances the spread of another it is not sufficient to merely examine this balance without appreciating the larger context and its particular needs and goals. To speak of a conflict between these two forces ignores the wider context: it misses the purpose of the balance which must fit into a larger context.

A simple example may help: the heart is a microcosm of the organism and the organism a microcosm of the larger problem. When electrical forces sweep in various directions over a portion of heart muscle the result at any instance in time is what is called a resultant vector. This complex construct is the product of a myriad of forces in balance with each other and ultimately assuring an orderly contraction of the muscle so that the right amount of blood to underwrite the organism's survival occurs. At any moment of time these forces can be seen as opposing each other to ultimately produce the mean vector. But such forces are not truly in competition with each other: rather, their harmonious balance is necessary for the heart's proper function which in turn is necessary for the organism's ultimate survival. Reducing what is going on to two or even to a few "opposing" forces is well and good in teaching electrocardiography: but such an insight must then be integrated into an understanding of the whole which such an instance itself underwrites. In pathological states, disorganization may occur: rather than a smooth balance among many forces, segments of muscle and opposing electrical currents now pursue their individual goals and chaos, malfunction and eventual death of the organism result.

When Aristotle considers the mean and sees it as a working out of disparate forces operating in a particular context he has a less conflict-laden perception of these forces than the usual sense of dialectic implies.[18] Marx, on the other hand, (or at least the way Marx is generally interpreted) sees such a dialectic as a struggle between material forces, each striving for their separate ends with both finding a merely temporary resolution only in an ongoing struggle. It is a struggle between two forces in which each seeks its own individual goal; unable to overpower each other they resolve their problem in a temporary truth which is merely a prelude to another struggle. Homeostasis, on the other hand, instead of seeing a struggle in which the contesting forces have disparate goals and use separate means, is generally conceived as a balance between a myriad of forces working towards a common telos or goal.

The modern notion of homeostasis applied in the framework of natural process was initially conceived by Claude Bernard, who in turn owed much to the earlier Pfluger and Fredericq.[19] Claude Bernard originated the notion of what he called the "*milieu intérieur*," the internal environment which seeks to maintain stability in response to inner as well as to outer (*"milieu extérieur"*) forces by means of a dynamic balance later termed "homeostatic" by Cannon.[20,21] The notion of such forces has been found useful to the understanding of ecological process.[22] In this book I am suggesting that the concept of homeostasis may be usefully applied not only to such natural systems but likewise that it can find great usefulness in looking at communities and their development.

Sociological phenomena, philosophical concepts, and ethical perceptions are activities necessarily engaged in by biological organisms and, therefore, while by no means reducible to biological process are inevitably associated with and linked to such process. To speak of such activities outside the context of biology is to ignore the framework within which, inevitably, biological organisms must grapple with these questions; to reduce these activities to merely biological processes, however, is to take a purely mechanistic view and, therefore, to make an entirely deterministic claim.

When I speak of the process of homeostasis as balancing communal and individual interests I imply that individuals and communities share common goals and work toward common ends. Even beyond this, I suggest that when they work only toward their own goals and ends they will, in the process, inevitably defeat the very ends they seek. This is a pathological state of societies in which disorganization occurs: rather than smooth balance among many forces, individuals or segments of population now pursue their individual goals and chaos, malfunction, and eventual death of the community result.

When communities ignore the interest of their individual members for individual flourishing and self-expression, solidarity is threatened. Infants are nurtured and protected so that they may differentiate themselves from the world about them and come to begin to recognize their selfness; their initial sense of autonomy inevitably must develop in such a setting. As the infant's autonomy emerges and as infants begin to recognize and strive for their individuality they are in need not only of further physical protection with all that being physically protected entails, but likewise are in need of nurture in an educational sense. Such education, be it preparation to assume a role in a primitive tribe or education to assume a role in a modern community, is an ongoing process engaged in by the community. It is aimed at providing the possibility for optimal development of basic talents so that individuals can be fulfilled in their chosen life activities and so that communities, in turn, can flourish, grow, and develop. Individuals and their communities are entirely dependent upon each other. Separating the concept of community from the notion of the individual or abstracting the notion of community from the reality of individual existence may be abstractly or analytically useful in better understanding particular problems; it may give us useful information or provide insights. However, separating these concepts does not directly help in solving the problem until the insights gained are applied to the problem at hand.

If one assumes that individuals can first define and then pursue their interests separately from the community in which such interests occur, or if one assumes that communities can define or develop their existence unmindful of their individual members, one makes the mistake of ignoring such an interrelationship. Communities and their members are inevitably enmeshed. When individuals (or groups within the community) ignore their community in pursuit of purely selfish interests they will gain a pyrrhic victory bought at the expense of their own destruction. On the other hand, when communities ignore the legitimate striving for self-expression and self-fulfillment of their members (or of groups of their members) so that the dead hand of uniformity produces a homogenized society, they too will gain a pyrrhic victory and will destroy themselves. Communities and the individuals within them are entirely dependent on each other's interests; separating the interest of one from that of the other is conceptually interesting and analytically useful. It is a separation of interests which can help enrich our understanding and help chart our future directions. But ultimately such separation must be brought together in the full realization that the interests and therefore the ultimate fate of communities and of the groups and individuals within them cannot be defined apart from one another.

FROM NURTURE TO SOLIDARITY

For Hobbes, any collective can be reduced to the individuals of which it is composed. Collectives are collectives because of a series of individual agreements, understandings, and private actions independent of each other and not rooted in any notion of community.[9] For Locke, this essentially individualistically based notion of association persists even when his ideas of mutual obligation far transcend the Hobbesian notion of merely non-harm.[23] Even Rousseau still preserves the priority of individuals over communities in his understanding of social contract.[24,25] Indeed, classical contractarianism and its modern counterparts (for example Rawls[26]) requires such an individualistic point of view no matter how more- or less-broadly based it may be.[27] In this century Popper continued this individualistic notion of social entities: to him social entities are purely theoretical constructs and they are comprehensible only in terms of individual relations, obligations, and actions.[28] Nozick presents the extreme point of view in this respect when he argues, from a very Hobbesian perspective, for a society based purely on individuals bound merely to respect each other's freedom but having no obligations beyond this.[9]

Solidarity is the cement which holds associations of persons together. Such associations stay together because of the force exerted by that glue. In a Hobbesian sense, as well as in the sense in which most social contractarians view association, freestanding persons come together to enter into a contract. They are bound together by their individual interest in such a contract, say in the contract not to harm each other and to allow the other to freely pursue his/her goals provided only that these goals do not impinge on the free exercise of others to do the same. Knowing that they are able to pursue this goal in relative safety provides the cement which enables communal survival. Such a contract certainly provides some glue especially as long as at least most members of such an association prosper; when, however, a significant number find that they have basic unmet, and as individuals largely unmeetable, needs, things change. Persons in dire want are not greatly comforted by the realization that they are free to speak or to go about their business without hindrance from others; persons who because of a lack of resources are unable to avail themselves of the fair opportunity range their society has to offer are not greatly helped by the suggestion that they are quite free to develop and will not be hindered in developing their personal talents. Being told to pull oneself up by one's bootstraps requires boots, straps, hands, strength, and the knowledge of how to pull. When one lacks boots, straps, or strength, being told to pull oneself up by one's bootstraps is cynically being asked to defeat the laws of nature. Societies in which basic resources to underpin life and to make the fair opportunity range realistic to all are missing will have little solidarity. Even a cursory reading of history will support this statement.

The suggestion I shall make throughout this work is that true communities do not correspond to a classical social contractarian model: they are not associations of free contractors but are entities into which we are born and to which our continued existence owes an obligation. Social contractarians, of course, do not hold their model to be an historically realistic one; rather they consider it to be a useful construct for exploring their ideas. Unfortunately, such a model when used to deduce theories of mutual obligation suffers from the fact that the initial contract, even when pictured in such a way, did not come about in such a fashion and most certainly is not in today's world perpetuated in such a way.

Social contract theorists who explain community as the free expression of individuals coming together to shape whatever form of contract their theories require, neglect the fact that individuals themselves were necessarily shaped by the community and that they must, in some sense at least, be understood as an expression of concrete social universals. Instead of seeing individual action as initially shaped by the community in which persons developed their individuality, social contractarians generally see social action as a function of individual goals.

In the way social contract theory sees individuals as free-standing entities whose values, goals, and desires are the product of self-choice, individuals simply and in reality do not exist. In having a peculiar genetic make-up individuals are peculiar and (except in the case of identical twins) unique onto themselves; but such individuals cease being such beings as their individuality and autonomy necessarily emerges in the embrace of community. Their genetic peculiarity is inevitably shaped, modulated, and conditioned by their community until what is and what is not nature and what is and what is not nurture are so intertwined as to be virtually indistinguishable.

Social contract theories which attempt to see persons as abstracted from their social milieu and which envision man as somehow emerging in an asocial state of nature in which persons were freestanding, abstract persons from their necessary biological roots of nurture and communal shaping. It is what, to paraphrase Jonathan Moreno could be referred to as the "myth of the asocial individual."[29] Individuality develops in the context of community and is inevitably shaped by this experience; except when very narrowly and myopically conceived, individuality is not in competition with community but rather requires community to fulfill the potential and possibility of its genetic individuality. Rather than the relationship being purely one of competition between the claims of beneficence and the claims of individuality as I have argued in a past work,[1] there is a necessary interrelation in which a homeostatic balance assuring communal and individual survival occurs. A balance of this sort is conducive to communal solidarity, evolution, growth, and ultimately to survival. This balance results and is expressed in solidarity.

One needs to define "community." Various types of collectives or associations exist, not all or even most of which can be called "communities." Differences between mere collectives or associations and true communities are critical to our discussion.[30] I shall divide human associations into three categories, fully aware that these do not exist in watertight compartments but that there are a variety of intermediate forms. For the sake of discussion, I shall divide such associations into (1) relatively simple associations pursuing a single or a small set of related purposes; the German word *Verein* best suits this type of association; (2) intermediate forms which have a more sophisticated set of shared goals and for which the English word "society" does not quite substitute for the German word *Gesellschaft*; and (3) a more encompassing form which can be termed "community" or

Gemeinschaft, in which a broad set of values and goals are shared and in which the shared value and goal of community itself plays a central role. Lose associations of people constantly coalesce only to again break apart. Tighter associations break apart less easily. Solidarity is the force of cohesion which cements communities together and which prevents their rupture. The differences between the different types of collectives or associations, their interrelationships, and the obligations they have to each other and to their members will be largely the topic of this and the next few chapters.

More or less lose collectives or associations (*Vereine*) are formed for a more or less transient and often but not necessarily single purpose by the individuals composing such associations. Examples of such associations (there is no really good English word for this, the German word *Verein* is the closest word for this concept) are associations or clubs formed to pursue an activity of interest to its members, such as football or chess clubs, bird-watching groups, or study groups of students preparing for an examination. The critical attribute is that such groups or associations are formed by individuals voluntarily coming together for a specific purpose: the cement holding the group together is the pursuit of the purpose and the members may otherwise share few common interests or goals.

Collectives or associations I shall call *Vereine* are knit together by the value the members have for the goal of the association. Such *Vereine* may be short lived or they may extend over history with members coming and going as interests and perceived needs of the individuals who compose the club change. A chess club is a chess club because of its members' interest in playing chess. The club is the means which in the eyes of its members makes the activity possible, or at least which makes the activity more satisfactory to pursue. Members see the club not as intrinsically valuable (not as valuable in itself) but merely as instrumentally valuable: as valuable because it serves the goal of playing a better game of chess than would, at least in their opinion, be possible without it. If a member's interest in chess changes or if what is perceived to be a better game of chess can be found elsewhere a member is likely to leave the club. The solidarity of such a *Verein* is fairly weak; many things may cause the club to disband or its members to leave.

Many such initially temporary associations may, over time, develop other attributes. As the members get to know each other better, other goals besides simply playing chess may be added, a tradition may evolve, and the club may, in fact, outgrow its initial nature and develop more cohesion and solidarity. The health and stability of the club may take on a value of its own (may attain some intrinsic as well as instrumental value): the meaning that such a club has in the lives of its members may transcend the initial value of offering an opportunity to play chess. Apart from the value of playing chess, the *Verein* may slowly begin to evolve into a more stable form of association. As more goals are shared and eventually as the persistence of the club becomes a goal in its own right, solidarity is less tenuous and stability is more assured. Individuals, however, have generally voluntarily come together to pursue a common interest rather than being, as it were, born into the *Verein*. True, some membership may be virtually passed on from father to son or mother to daughter. When that, however, is the case, the *Verein* is well on its way to becoming a different kind of association.

More complex associations or societies (*Gesellschaften*) are knit together by a larger and more sophisticated set of shared values and goals. They stand between mere associations (*Vereine*) in my former and communities in my later sense. Civil organizations such as cities, states, or countries may be examples. Their ends or goals are far more complex than those of mere associations and rudimentary communities may readily but not necessarily evolve from such associations. In general, however, such societies are still formed either by individuals themselves or, at times, consist of the coming together of more uni-purpose associations who because of shared needs or interests have flocked together. Cities, states, or municipalities may merely be societies or they may, in some instances, be on their way to becoming or may have already become real communities. Birth or voluntary individual action may be part of the formation of such entities: persons may be born into or move to a new city or country and become its citizens. Or membership may be by virtue of belonging to a smaller association which is part of the larger. Because of the more complex nature of their goals and because they are far more deeply a part of the life of every one of their members, societies have much more stability than *Vereine*. Their existence as a goal in itself rather than their existence merely as a means for fulfilling one or several of many ends is foreshadowed if not already sometimes present in the *Gesellschaft*.

In the sense in which I use the term here, communities (*Gemeinschaften*) have a much deeper foundation and in some respects have quite different goals. Frequently, albeit not necessarily, communities (*Gemeinschaften* as opposed to *Gesellschaften*) are something persons are a natural part of, are born into, and are not truly dissociable from. Literally the word *Gemeinschaft* means a "creating together," not merely working together on a particular problem but literally creating (*schaffen*). What makes communities communities is, as we have said, the fact that they include the notion of community itself as one of the base values and reasons for their coherence. Literally, communities work together to create their present and to shape their future in a common effort in which all equally partake. Members of a true community or *Gemeinschaft* share values and goals which are not merely individual interests which may, at a given time, happen to coincide. They share values and goals which have become communal values and goals for whose realization community itself is necessary so that eventually community itself becomes a goal and a value in its own right.[31,32]

Community has a pervasive intrinsic as well as an instrumental value. The raison d'être of community, in part at least, is community itself.[1,31] It is evident that the solidarity of lose associations (*Vereine*) is small: if individuals change merely one of their interests, if they find that there are too many other differences between them and the other members, or if they are otherwise distracted, they will leave the association. If many individuals do this, the association stops existing. Such associations are, in a sense, external to the individuals who compose them: they are not essential to the way individuals identify or characterize themselves. Communities in some sense are internal: the way individuals identify themselves is to a large extent and often tacitly through the community. Societies (for want of a better word, those more complex associations which are not quite communities) by virtue of sharing more interests and goals stand in an intermediate position between mere "Verein" association and community: by virtue of the complexity of goals and interests members have a greater external and internal stake in them. Their self-identification may be linked with these societies albeit such linkages still tend to be fairly superficial, practical, and less tacit or internalized.

The differences between what I have called *Verein, Gesellschaft,* and *Gemeinschaft* are not watertight differences. One constantly can observe intermediate and transitional forms. The borderlines in reality or conceptually cannot be strictly drawn. Nor is development necessarily in a direction from *Verein* to *Gemeinschaft.* Former *Gemeinschaften* may falter, a *Verein* may develop into a *Gemeinschaft,* and a *Gesellschaft* may begin to develop the attributes and ultimately become a true *Gemeinschaft.* The differences I have sketched are conceptually useful but all these states are (or are potentially) dynamic.

When societies remain societies rather than developing the attributes of community, the glue of solidarity is relatively weak. Societies, such as the United States, may serve as examples. Unmet needs as well as real and perceived gross injustice produces a state in which a vicious circle is set up: individuals feel a sense of betrayal as in the midst of an allegedly individualistic society they find themselves unable to develop their individual talents or to pursue their individual goals and interests. Such persons feel that they have been betrayed and "sold out" by what they regard as at best a society. It is a society largely external to them with little instrumental and less intrinsic value. Their own small community of the disadvantaged may be the only community they know: the only structure or entity worth preserving for its own sake, the only one having some intrinsic worth. And often not even that is the case. They see their individual selves or their community pitted against the larger society of which they are told they are a part. Such a society, however, is not one from which they have experienced nurture and to which they consequently owe obligations. On the contrary: what obligations they perceive are owed to their own community, now seen as distinct from and in conflict with the society from which they are alienated and into which they feel impressed. In consequence, the larger society of which such groups inevitably are a part lacks solidarity and is easily disrupted. Such societies instead of flourishing, growing, and evolving, must ultimately either change radically or wither and die.

Solidarity with one's community is, I have argued, based on a number of factors: the implicit realization that my community and the persons within it will refrain from harming me directly allows me to pursue my particular goals in considerably more freedom than I could have if such assurances were not at hand. The situation on American streets (a situation in which persons have good reason for fearing others) illustrates this point. Persons who must go about their business in perpetual fear of possible harm are unlikely to go about their business as successfully as they would if such fears played little role. And, in fact, this is well illustrated by the situation at hand. Persons in many if not all cities in the United States are best advised to avoid many areas in their cities or to refrain from going out on foot after dark. The danger of bodily harm is ever and very realistically present. Solidarity with the community which affords little protection from harm is slim.

There is more to feeling secure than knowing that my personal freedom will not be limited or that I will not be done direct bodily harm. My personal freedom can be of value to me only if other conditions are met. In order to enjoy my freedom more than lack of incursion by others is needed. At the very least I must feel confident that when trouble strikes I will be helped: whether such trouble comes to me at the hands of blind fate (the natural lottery) or whether it comes to me deliberately at the hands of others. Knowing that others will not hinder me in pursuing my goals or in unfolding my talents is certainly one of the first conditions in my ability to do so and such assurances produce a certain solidarity with the community which holds such a promise. But I am not truly "free" to pursue my goals and unfold my talents if my basic biological or social needs remain unmet. The starving, the homeless, or those denied equal education or medical care may be "free," but such freedom is a bogus freedom, a cynical commentary by those who control the resources and who do not wish to part with any of them. When such a state of affairs exists, as it does in the United States today, solidarity will be minimal.

I have claimed that less complex associations such as the "Verein" are, in a sense, external to the individuals who compose them: they are not essential to the way individuals identify or characterize themselves. When the disadvantaged feel apart or alienated from, or even actively hostile to, society they are and remain external to society and solidarity cannot develop. When persons are not disadvantaged but when societies play a role in assuring basic necessities for all and in an equitable manner attempt to provide all with a fair chance at the opportunities such societies have to offer, such societies are well on their way toward becoming communities: structures with which the members identify themselves and through which they can best accomplish their goals. The society which nurtures its members, not only nurtures them sufficiently to allow their biological survival but nurtures them so that they can truly develop their talents and pursue their goals, will be a society well on its way to being a true community: a structure internalized by its members and a structure in which community itself is a critical value and goal in its own right. Such communities will see a homeostatic balnace between individual and communal goals: a balance in which values, goals, and strivings overlap and complement each other.

REFERENCES

1. Loewy EH: *Suffering and the Beneficent Community: Beyond Libertarianism.* Albany, NY: SUNY Press; 1991.

2. Dennett DC: *Elbow Room: The Varieties of Free Will Worth Having.* Cambridge, MA: MIT Press; 1985.

3. Daniels N: *Just Health Care.* New York, NY: Cambridge University Press; 1985.

4. Mandeville B: *The Fable of the Bees.* Harmondsworth, England: Penguin Books; 1970.

5. Darwin C: *The Descent of Man.* New York, NY: H.M. Caldwell; 1874.

6. Tawney RH: *Religion and the Rise of Capitalism: A Historical Study.* New York, NY: American Library; 1954

7. Kautsky K: *Foundations of Christianity* (Henry F. Mins, trans.). New York, NY: Russell; 1953.

8. Weber M: *Die Protestantische Ethik und der Geist des Kapitalismus.* Gutersloh, Deutschland: Mohn; 1981.

9. Hobbes T: *Leviathan.* New York, NY: Collier; 1962.

10. Nozick R: *Anarchy, State and Utopia.* New York, NY: Basic Books; 1974

11. Engelhardt HT: Morality for the Medical Industrial Complex:

A Code of Ethics for the Mass Marketing of Health Care. NEJM 1988; 319(16): 1086–1089.

12. Rachels J: *Created from Animals: The Moral Implications of Darwinism.* New York, NY: Oxford University Press; 1990.

13. Springer-Loewy RA: An Alternative to Traditional Models of Human Relationships. Cambridge Quarterly 1993 (in press).

14. Rousseau JJ: *Emile: ou, de l'Education.* Paris, France: Garnier Freres; 1957.

15. Pellegrino ED and Thomasma DC: *For the Patient's Good: The Restoration of Beneficence to Health Care.* New York, NY: Oxford University Press; 1988.

16. Dworkin G: Paternalism. Monist 1972; 56: 64–84.

17. Feinberg J: Legal Paternalism. Canadian J Philosophy 1971; 1: 105–124.

18. Aristotle: Ethica Nicomachea. In: *The Basic Works of Aristotle* (R. McKeon, ed.), New York, NY: Random House, 1971.

19. Langley LL: *Homeostasis.* New York, NY: Reinhold Publishing Corp.; 1965.

20. Bernard C: *Introduction à l'étude de la médicine expérimental.* Paris, France: J. B. Bailiere; 1865.

21. Cannon WB: *The Wisdom of the Body* (2nd ed.). New York, NY: Norton Publishers; 1939

22. Trojan P: *Ecosystem Homeostasis* (I. Bagaeva, trans.). The Hague, Netherlands: Dr. W. Junk Publishers; 1984.

23. Locke J: *Second Treatise on Government* (C. E. Macpherson, ed.). Indianapolis, IN: Hackett Publishing; 1980.

24. Rousseau JJ: *Du Contrat Social* (R. Grimsley, ed.). Oxford, England; Oxford University Press; 1972.

25. Rousseau JJ: *Discours sur l'Origine et les Fondements de l'Iné-galité parmi les Hommes.* Paris, France: Gallimard; 1965.

26. Rawls J: *A Theory of Justice.* Cambridge, MA: Harvard University Press; 1971.

27. Weber M: *Grundrisz der Sozialökonomie—III. Abteilung: Wirtschaft und Gesellschaft.* Tübingen; 1925.

28. Popper K: *Conjecture and Refutations: The Growth of Scientific Knowledge.* New York, NY: Harper and Row; 1968.

29. Moreno JD: The Social Individual in Clinical Ethics. J Clinical Ethics 1992; 3(1): 53–55.

30. Tönnies F: *Gemeinschaft und Gesellschaft.* Darmstadt, Deutschland: Wissenschaftliche Buchgesellschaft; 1963.

31. Oakshott M: *On Human Conduct.* Oxford, England: Clarendon Press; 1975.

32. Buchanan AE: Assessing the Communitarian Critique of Liberalism. Ethics 1989; 99: 852–882.

CHAPTER 5

Interrelating Communities

In prior chapters I have focused on developing the concept of suffering in the context of a notion of community which grounds community in the nurture necessarily experienced by all individuals prior to the emergence of any possible sense of selfhood. Autonomy, according to this point of view, of necessity emerges in the embrace of beneficence. I have differentiated between various types of associations arguing that an association can be a community (*Gemeinschaft*) only when such an association accepts and internalizes the existence of community itself as a transcendent goal in its own right. Further, I have argued that accepting these notions entails certain beneficent obligations. My claim has been that obligations of this sort can be grounded in far more than merely deductive logic. If one accepts beneficent obligations and, therefore, if one concerns oneself with social justice, one inevitably has interests in social justice with the legitimate interests individuals have to be as free as possible.

Competition between individual and communal interests is, I believe, a narrow way of conceptualizing problems of social justice and individual liberty. Competition is a narrow way of conceptualizing these problems because these problems go to the very marrow of human relationships, human obligations, and human social structure. One cannot reduce such fundamental human concepts to competitive struggle without trivializing them. Instead of a dialectic or competitive model, I have suggested that the relationship of individuals with their community is one of homeostasis in which inevitably, rather than vying with each other, individuals and communities must share some important fundamental and common goals. Homeostasis in organisms, species, and cultures enables sufficient stability so that progress and evolution of such organisms, species, and cultures and ultimately their survival is made possible; competition between narrowly conceived individual interests does not provide this kind of stability and, therefore, does not serve to underwrite evolution, progress, and survival in the same way. Solidarity in a community provides sufficient cohesion so that homeostasis can function; in turn, by allowing adjustments within a preset range of values, and by allowing experimental readjustment of the range ultimately for the benefit of all, homeostasis supports solidarity. When greater rather than lesser equity in access to basic needs (including the needs individuals have for flourishing as persons and for developing their own talents) exists, cohesion and solidarity are firmer.

In a world in which mutual needs and almost instant communications have made peoples and nations interdependent, the relationship between individuals and their particular community is inevitably enmeshed in a wider set of relationships which ultimately no individual and no association can escape. In this chapter I want to examine some of the aspects of the relationship among various kinds of associations and communities. In doing this I will argue that differentials in capacity exemplify the relationship between individuals as well as among mutually dependent associations, and I will expand the notion of community to show that the relationship among various associations bears a striking similarity to the relationship between the individual and his/her particular community; such a relationship includes a similarity of mutual obligations in which the mutual meeting of basic needs is central. In claiming that the tacit model we use structures the way we see relationships, I will advance the claim that a homeostatic model is a more fruitful and realistic model with which to examine relationships among various associations than is a crassly competitive one. I will conclude by showing that far from producing a homogeneity of communities throughout the world, a relationship of this sort would foster the development of individual communal attributes and cultures. I shall claim that fostering the development of individual communal capacities and attributes is as much in the interest of the larger as it is in the interest of the smaller communities. While I will weave practical examples throughout this discussion, such examples can, of course, be no more than a tentative sketch of the problems which need or can be addressed; hopefully, however, the examples will stimulate further inquiry.

INTERDEPENDENCE AND ASSOCIATION

Communities, no more than individuals, can, at least in today's world, exist in isolation. Without other communities, particular communities cannot define themselves. I shall argue that the survival of any particular association or community depends not only on its own internal solidarity but likewise that the survival of such collectives is a function of the relationship particular associations or communities have with others. In examining such relationships, I will again stress that the concept of homeostasis provides a natural and realistic framework in which relationships can fruitfully evolve and grow.

To achieve the goal of community, solidarity and individual flourishing is to hold suffering to a minimum. I have argued that (1) to meet such a goal all individuals must have equal access to first order necessities (those things needed to sustain biological existence) as well as to second order necessities (those things essential for individuals to fully develop their talents in a given social setting); (2) in societies in which some groups have been historically disadvantaged, some form of effective affirmative action for the historically disadvantaged, likewise, arguably is a second order necessity; and (3) communities can reasonably be expected to see to it that all individuals within their society have full access to first and second order needs before allowing other members of the community to enjoy opulence, even if providing such access results in restricting some of the freedoms (by, for example, taxation) of those who are better off. Restricting freedoms in this way ultimately benefits not only those who now lack equal access as well as benefiting the community itself but, likewise, ultimately helps sustain individual freedom for all.

A social homeostatic system requires internal adjustments so that all persons within such social systems can sustain their individual lives as well as achieve a reasonable unfolding of their individual talents. This, of course, implies that every effort to supply first as well as second order needs must be made. Social entities which provide such necessities are apt to produce social cohesion. Communities by failing to provide access to basic needs when they could do so weaken their own solidarity. When some live in poverty while others enjoy opulence community is threatened: when community perishes, the necessary condition for everyone's freedom as well as for individual flourishing is eliminated.

Libertarians argue that the world is hopelessly pluralistic and that such pluralism, without an initial almost Hobbesian contract of mutual non-harm, inevitably would lead to hostility. Peace can be assured only by coexisting in a framework of mutual respect for freedom. Freedom and respect for as absolute freedom as is consistent with the freedom of all others for like freedom, is the basic and indeed is the sole requirement of morality.[1,2] Only by regarding freedom as the necessary condition for relationships can a Hobbesian war of all against all be avoided. Without such a notion of the overriding moral power of freedom (unless we make freedom into a condition rather than merely into a value of morality) diverse visions of the good would inevitably clash and lead to hostilities.

Libertarians are quite right when they consider respect for freedom to be a necessary condition for morality. But, as I have tried to show, libertarians go far beyond considering freedom as merely a necessary condition: They consider freedom not only as the *sole* necessary condition but indeed they also consider freedom to be the sufficient condition for relationships. From a libertarian perspective, beneficence may be desirable (though quite why other than for aesthetic or traditional reasons beneficence would be desirable is far from clear) but outside specific moral enclaves beneficence has no morally binding force and, therefore, can never be an enforceable moral obligation. Persons, by virtue of being persons, have no beneficent obligations except insofar as beneficent obligation is entailed by their membership in a particular voluntarily joined and adhered to association. Except by contract or treaty communities (or separate moral enclaves) have no beneficent obligations to other groups or associations. Their obligation is to respect the freedom and integrity of these other groups and to strictly adhere to freely entered contracts or treaties. A responsibility to come to each other's aid (unless doing so has been explicitly stipulated by contract or treaty) does not exist.[1,2]

From the libertarian perspective, persons have no beneficent obligations.[1,2] They are required only to adhere to freely entered contracts and to refrain from harming each other. In turn, communities have no specific obligations of beneficence toward their members. Their only function is to provide a peaceful setting in which mutual non-harm is enforced and liberty safeguarded. Governments, from a libertarian perspective, are instituted to protect liberty and to enforce freely entered contracts. Assuredly governments cannot diminish the liberty of one to benefit another. Being beneficent is a matter of personal volition or a requirement of membership in certain peculiar moral enclaves defined in part by such a requirement. A community founded on such libertarian precepts is, of course, one in which capitalism and entrepreneurialism will flourish to the benefit of those who win in this competition and to the detriment of those who inevitably must lose. As long as the rules are followed, the losers have no just cause to complain.[3] And, according to libertarian doctrine, the rules aside from rules of refraining from overt harm to each other and of meticulously adhering to the rules of freely entered mutual contract are few.

Individuals are social beings which exist in and are enabled by community. Without community individuals cannot define themselves, let alone find true fulfillment. Individual action is inevitably social, just as communal action inevitably affects individuals. The social and the individual while conceptually separate are not in reality separable. Social action inevitably takes place in a variety of associations. Associations are, in a sense, corporate entities; but just as individuals are not separable from their social context, associations likewise exist in an inevitable wider social context in which they must relate with and to others.

Collectives or associations have been differentiated and discussed in the fourth chapter. *Vereine* may evolve into *Gesellschaften* (or societies) when, by and of necessity, they develop certain shared goals. The association itself may initially not be one of the transcendent goals shared in such an association. Loosely fashioned associations (associations such as the *Verein* or even the beginning of the *Gesellschaft*) see the goal of association purely as an instrumental end: without their particular association they cannot as easily pursue their particular goals and interests. As time goes on and shared goals expand, association itself may become one of the important, shared, and ultimately transcendent values. When this occurs, such associations will approximate true communities.

Communities are not equivalent to the state: states may or may not be communities in the sense I have spoken of community (*Gemeinschaft*) and communities more often than not are not states. A state may be a very artificial association created by external forces, as when an artificial state is arbitrarily carved out in the course of settling a conflict (many of the states created in the Middle East by various conventions after World War I serve as examples); states may be associations imposed externally; states may be more organic units; or, at times, states may be or may come to approximate communities in the true sense.

In today's world associations are inevitably enmeshed with each other. This inevitable mutuality is what makes it most difficult to delineate what may properly be "purely an internal affair" from what ultimately must concern all, just as it is difficult to delineate when what I do is entirely my private affair from when it impinges on others and on my community. When John Donne wrote "send not to ask for whom the bell tolls, it tolls for thee," he implied about individuals and their association with each other what today holds with at least equal force when it comes to diverse associations and their fates. The prosperity or death of another association or community, no matter how distant or how close to us, eventually and inevitably affects us all. In a very immediate or in a more removed sense we all are involved with each other.

The basis of obligation is relationship. The condition of obligation is ability. Unless things are actually or potentially, directly or indirectly, in some relationship to each other obligations cannot come about. Unless the capacity to affect one another exists, the concept of obligation is moot.[4] Having an obligation to someone or something implies, among other things, both a relationship and a capacity. An obligation to help my friend (or to help a stranger) exists because of the relationship I have with my friend (or with the stranger). Such an obligation becomes operative when capacity exists and help is needed: in other words, it becomes operative when one of us is relatively weaker or stronger than the other. I also have an obligation not to lie, steal, murder, or write graffiti on the wall because of my relationship to others (others who are of primary or secondary worth) and because of my capacity to do these things. Since I have the capacity to lie, steal, murder, or write graffiti, others who I would lie to, steal from, or murder (or objects which I might decorate with graffiti) are vulnerable. A relationship and the ability to do something are the grounds of obligation.

Having a relationship and an ability alone, however, does not necessarily entail an obligation. I may have a relationship with a person and I may have the ability to buy him/her a ticket to the opera: that, most would agree, does not under ordinary circumstances obligate me to do so. On the other hand, I may meet a starving person and have the ability to buy him/her food: many would say that an obligation for me to do so, rather than to allow him/her to starve, exists. Obligations may be grounded in a prior promise: if I had promised to buy opera tickets for my friend the prior contract (or promise) and our relationship would create the obligation; my capacity to buy the tickets would render it operative. Or obligations may be grounded in need. Obligations to supply a starving person with the means to meet first order necessities when it is possible to do so do not, if beneficence is to be acknowledged to have significant moral force, require prior explicit contract: it is our common heritage as recipients of nurture and beneficence and our common understanding of a beneficent community which provides the (tacit or implicit) contract. To be a human in the true sense in which the term is used implies beneficent obligations (see chapter 3). To, when that is possible, help someone in dire need is an implied promise grounded in the beneficence demanded from our shared humanity and experience as well as in the duty to include the ends of others among my own ends.[5] My being able to rely on help by others (and their being able to rely on me for my help), as well as my and others' tacit acceptance of such an implied promise and of the obligation such a promise entails promotes solidarity and provides social strength.

A relationship between myself and a starving person is created not only by our meeting but symbolically by our being contemporaries on the same planet; the better I know the person, the closer the relationship, the more (or, at times, the less) may my obligation be. The fact of relationship as well as my capacity to affect that other creates the obligation. Such an obligation would be grounded in an ethic accepting beneficent obligations: at least the obligation to, where possible, provide for the first order necessities of my neighbor. The nature of the relationship may, furthermore, strengthen or weaken the undeniable obligation: needs being similar, my obligation to my wife who has always unstintingly helped me and whom I love is greater than is my obligation to the person I have never met; my obligation to the person I have never met may be greater than my obligation to another who has done me deliberate and persistent harm. But the obligation (strengthened or weakened but an obligation nonetheless) exists by virtue of the other's need and of my capacity. Obligations, however, are moot without my capacity to discharge them: if I have no resources, the condition for my obligation, but not the obligation itself, is gone. The persistence of the obligation (even when it is rendered moot by my lack of capacity) acts as a stimulus urging me on to attempt to develop the capacity to help.

An obligation is created by, among other things, a relationship and the capacity to do or to refrain from doing something. One might argue that we have no actual relationship with our environment or with tomorrow and that, therefore, acting responsibly when it comes to matters which have no effect on actual others even when we have the capacity to do so can not be construed to be an obligation. Why worry about the ozone layer, the Amazon or an endangered species? I shall argue, as has Hans Jonas, that we have responsibilities which are deeply connected with our ever increasing power and capacity to permanently affect such things. It is the totality and permanence of our power which is, in part, what produces such a responsibility. When our actions only temporarily affected a limited number of persons, our responsibilities were far different.[4] We have a responsibility to tomorrow because others who lived yesterday enabled our existence today. This argument is akin to my argument that it is our common experience as infants of being nurtured and beyond this our common experience of beneficence which in part underpins our beneficent obligations. How we act today may be critical for those who live tomorrow and our relationship with tomorrow is created by the relationship we ourselves have and have had with our yesterdays. When, furthermore, our actions have the capacity to destroy tomorrow itself, our obligation to maintain a tomorrow for others—since others yesterday helped maintain the possibility of today for us—becomes an important issue.

The fact that I have the capacity to do or not to do something, while it does not by itself create an obligation, nevertheless is at the root of my obligation. Vulnerability interrelates us. My obligation to rescue someone when I easily can do so (an obligation libertarians would deny exists) rests on this very fact. I have argued that beneficent obligations are generally (but perhaps not necessarily specifically) binding not only because not to accept them would, as Kant rightly claims, "cause the will (or volition) to conflict with itself" (p. 54), not only because not to do so would fail to include the ends of others among my own,[5] but also because all of us inevitably are enmeshed in a personal, species, and cultural history of beneficence. Our own existence at critical times in our lives and perhaps again in the future have and will depend on it.

Libertarians deny Kant's claim that to will a world without beneficence would force the will to contradict itself. Rather, libertarians claim that this argument is made from inside a particular moral perspective which already assigns a high value to charity and beneficence. Such a claim, they believe, denotes a "lack of imagination."[6] I will grant that, as Kant acknowledges, it is not strictly logically necessary to will beneficence: one could, and not contravene strict logic, will a world in which beneficence did not exist. (Although as Kant certainly emphasizes, failing to include another's ends among one's own denotes disrespect and would conflict with at least one formulation of the Categorical Imperative.) My imagination goes far enough so that I can conceive a world without beneficence; it also goes far enough to realize that not only would such a world not be one in which most (sane) persons would want to live but that it is a world in which solidarity and social cohesion would be sorely wanting. Such a world would threaten to be a world at perpetual war with itself. It would lack stability and could not even hope for solidarity.

I have argued that our obligations and our sense of community are, at least in part, grounded in our early and necessary experience of nurture. Without initial nurture to ensure our physical survival and later beneficence to allow our flourishing none of us would have survived to value freedom. The necessary condition for our capacity to value freedom or anything else rests on that experience. To will otherwise is to will one's own nonexistence: and that, I believe, would be a case of the will conflicting with itself. It would entail a willing away of the ground of one's will. Likewise it would, in many instances at least, will away the ground of one's freedom. Freedom without the basic essentials necessary to support life and flourishing is a peculiar and at best a stunted freedom. Much as libertarians will deny this, the libertarian argument is and is inevitably itself an argument made from within a particular moral perspective: The libertarian perspective of a starkly atomistic and individualistic world. An attempt to argue without a perspective is inconceivable: it is not something humans can do. It is akin to judging without a framework for judging. But that is precisely the problem: judging without a framework for judging, or arguing without a perspective, inevitably is likewise a framework or a perspective. In the human condition that seems inescapable.

Associations have obligations to their individual members. The individuals likewise have obligations toward the association and toward each other. Just as is the case with individuals and their obligations, capacities, vulnerabilities, and relationships condition the obligations communities and individuals have to and with each other. By virtue of the fact of relationship and of vulnerability and capacity, associations are obligated to their members and the members are obligated to their association. The nature of the association conditions the relationship. A *Verein* (an association formed to pursue a given common goal, say play quartets) has very narrow obligations to its members. When the *Verein* is small enough, such obligations can be almost (but not quite) reduced to the obligations individual members have to each other. Beneficence is not generally an obligation taken on by the association in the process of forming the usual type of *Verein*, though, as the *Verein* grows and closer relationships form, such obligations may tacitly be assumed. *Vereine* internally operate, and operate well and legitimately, on a libertarian model of mutual non-harm and explicit contract. Their relationships with other *Vereine*, and with the larger associations within which they are embedded, likewise, tend to be more contractual and superficial. They do not, as I will argue shortly, generally formulate and evolve further goals. When they do, they are well on their way to becoming more complex associations and to having more complex obligations.

Individuals in any association, if my previous sketch of obligations has any merit, do have beneficent obligations toward one another. Such beneficent obligation is, however, one which exists regardless of the association. By virtue of having probably formed closer human bonds with my chess partner than I have with the man sitting next to me at the lunch counter, my obligations to my partner may be more extensive. But that neither means that my obligations to the man next to me at the lunch counter are purely those of non-harm nor that my greater obligations to my chess partner are defined or definable by our being members of the same *Verein*. The *Verein* merely has created a setting in which deeper relationships are likely (but do not have to) occur.

I want to make myself quite clear at this point: in differentiating between *Verein*, *Gesellschaft* (society), and *Gemeinschaft* (community) I am not implying a necessary difference in size. In general, but not necessarily, a *Verein* will be smaller than either a *Gesell-* or *Gemeinschaft*. But an association of persons committed to one or a very few goals and having little interest in the integrity of the association outside these immediate goals could, in fact, be quite large: for example, an international business venture committed to the sale of condoms or automobiles. When I speak of "size," of the smaller relating to or fitting into the other, I have more than physical size in mind: it is largeness as well as complexity of design and complexity of meaning rather than physical largeness that I am after.

Associations may share one or a very small set of values and goals (*Vereine*); may be more complex and share a more complex set of values and goals (and be *Gesellschaften* or societies); or they may share a very complex set of multiple values and goals among which the integrity of the association itself becomes an overarching and critical goal and a value in its own right. Such organizations are what I have called *Gemeinschaften* or communities.

When associations become more complex than mere *Vereine*, they begin to find that the association itself is not only united by a set of values and goals but that the association begins to generate and formulate new values and goals. Such an association may still be a *Gesellschaft*: while the integrity of the association is of greater importance to its members, such an association is still mainly of importance in meeting specific goals and only to some extent important in formulating new ones. By the time a *Gemeinschaft* comes into being it plays a far more organic, dynamic, and significant role in the formulation and generation of an evolving set of values and goals. The *Gemeinschaft* now is not only of critical importance to all within it; it has developed an organic life of its own. It is a life not only necessary for pursuing the values and goals which unite the *Gemeinschaft* but also necessary so that new values and goals can be formulated, enunciated, and pursued. Community, in that sense, is now the essential ground of individual existence. Within the overarching goal of community further values and goals are enunciated, tested, and determined. In this way, community itself assumes a "prior value": prior, that is, to the possibility of formulating coherent goals and of living productive lives. Homeostasis enables evolution, growth, and ultimately survival in a dynamic world. Homeostasis, to be effective, requires more than action within a proscribed status quo: evolution, growth, and survival requires the formulation, testing, and eventual pursuit of new values and goals.

Some *Gemeinschaften* (communities) go even a step beyond the description of the *Gemeinschaft* I have given. I have in mind here some religious communities as well as some secular examples such as the kibbutzim in Israel or Owen's early New Harmony experiment in Indiana. Such communities are not a *Gemeinschaft* in the sense I have painted here. Such communities share an overwhelming commonality (often almost an identity) of values and goals so that their members, in many senses, are virtually homogenized. Often such communities are much less dynamic: Their values and goals are much more static. Such communities (while assuredly they are *Gemeinschaften*) are *Gemeinschaften* in a different sense than the sense I have and shall continue to use here. Often quite purposively such communities (one can here think of monastic orders or some of the Amish communities in the United States) deal as little as they can with the outside world, sometimes because they fear contamination, sometimes because their beliefs demand this, and sometimes because of outside hostility.

Persons are usually totally committed to communities of this sort. Their relationship with each other is not only modulated but is defined by the community of which they are a part. There is little give and take in such communities: rather than being solid and cohesive, communities of this sort tend to be static and frozen, committed to the same goals and values year after year. The range of values which acts as the framework in which the homeostatic system operates is narrowly set. Resetting this range of values is almost impossible since deviation from the narrowly defined range of norms is not looked upon as innovative, experimental, or even interesting, but rather is looked upon as almost treasonable. One who tries to innovate and who questions such norms is apt to be ejected. A homeostatic balance in which differences are weighed, adjudicated, and settled in an ongoing and interactive manner by all concerned is not possible outside a very narrow range. The value of community is not just a transcendent value which unites such communities but rather tends to become a straight jacket preventing evolution and growth. Such communities are stagnant rather than dynamic in the sense of striving and developing new goals and experimenting with new ways. They pay a heavy price for a solidarity and cohesion which, instead of supporting individual development and expression, is cloying and ultimately stifles individual development and expression. For that reason these communities are apt to stagnate and often do not survive. But even such associations are critically dependent upon the inevitable relationships they must have with others. Unable to adapt to any way but their own and unable to compromise, work with, or often even tolerate other values and goals, they are apt to be crushed. When I speak of *Gemeinschaften* or communities in this work I do not have such associations in mind. Rather, I have in mind associations which, while they hold the very existence and flourishing of community as a transcendent value and goal, in the process of being actively engaged in evolving new values and goals are far from insisting on dull uniformity. On the few occasions when I shall have cause to mention such monolithic communities and even though I am fully cognizant of the fact that they may be secular as well as being religious, I shall, for want of a better word, refer to them as "cloistered" or "monastic" communities.

If the differentiations made between *Verein, Gesellschaft*, and *Gemeinschaft* are conceived as watertight differentiations they will serve little purpose. One type of association does not at some point suddenly become another type any more than at some point one species suddenly springs forth from another. While we may, for the sake of convenience and classification, set up specific criteria and create convenient models, we set up these criteria in full realization that such criteria are definitional and social conveniences rather than being "facts of nature." The progression of social associations from the least to the most complex proceeds in an evolutionary and often in a quite tentative manner.

A simple association (the *Verein*) may remain a simple organization devoted to a specific or a specific small set of values and goals. Often, however, as relationships among the individuals of such a *Verein* as well as relationships with other like associations and with the wider world in which the *Verein* is embedded develop, the *Verein* takes on a greater value in its own right. The *Verein* is now more than merely the possibility for pursuing one small goal or one small set of goals of life, say playing chess or Mozart quartets or doing these things and having coffee and cake. Through other social associations a *Verein* begins to fill a wider need: maintaining the association begins to assume importance in its own right regardless of the original goal. In part this greater importance is due to the development of individual relationships among the members; in part it is because of the inevitable relationships such associations form with wider social structures; in part it is because, tacitly or explicitly, such associations have begun to evolve new values and goals; and in part the importance begins to transcends the sum of these parts. As the *Verein* develops into a *Gesellschaft* and eventually into a *Gemeinschaft*, it not only takes on greater importance: in developing this greater importance, relationships external and internal to the association have changed as, inevitably, have its individual and corporate obligations.

When a *Verein* begins to grow in complexity, begins to fill wider needs, and takes on various new values and goals, it evolves into what can now be recognized as a *Gesellschaft*. Eventually, tacitly perhaps more than explicitly, this changing association develops its own integrity as a value in its own right. To sustain growth and evolution, such societies must begin to formulate, enunciate, and evolve new values and goals. With these evolving new internal values and goals and with this changing internal relationship, external relationships and with them external obligations likewise change and grow.

A *Gesellschaft* (or society) is a far more organic association than is a mere *Verein*. When a *Gesellschaft* becomes a *Gemeinschaft* this process has continued. The value and goal of its own integrity and existence and the capacity to formulate new values and goals is a much stronger one. Obligations grow with this assumption: solidarity in a *Verein* depends on the continued desirability of a particular or a small set of particular goals and values; in a *Gesellschaft* the more numerous, intricate, and interwoven values and goals begin to require that the goal of preserving the *Gesellschaft* assumes some importance. In a *Gemein-schaft*, the goal of maintaining the *Gemeinschaft* itself becomes an overarching and transcendent goal for all of its members.

The interrelationship among the three types of associations or collectives sketched cannot, of course, be strictly compartmentalized. Not only is there no definite place at which one type of collective can be said to end and another type of collective can be said to begin, but as collectives continue to develop they may develop in either direction. Moving from *Verein* to *Gemeinschaft* is not a one way street in which collectives by some sort of *volente general* strive to approach the ideal of *Gemeinschaft*. Rather, movement is a fluid, dynamic process in which one can rightly and with justice claim that a given collective is more or less of a *Gesellschaft* or more or less of a *Gemeinschaft*: that is, that it has gained or lost certain aspects of one or the other and so forth. As new values and goals develop or as the priorities of one goal or value over another changes, a certain type of collective may experiment with approaching more one or more the other. A true community may decide to experiment with adopting certain features of a *Gesellschaft* or the opposite may occur. One can see this, for example, with some of the drift toward the right which has occurred and which is being toyed with in some Scandinavian societies: as they do this, they inevitably move from being more of a *Gemeinschaft* to being more of a *Gesell-schaft*. Market economies, as contrasted to more socialized ones, have a different set of homeostatic set-points. They are generally more *Gesellschaften* than they are *Gemeinschaften*. Collectives which are more socialized like the Scandinavian states may decide to experiment with adopting more features of a *Gesell-schaft* by approaching market states like the United States; or the converse may occur.

In a truly democratic society, this capacity to alter set-points, to experiment, learn, and adapt, is one of democracy's many strengths. When democracy fails while the technical trappings of democratic process remain, the ability to internally formulate new values and goals and the capacity to alter homeostatic set-points also fails. The more truly democratic a society (the more the *volente general* can be freely, informedly, and democratically evolved and expressed) the better its homeostatic capacity; the more democracy becomes a sham, the less can effective homeostasis continue. When the technical features of democracy remain but democracy itself has become meaningless (when elections are technically honest but no real choice exists or/and when the electorate is ill-informed or indolent) values and goals are no longer set by the *volente general* but are easily manipulated by external or internal power structures.

A state of affairs in which technical features of democracy remain while democracy itself has become questionable can be observed under a variety of conditions. In the former Soviet states elections were a farce: The electorate had no meaningful choice, information was contrived, and whatever *volente general* existed was not to be expressed through existing channels. Rather, the *volente general*, inchoate in its being but enunciated by many intellectuals who opposed the system and who paid the price, ultimately expressed its way and showed its power by destroying the system. In the United States today, elections are technically honest: those who vote have the legal right to do so, the process is secret, and the results are not manipulated. But in the United States today, while elections are honest, they likewise have become a farce: candidates are perforce funded and, therefore, ultimately controlled by capitalist interests, information is manipulated by the media which are also largely controlled by the same interests, and the general education of the electorate is acknowledged to be deficient. Intellectuals and others may speak out but they are generally ignored. Under such circumstances not only does a *volente general* have a difficult time being expressed, a *volente general* is difficult, if not indeed impossible, to form. Instead a seething and restless dissatisfaction which has little direction and little unity of purpose takes its place. Individuals may regret the state of affairs but individuals remain individuals who have little sense of community and, therefore, little hope of communal action.

In general, socialized communities, say on a Scandinavian model, will be closer to *Gemeinschaften* while market based collectives inevitably will be closer to *Gesellschaften*. Indeed, as market-based collectives become less and less accepting of beneficent obligations, as poverty increases and as individual aspirations consequently become, except for those who can commandeer the price, a sham, such *Gesellschaften* begin to lose interest in community as a goal in its own right and approach a *Verein*.

As a *Gesellschaft* moves toward a *Verein* obligations are definable by mutual non-harm and rigid adherence to freely made contracts. As *Gemeinschaft* becomes extreme it assumes the trappings of a monastic community in which rigidity prevails and is enforced. In a political sense, neither is viable. In one case, members who lose interest or belief in the goal are ejected; in the other case alienation is inevitable and individuals leave by themselves, refuse to participate in the necessary working of the collective, or unite in a new collective whose purpose, understandably, is destruction of the old.

Different notions of obligation can be traced to different conceptions of community: in a *Verein* obligations of mutual non-harm and of freely entered contract scrupulously discharged may almost suffice to get on with the goals of such an association. When a *Verein* evolves until a more complex association is formed, scrupulously adhering to contract is far more difficult. The various values and goals necessarily interrelate; the ability to adhere to one value or to meet one goal more and more frequently conflicts with other values or goals. Interests, therefore, begin to coalesce or, at times, to conflict. The obligation simply not to harm one another and to adhere to one's particular contractual arrangement outside the framework of other contractual arrangements which others may have no longer works. My ability to live up to my contract (and my partners ability to live up to his/her side of the bargain) inevitably depends upon complex factors extrinsic to ourselves and to our particular contract. The health of the entire enterprise, therefore, assumes greater importance and my neighbor's weal and woe is of increasingly more direct concern to me.

Libertarians will argue that it is precisely this complexity which necessitates a "backing away" from each other. Individuals as well as associations, libertarians claim, are often "moral strangers" to each other: persons or groups of persons who have entirely different views not only regarding the morality of particular endeavors but also persons or groups of persons who completely fail to share any common moral or philosophical framework in which such differences can be worked out.[6] When persons or associations meet as "moral strangers" a neutral framework of discourse and adjudication must be found if a resort to force is to be avoided. No matter what their own other personal beliefs may be (they may, for example, have a strong personal bent toward acting beneficently and may, in fact, belong to a moral enclave which enjoins beneficent action on its members as a condition of membership), libertarians will see individual and communal interests not as much as coalescing but as inevitably clashing. Communitarians, on the other hand, see a coalescence of such interest. In this respect the dispute between communitarians and libertarians is an argument akin to the argument as to whether a glass is half full or half empty.

Inevitably, as larger associations develop and as associations relate with other associations (just as when individuals relate with other individuals) some interests will correspond and others will clash. When interests correspond, associations (just like persons) will tend to join together. It is, however, rare that persons or associations find all of their interests either corresponding or clashing. When some interests clash and others correspond one can begin to solve this problem by backing away from each other and seeing a solution in purely respecting everyone's liberty and, perhaps, trying to arrange all matters by explicit contract. Or one can start to solve the problem by beginning to work at a solution and by seeing such a state of affairs as one necessitating a homeostatic balance in which differences are weighed, adjudicated, and settled in an ongoing and interactive manner by all concerned. Such a process promises enough stability so that the range of values which acts as the framework of homeostasis can be set and reset in a variety of innovative and experimental ways so as to allow a fair adjustment of interests and values. The drive for seeking such reconciliation lies in the interests of individuals as well as in the interests of the community itself: one cannot prosper without the other. Process no less or perhaps more than actual framework, content, or contract is of essence if peace is to be maintained.[7]

Associations have inevitable relationship with other associations and, eventually, in a complicated and interrelated world no one and no association is entirely immune from what affects another. When persons or associations have relationships and abilities to do or not to do something they, at the very least, have the minimal obligation not to cause each other harm. Necessary and fundamental as such a minimal obligation is, it does not suffice to exhaust the whole complicated skein of explicit and tacit obligations underwriting a variety of relationships.

I suggest that "moral strangers" (whether they are strangers as persons or strangers as communities) can find resolution in more than merely the libertarian point of view. Respecting each other's freedom and refraining from harming each other does not suffice to sketch the extent of what may eventually makes us moral friends. To be moral friends (rather than moral strangers, or, to widen the metaphor, to be, while not moral friends, at least moral acquaintances) shared values and goals beyond the value and goal of strict respect for freedom are needed. I have claimed and will continue to argue that suffering or the prevention and amelioration of suffering can provide at least one such transcendental value and that the prosperity, evolution, and survival of community itself can provide such a goal. With these as values and goals, moral acquaintances can strive to formulate, enunciate, and evolve new shared values and goals so as to become better acquaintances and even, on occasion and as mutual understanding thrives and develops, approximate being "moral friends." Such a process, accomplished within the embrace of a flexible and well-functioning homeostatic system in which mutual respect and mutual beneficence reinforce each other, can allow individuals to flourish, can permit individual communities to develop themselves, and can, ultimately, allow a larger world community to function.

I shall claim that persons can only truly be "strangers" when they have utterly no conception of each other's needs, interests, or values. The same is the case among associations. In truth, however, no one individual or association is a complete stranger to another since we all share some very fundamental needs, interests, and values. To say that I "know nothing" about my neighbor (or about any other sentient creature) may be meant as a metaphor: essentially it is hyperbole denoting that what I know is *nothing beyond* these fundamental needs, interests, and values which I assume as a basis for our being. Such a statement assumes a given and universal plateau of what we know. More accurately it would have to read: "beyond knowing that this creature shares with all other creatures certain fundamental needs, interests, and values and beyond knowing what at least some of these fundamental needs, interests, and values are, I know nothing." But just as the metaphor of "knowing nothing" is only accurate or meaningful when modified in this way (when, in other words, it takes the enormous fundamental mass of shared needs, interests, and values as a given), the metaphor of "moral strangers" is also only useful when it implies that "beyond some very fundamental shared views concerning moral or philosophical frameworks these persons or associations know nothing about each other."

I do not deny differences, often vast differences, among different individuals and different associations. What I claim is that despite these differences fundamental similarities beyond the similarity of the desire for personal freedom (the desire to be "left alone" by the outside world) exist and that, therefore, obligations beyond the simple obligation of mutual non-interference can be carved out. While a wide latitude for individual differences concerning the morality of particular endeavors must be assumed and assumed to be irreconcilable, some rather fundamental concerns can certainly be fruitfully addressed. We (or associations) are not truly "moral strangers" to each other; at the very least we are morally acquainted. To be morally acquainted implies that persons or associations must: (1) have (since they will expect this from others) a great deal of respect for a broad range of divergent views; (2) be willing to develop such views within a broad common human framework of shared experience; and (3) share at least some similar needs, values, and interests. In addition it is most helpful if such persons have a sense of humor with and through which they can view their differences in a broader and perhaps more generous light. Beyond being more or less close moral acquaintances, being moral friends implies a very large commonality of shared interests, values, and points of view. Truly being "moral friends" is probably possible only in the type of homogenized and cloistered communities discussed before.

Some associations such as highly disciplined parties (or religious groups) are very similar to such cloistered communities. In such organizations "party discipline" and absolute obedience to dogma replaces any attempts at innovation or often even of free discussion. Homeostasis has a very narrow range of values in which to operate and generating new goals and values is difficult if not indeed impossible. Such communities (secular or religious) have little respect for their members' freedom of thought and expression; they look at other points of view at best with a sort of condescending pity (other communities or belief systems are misinformed) or, at worst, will seek to suppress, stifle, or destroy them. Tolerance (other than a sort of situational tolerance forced by a lack of power) for other ways of thinking or living is not a hallmark of what I have called cloistered communities. A sense of humor is almost never a part of such communities. Communities of this sort tend not to be viable; in the long run their inability to evolve and adapt leads to their own destruction.

Respect for other points of view, and for other historical perspectives from and in which such points of view developed, is part of a common framework of cooperation. Such a statement does not, however, imply that "anything goes." It implies that to judge others and their moral viewpoint one must understand their history as well as the material conditions under which they live. One also must clearly differentiate between judging persons as blameworthy and judging actions as wrong. The Babylonian peasant who sacrificed his first-born to Moloch so that the village might live was not an evildoer even though the action of child sacrifice would, from today's moral perspective, be most likely condemned![8]

In the modern world collectives eventually must relate to each other. Such a relationship may be a fairly remote and indirect one, as when a sports club in Uruguay relates with a string quartet in Finland. But since an Uruguayan sports club must in one way or another relate to Uruguay, the string quartet must relate to Finland, and Finland and Uruguay eventually (and even if indirectly) must relate with one another if such a relationship exists. When collectives relate to each other, they can relate in a minimalist fashion (accepting only obligations of mutual non-harm) or they can relate in richer and more encompassing ways.

Collectives larger than mere *Vereine* are complicated organic structures whose assortment of goals and values and whose varying capacity to generate new values and goals mark them as either *Gesellschaften* or *Gemeinschaften*. There may be some argument about which of these an association is and, indeed, some may have an intermediate structure. What is important for now is that the complexity of their structure and the richness of their values and goals creates a variety of interfaces through and with which relationships with other collectives are modulated.

Like interrelationships among individuals and akin to the

relationship between collectives and the individual built on a minimalist model, interrelationships among associations can be conceived on a minimalist model in which mutual non-harm is the sole obligation associations have toward each other. Even when one considers only the *Verein* such pure minimalism would be hard to sustain. *Vereine* are ensconced in a larger community and since the life and prosperity of that larger community is essential to the existence of the *Verein,* the *Verein* has obligations toward the community transcending mere non-harm. When collectives are more complex, their obligations likewise become far more complex. Here too obligations depend upon relationship, vulnerability, and capacity.

A minimalist model of relationships between various collectives has similar problems to a minimalist model of relationships among individuals or to such a model when it comes to relationships between persons and their particular community. From a Hobbesian point of view a compact to refrain from mutual harm requires an all-powerful sovereign. Without such a sovereign the vulerability of one is likely to be exploited by the strength of another. To maintain the freedom of each community, arbitrary tyranny ruling such larger associations would have to be accepted. Those of us who seek a democratic and flexible world government able to enforce its will hardly have that in mind. To be workable an association of various collectives into an initial world *Gesell-* and an eventual world *Gemeinschaft* must have richer possibilities and larger goals. Homeostatic ways of working out mutual interests are not possible in a model in which competition must reign supreme nor in one in which democratic process is replaced by autocratic action.

Unless *Gemein-* or *Gesellschaften* share things beyond a common goal of being left alone to get on with their own interests and values the hope of ever forming a world in which peaceful cooperation rather than mere tenuous coexistence exists is slim. Such a state of precarious mutual coexistence must either be enforced by an all-powerful and eventually arbitrary and perhaps tyrannical sovereign or must exist by virtue of a state of mutual terror. The former has been the goal of world conquerors from Caesar and the Pax Romana through Hitler, and such sovereignty may be the unwritten agenda of the "new world order" in which a thinly veiled Pax Americana would reign. History has shown that such states of peace benefit a few at the expense of many and, beyond this, has shown that they simply do not work in the long run. The state of mutual terror (as exemplified by the "peace" called the Cold War) is likewise neither a desirable nor a permanently possible one: sooner or later one or another, thinking themselves "ahead," is bound to strike. The hope of each side to eliminate mutual terror and, instead, establish peace through tyranny of one or the other is an eternal temptation for both.

When collectives interrelate on a richer model wider possibilities open up. The argument that war is a natural state of affairs or that it is the necessary moving force of history (as Hegel thought) is an argument akin to the thought that of necessity persons must be in eternal conflict with each other. Kant saw very well that this was not the case: he saw war (even though frequent) as unnatural and a federation of states without boundaries to be the ultimate end toward which humans should and would strive.[9-12] A relationship among collectives very well can fit the Kantian formulation of not using others merely as a means but always also as ends in themselves. Collectives rightfully can expect mutual respect and such mutual respect must be based on more than mutual terror. Persons are social animals and, as Kant rightly stressed, community is the necessary condition for their thought and existence.[11,12] Beneficent obligations among collectives can be established by a line of reasoning quite similar to that for beneficent obligations among individuals. Communities, if they are to respect each other, must seek to incorporate the ends of their neighbors among their own ends. Community is the laboratory in and through which humans work out their problems. Such a working out between collectives requires shared values, goals, and interests beyond the interest of merely being left alone. Collectives are not (in the sense of sharing no framework of goals, values, and interests and, therefore, no ethical framework) "moral strangers" to each other.

Establishing a common framework among persons or associations depends upon delineating those needs, interests, and values which all by virtue of their common nature must share. All sentient beings by virtue of being sentient beings share at least (1) a common structure of the mind which forces them to arrange experience in certain categories and to see at least certain basic propositions as compellingly logical or illogical; (2) a desire to avoid suffering; (3) the necessity to have certain biological conditions essential to continued life met; and (4) an interest in utilizing their talents and pursuing their interests (whatever these might be) to the fullest. Associations, likewise, hold certain things in common. Being composed of sentient beings, they share: (1) a commonality of thought process (even though the content of their thinking may be starkly different); (2) an interest in minimizing suffering; (3) the necessity to have those things vital for the association's survival met; and (4) a desire to fulfill whatever their self-conceived mission might be. This does not make of persons who do not know each other moral friends or of associations which have little reason to be in contact allies; it does not say much beyond quite primitive ways of seeing the world, is moot about specifically what promotes suffering, what specific things may be needed to sustain life, or what talents and interests are to be pursued. But it does say that even persons or associations which know little about each other know a good deal more than "nothing."

I suggest that moral acquaintances (whether they are acquaintances as persons or acquaintances as communities) can find resolution in more than merely the libertarian point of view. Respecting each other's freedom and refraining from harming each other does not suffice to sketch the extent of what inevitably approaches making us moral friends. To be moral friends or at least moral acquaintances (rather than moral strangers) we need shared values and goals beyond the value and goal of strict respect for freedom. I have claimed and will continue to argue that suffering or the prevention and amelioration of suffering (among other things by meeting basic needs) can provide such a transcendental value and that the prosperity, evolution, and survival of community itself provides such a transcendental goal. With these as values and goals, moral acquaintances can strive to formulate, enunciate, and evolve new shared values and goals so as to become better acquaintances and even, on occasion, to approximate being moral friends. Such a process, accomplished within the embrace of a flexible and well-functioning homeostatic system (a system which provides sufficient stability to allow evolution, growth, and the emergence of new values and goals and a homeostatic system in which mutual respect and mutual beneficence reinforce each other) can allow individuals to flourish, individual communities to develop themselves and can, ultimately, allow a larger world community to function.

So as to approach achieving the goal of world community, solidarity, and individual flourishing, suffering (whether it be the suffering of individuals or the "suffering" of associations so that their members do not suffer) must be held to a minimum. Associations have obligations to each other which are not entirely different from the obligations individuals share with each other and with their community. To hold suffering to a minimum on a world scale requires similar conditions of interrelationship as those conditions which pertain to interrelationships between individuals and their community. In the modern world, individuals are powerless without the community which provides either active or tacit support. Likewise associations without the active or tacit support of others cannot long endure.

Different associations have different strengths and weaknesses and, therefore, different capacities and vulnerabilities. They share a variety of closer or more distant relationships with each other. From these vulnerabilities, capacities and relationships their various obligations can be seen to emerge. When *Gesellschaften* (societies) or *Gemeinschaften* (communities) interrelate with each other, certain basic obligations similar to obligations individuals have emerge. At the very least and where the capacity on the one hand and the need on the other hand exist, such associations have the obligation to (1) respect each other's different values and aspirations within a framework of mutual non-harm; (2) see that first order necessities are, where possible, met and if possible to help meet legitimate second order needs so as to permit such communities to develop; and (3) rectify prior historical disadvantage (national exploitation of one by another) by advantaging the historically disadvantaged until reasonable parity is achieved. (For a discussion of first and second order needs see Chapter 6.)

It is not unreasonable to expect that all within a wider world community have full access to first and second order needs before allowing other communities to enjoy opulence and vast luxury, even if providing such access results in restricting some of the freedoms (by, for example, taxation) of communities who are better off. Restricting freedoms in this way ultimately benefits not only other communities but ultimately benefits all. A general lack of prosperity and opportunity not only threatens prosperity but also threatens freedom. Social homeostasis requires internal adjustments so that all communities within the system can sustain their lives and so that communities within the system can achieve a reasonable unfolding of their specific communal talents. In a world in which all communities are necessarily affected by the fate of another a functioning homeostatic system requires a balance between the specific interests of one community and the specific interests of another. Without this balance social cohesion and peace remains an unrealized hope for all. Failing to provide access to the basic needs of all makes world solidarity impossible. When some societies live in poverty while other societies enjoy opulence, cohesion, even cohesion sufficient to prevent war, is impossible; when the idea of community perishes, the necessary precondition for peace, for freedom, and for individual flourishing is eliminated.

COMPETITION, HOMEOSTASIS, AND COMMUNITY

In the preceding work I have tried to show that the relationship among various associations or communities bears a strong relationship to the way in which individuals relate among each other and with their community. Things are not quite that simple, however. Individuals belong to a large number of interrelated and often quite diverse associations of various complexions and complexity. An individual may belong to several *Vereine*, *Gesellschaften,* or even *Gemeinschaften* which do not always have entirely reconcilable values, goals, and interests. An individual may, among other things, be an obstetrician, a Catholic, a member of a string quartet, and an Italian. Another may belong to one or more of these but also belong to others. An association likewise can have a multitude of overlapping and diverse identities, interests, and commitments. Such a state of affairs may often involve a measure of cognitive dissonance for the individual as well as for the association.

Associations and individuals relate in complex ways with other individuals and associations. Some interests and values are shared, others are quite different from each other. It is this complexity of values, goals, and interests which prompts libertarians to despair of finding a common morality other than strict respect for the freedom of all so as to keep the peace. A peaceful community, libertarians will insist, can be kept peaceful only by making freedom a condition of morality rather than making it merely one among several values. Beneficence cannot be accepted as a universal value by libertarians (even when, as some libertarians will, they personally regret not being able to make beneficence a universal value) because an obligation to be beneficent necessarily will, at some point, interfere with liberty.

The libertarian model is necessarily a competitive one. To achieve my aims in life in a world where none are obliged to come to my help implies that I shall have to compete, perhaps even to compete savagely, with others. Competition, in such a model, is not only acceptable but may, in fact, be desirable. Competition not only assures that those who are the fittest will survive and procreate (and thus will allegedly strengthen the race) but, competition likewise provides a setting in which all goods and services can be provided cheaply and efficiently. Interlocking contracts among individuals and associations fix mutual obligation and responsibility to the benefit of all. The buyer of goods and services will seek to buy the best product at the lowest price; the seller, so as to attract as many buyers as possible, will be motivated to improve goods and services. Thus, the best possible goods or services can be provided at the lowest possible cost. Entrepreneurialism in its widest sense, libertarians will argue, is not only an acceptable way of life: entrepreneurialism can well serve as the basis of community and of morality.[13]

Even when near-libertarians grudgingly accept some minimal beneficent obligations (true and staunch libertarians cannot even go this far), they inevitably see a fierce struggle between communal and individual interests. At best, individuals may be granted certain entitlements by virtue of being destitute: entitlement is certainly not by virtue of being members of community. Charity, grudging charity at that, rather than beneficence is accepted simply because providing minimal help for the destitute may help to maintain peace. Such help, in a sense, is not accepted as a moral obligation but is either given as a form of self-protection or, at best, is felt to be supererogatory.

The misconception of social Darwinism on which the presumption that the race is strengthened by allowing the least fit to be cast off rests has previously been discussed (see preceding chapters). It is a misconception which, among other things, rests on the belief that (1) economic success is generally a proper measure of fitness; and (2) that this particular fitness is somehow genetically transmitted. There is a serious flaw in such an argument when it comes to applying it to modern, sophisticated, and industrialized nations. Aside from the fact that economic success does not necessarily equate with being outstandingly talented or bright, it is well known that the brightest and most talented parents (those who supposedly would "succeed") do not necessarily have the brightest or the most talented children. Often the children of such parents have no greater talents (and often they have far lesser talents) than do the children of less successful parents. In highly competitive (Capitalist) societies, the children of the economically successful (even when these children are not particularly talented, highly motivated, or hard working) will have opportunities denied the children of those who have been less successful in the economic race. The children of those who were less successful or even of those who failed abominably in the economic race may, in fact, be brighter, more talented, and harder working. But unless they are far brighter, far more talented, and far harder working they, in turn, will be unable to compete successfully with others whose parents can buy opportunities (e.g., better education or health care) denied to those who are poor. Even if one were to accept a misconception of social Darwinism and believe that societies are strengthened by allowing those who do not succeed to fend for themselves, the incredible waste of individual talent in Capitalist societies speaks against the practical usefulness of such a world-view.

The belief that competition necessarily provides a setting in which goods and services are likely to be provided most cheaply and most efficiently is, in some cases at any rate, another misconception. Assuredly when it comes to goods and services consumers are familiar with or goods and services which they do not critically need a lot can be said for this proposition. Within limits, the market (when supervised sufficiently to see to it that consumers are not misled) can produce a better selection of many things. When, however, it comes to supplying other things, the market has proven to be singularly inefficient. Consumers cannot, for example, judge the quality or often even their need for medical services (or for education) nor can they be expected to be good judges of the quality of medical services or of education. Consumers of health care are often critically in need of services (their life may be at stake), are frightened, or are in pain. Consumers of education are often ignorant of precisely what it is they need and are generally able to judge quality only after the fact. Their capacity to judge education or health-care matters (especially ahead of time) is seriously flawed. Choosing from among a variety of diagnostic or therapeutic options (or choosing among schools or types of preparation) is not quite like choosing from among different breakfast cereals or even motorcars. Further, a mistake in the choice of motorcars or breakfast cereal is unlikely to seriously affect a person's future life or happiness.

The American health-care system, based firmly on the market, is the world's most expensive as well as being one of the world's most inequitable and inefficient. Much of the system's technology is used as a bargaining chip in competition among health-care providers. When it comes to selling shoes or pears the market may function well; when it comes to essential commodities it does not and cannot. Competition can work fairly well when persons or corporate entities are fairly evenly matched; when the vulnerability of one is out of proportion to the capacity or strength of another, competition in its true sense is not possible. Competition then becomes a form of piracy. When competition becomes the basis of society instead of being an accepted way in which some things within society are allowed to function, society is ultimately the loser.

In a past book, I suggested that a dialectic model may be useful in describing the balance between individual liberty and social justice (between valuing freedom and valuing communal beneficence). Such a model sees the two limbs of the dialectic as competing with one another. The particular value societies attach to issues of individual liberty and to issues of beneficent action emerges from the synthesis of this tension. Particular societies are defined by the way in which they resolve this tension: in the United States, for example, resolution strongly favored individual liberty at the expense of social justice; in the former Soviet states, resolution favored social justice at the expense of individual liberty. And yet, individual liberty is not possible or meaningful unless the basic necessities of life are met, and meeting the basic necessities of life without assuring individual liberty, while creating the conditions for existence, fails in making such a life a life worth living.[8]

The model of the dialectic inevitably is one of competition: a power struggle between two opposed forces each pursuing its own values, goals, ends, and interests. It is a tension in which community inevitably is juxtaposed to the individual and individuals see their individual lives as a struggle against the forces promoting community. Each, in a sense, is seen as threatening the other's interests. Interests are in opposition and, therefore, in competition with each other.

Such a view helps formulate a relationship between the individual's striving for maximal liberty and the community's striving to promote the well-being of its members. Such a view formulates this relationship in a way in which competition can (and historically has) run amok. In resolving the dialectic, societies have often come perilously close to one or the other limb. When individualistic societies define and value freedom and human rights outside the context of social justice or societies value social justice without regard to individual rights a situation not unlike the situation in the capitalist United States or the Bolshevik Soviet Union emerges. The dialectic model sees resolution in a perpetual and inevitable struggle of two necessarily opposed forces seeking their own particular goals. Implicitly the goals of each are not only different but indeed in conflict.

When communities no longer are seen as being of prior or of secondary worth to their members because, on the one hand, they no longer are felt to present the possibility of formulating new goals and, on the other hand, no longer create the possibility of fulfilling goals, such communities no longer will be accepted as a value in their own right. Such communities can fail either by failing to meet the social needs of their members (Capitalism) or by failing to provide the possibility for individual flourishing (totalitarian forms of Communism).

The model we tacitly use structures the way we see relationships. A competitive model sees persons or associations cooperating only when respect for freedom or explicit contract or treaty demands it. Societies, just like individuals, are (short of doing each other explicit harm) free to vie with each other. One's individual or corporate neighbor is entirely at liberty to enter or not to enter into a contract or treaty. Such a model does not see obligations as emerging from vulnerabilities, capacities, and relationships. As long as mutual freedom is respected and allegedly freely entered contract is affirmed morality is preserved. Such a model, however, flies in the fact of human needs and vulnerabilities. The freedom of a contract or treaty between persons or associations of vastly different strength is a kind of freedom inevitably advantaging those who are already advantaged vis-à-vis those who are not.

A competitive model, moreover, ignores some other important considerations. In the modern world the relationship of individuals to their community and of the various associations or communities with each other inevitably necessitates at least some similar goals. Without a strong community which supports them, vulnerable individuals cannot flourish and in turn contribute their talents to the community. Without a strong world community (at least a community in the sense of having a high interest in its own existence) vulnerable associations cannot flourish and, in turn, contribute their particular and peculiar talents.

I shall argue that a homeostatic model is a more fruitful and realistic model than is a crassly competitive one not only for examining the relationship between individuals and their community but also for examining relationships among various associations. Homeostasis does imply a certain amount of inner tension. In biological or ecological models such a tension, however, is a tension which pursues not only its own mission but which above all pursues a goal common to all concerned. In a biological model, for example, insulin modulates blood sugar but it does so in the interest of maintaining overall balance rather than in the interest of dominating. If one can speak of insulin as having an interest, it is an interest served only within the framework of survival and of the greater good. In an ecological sense, when wolves live by hunting caribou they do so within the framework of a greater good which, if not served, will destroy them. When wolves decimate reindeer herds so that few survive, wolves will go hungry themselves and the ecological system will be tilted out of balance. The health of the system is necessary for the health of the individual: this is as true in ecological as it is in biological or social systems. Biological, ecological, and social health is served best not by rampant opposition in which one force subdues another but by these forces pursuing their own interests only within the framework of the common goal.

Homeostasis seeks to maintain stability within a system and to allow its measured development. In doing so it provides the proving ground for experimentation: biological, ecological, and social. The relationships of individuals with their community or of communities with each other are best seen not as competition in which one or the other "wins" but as a cooperative venture in which all pursue a common goal. Such a common goal is only served when a proper balance between communal and individual interests (or when a proper balance between various interrelated associations) pertains. Such a goal is defeated when one or the other "triumphs": such a triumph is a Pyrrhic victory, one ultimately guaranteed to make everyone the loser.

Biological and ecological homeostasis differ in some respects from social homeostasis. Biological and ecological homeostasis have a mechanistic quality: They have maintained themselves because nature works best in this fashion. When homeostasis fails (as when a tumor produces too much uncontrolled insulin or a species of predators exhausts its food supply) new adjustments are likely to be tried until the mechanism is swamped and either the organism or the species perishes. It is not a conscious thing in which biological mechanisms or ecological systems "go out" to act in this manner. Social homeostasis is only in part mechanistic; too many conscious forces operate to allow this. If, however, humans are indeed animals with the capacity to learn from their environment and to transmit such learning to their offspring, if, in other words, humans are not only animals which can reason but likewise are animals which can learn from the consequences of their history and reasoning, then homeostasis can be taken as a model from which one can learn and which one can consciously and fruitfully adopt.

Communities which are free to do so will devise their political structures to fit their vision of community and mutual obligation. In turn these political structures alter and affect the way communities view themselves and their obligations. Political structures, when conceived that way, are the experimental proving ground for such visions. If such a concept is to work in reality, then it in turn depends upon a prior limiting framework which assures communities and those within it the ability to work out their destinies in such a manner. Above all, such a concept is critically linked with the notions I have developed in the foregoing chapters. Without assuring the basic biological needs of all and without providing free access to those things needed for the full development of individual capacities and talents the necessary conditions for involving all members of the community in shaping community itself as well as community's destiny cannot be met. An uneducated, disinterested, and disaffected public is bound, as it has in the United States, to make a sham of democracy and of the democratic process.

Political structures are instituted by and among persons to secure their vision of the good life. Without such a vision, political power structures themselves will evolve their own vision which they will then proceed to superimpose upon the public. An uneducated, disinterested, and disaffected public is likely to accept such a state of affairs and can easily be led to embrace the vision presented to it by the political structure as its own. Such an imposed vision is apt to be introduced with and fortified by the rhetoric of patriotism. Those who wish to challenge such a procedure, those who would question the vision itself or those who would wish to bring about fundamental changes in the way such a vision operates are then easily labeled as unpatriotic or even considered to be treasonable.

The world community, if free to do so and not shackled by the narrow interests of powerful groups, likewise will devise its political structures to fit its own far more complicated vision of community and mutual obligation. In turn these political structures alter and affect the way the world community views itself and its obligations. Such political structures are the experimental proving ground for such visions. If such a concept is to work in reality, then it in turn depends upon a prior limiting framework which assures all communities the ability to work out their destinies. Without assuring the basic biological needs of all communities and of all within them and without providing free access to those things needed for the full development of specific communal capacities and talents the necessary conditions for involving all members of the world community in shaping itself and its destiny cannot be met. A disenfranchised, often uneducated, and frequently starving public in traditionally disadvantaged nations will be unable to participate in a democratic process. Eventually, unable to bear its burden any longer, it will lash out at what it with considerable justification recognizes as its oppressor.

HOMOGENEITY AND COMMUNITY

The fear that a concept of homeostasis will have a homogenizing influence on various cultures so that eventually a single and bland point of view will emerge has often been expressed. After all, the balance of homeostasis can be seen as leading to a stability which eventually homogenizes cultures by imposing a uniform vision of the good on all individuals and associations. The transcendent goal of community in its own right could, so it is sometimes argued, easily lead to seeing community itself not only as a transcendent value but as an ultimate and controlling good in itself. Community, rather than enabling the pursuit of individual (private or corporate) interests, defines, homogenizes and ultimately imposes such interests on and for all.

The fear of producing homogeneity or a homogenous "world order" is not dissimilar to the fear of imposing such a "world order" by totalitarian means. Fearing homogeneity is fearing the superimposition of a given way of living or thinking upon one by extraneous forces. I shall argue that a homeostatic concept of social development is least likely to produce either homogeneity or the totalitarian superimposition of alien values. If homeostasis is conceived as operating to promote the kind of stability which permits evolution, growth, and survival, homogeneity would be its enemy. A "world order" (if by that is meant a uniform way of looking at things or the domination of one by another) is not something which ultimately can foster adaptation, evolution, growth, or survival. A homogenous "world order" in that sense produces stagnation and thus maladaptation and death.

In a competitive model individuals (whether single or corporate) are free to pursue their own atomistic interests as long as they do not directly violate the right of others to do likewise. Unless the contending parties somehow see their own interests served by preserving their competitors they have no interest in preserving the competitor. Striving to preserve a competitor is done only when the survival of the competitor is seen as necessary for one's own welfare. Under such conditions competitors (but competitors in as reduced a form as compatible with one's own welfare) would grudgingly be preserved. Vulnerability is something not to be respected or to be helped out; vulnerability is here to be exploited. Obligations (except the obligation not to do explicit harm and to adhere to "freely" entered contract) are purely to oneself and to one's (explicit) allies. Since those who are vulnerable are apt either to be destroyed or to be kept as powerless as possible, such a model of competition is not one apt to encourage or to foster diversity. Someone with a different way of doing things or looking at things might succeed and dominate.

Success in a competitive system of this sort is inevitably defined in economic or physical terms: The strongest, the wealthiest, the most powerful are those said to succeed. When someone with a different way of looking at things or doing things follows a different drummer by defining success in a different way (when, say, diversity expresses itself in aesthetic, artistic, or purely intellectual ways), it is apt to be eliminated. Far from fostering diversity per se, a competitive Capitalist model, by defining success in its own way and by destroying those who see success differently, is apt to produce a very homogenous world indeed. It is a new "world order" ultimately and quite without conscience imposed by force, whether such force is armed or economic force.

Far from producing a homogeneity of communities throughout the world, a homeostatic relationship would, in its own interest of survival, evolution and growth, foster the development of individual communal attributes and cultures. Fostering the development of individual communal capacities and attributes in the long run is as much in the interest of the larger as it is in the interest of the smaller communities. Ultimately, a homogenized and entirely stable world in which no experimentation with new ways and no attempt at having new arrangements and options is made, is a world which cannot or can only poorly adapt to inevitable new circumstances. The concept of homeostasis does not function unless it includes the capacity to alter its own framework and limits. A homeostatic vision of community is inimical to a "world order" imposed by armed or economic force and is, ultimately, skeptical of such a concept itself.

Individuals, in order to survive beyond infancy, are totally dependent upon nurture. As they begin to first become aware of their selfness and eventually become more able to fend for themselves this dependency changes but does not vanish. Autonomy, as I have said, necessarily emerges in the embrace of beneficence. Once fledgling selfness and a striving for autonomy have emerged, however, children are far from self-sufficient. They require not only further physical nurture but likewise require the support of their immediate community so that they can learn to express their striving for self-expression in meaningful ways. As children grow older their requirement for help by and from others changes but in many ways does not diminish. This is especially true in a modern setting when preparation for life is more complex and takes many more years. Even though many of our children (especially in the United States) are betrayed by a system which cares little for their physical let alone for their intellectual well-being, to achieve even the minimal possibility of function requires communal help. Such dependency is the usual state of affairs throughout life: The community must provide the setting and the support so that individuals can flourish. What changes is that as self-awareness and autonomous function become more fully developed the person perforce assumes tacit and explicit obligations. As relationships deepen and capacities strengthen these obligations become greater until they assume the degree we generally associate with those of adults. Communal nurture and support is essential for individuals so that they can lead full and meaningful lives. Providing its members with those things needed to sustain life as well as developing individual abilities and talents so that individuals can lead full and meaningful lives, in turn, is essential so that the community can survive. The relationship between individuals and their communities, far from being a necessarily competitive one, is a relationship in which both seek to expand their role and in which both see that expansion as critically necessary for both. Goals coalesce and means must be tailored to fit such transcendent goals.

Associations relate with each other in somewhat similar ways. No association, be it a *Verein*, a *Gesellschaft,* or a *Gemeinschaft* can sustain itself let alone develop to its fullest capacity without the active or at least tacit support of others with which it interrelates. Associations by virtue of having relationships, vulnerabilities, and capacities which are unique to themselves have obligations to each other. Associations in their genesis (just like individuals in theirs) were and are dependent upon the initial and ongoing support of others. No symphony orchestra or chess club, let alone no county, country or nation, can exist without such critical interrelationships. When individuals deny all obligations to each other a war of all against all is apt to ensue; when they accept merely obligations of mutual non-interference a less threatening but far from cohesive association exists. Only when obligations of beneficence (however the particulars of beneficence are crafted) are accepted can solidarity begin to develop and thrive. When nations on this earth (often more *Gesellschaften* than

Gemeinschaften but frequently in intermediate stages) assume no obligations toward each other the threat of war is perpetual; when they, however grudgingly, accept mutual non-harm cohesion is far from assured. Mutual non-harm continues to offer (just as it does when it comes to individuals) the possibility of mutual exploitation short of war. The differences in vulnerabilities and capacities lend themselves to this. When this happens, resentment instead of solidarity and cohesion results.

The more powerful owe the weak help and support. Such beneficent obligations can be founded on the inevitable nurture and beneficence which all at one time or another have experienced and must continue to experience. No nation, no state, and no association can or ever has led a life of self-sufficiency in the modern world. It may be argued that there are societies (such, for example, as the Ba Mbuti[3]) which are totally out of touch with the rest of the world and to which such considerations simply cannot apply. Such an argument (and I would challenge that there are many societies or even tribes totally out of contact with others in the modern world) even if granted is uniquely uninformative when it comes to considering the world as it is (largely) constituted today. Associations, perforce, are not moral strangers; assuredly most are not moral friends. But at the very least they are moral acquaintances who know certain critical things about each other and who, by virtue of their common biology and humanity, share at least some critical values, goals, and attitudes.

The help and support the powerful owe to the weak ultimately strengthens all. Just as communities cannot flourish if individual members starve, go homeless, or are not permitted to develop their individual talents, the world community (far from a *Gemeinschaft* but hopefully moving beyond a *Gesellschaft*) and ultimately all within it are the losers. To the extent possible the powerful and prosperous owe the poor and the weak access to first as well as second order necessities; (briefly put, consisting of those things needed to sustain either biological or social existence at a satisfactory level and further defined in chapter 6); beyond this the powerful and prosperous who have often become powerful and prosperous by exploiting those who are now weak and poor owe a sort of "affirmative action" to those who have been historically disadvantaged. All within the prosperous and powerful world have drawn and, whether they want to or not continue to draw, advantage from the disadvantaging of these others.

The internal structure of an association is critically important to the way associations interrelate. When *Vereine* relate to other *Vereine* to *Gesellschaften* or to *Gemeinschaften* their relationship is of a different sort than it would be for interrelationships among other types of organizations. Members of a group which gets together to play chamber music will see the health of their organization important for meeting a personal and a specific need. When members lose interest in performing chamber music, or when playing chamber music is a less important value than is something else, the association (unless it has grown beyond a *Verein*) and its health is no longer of great interest to them. Making the organization a value and goal in its own right is entirely dependent on a specific and, at times, transitory interest. A *Verein* is not an association valued in its own right but rather is valued merely for the particular interest the association enables. An interest in maintaining the organization depends on a specific or a narrow cluster of specific interests. One *Verein*'s compassion for another is apt to be far more aroused when both are pursuing similar values: two organizations devoted to performing classical music (say four persons joining into a quartet or another group joining into a chamber orchestra) are apt to have a far warmer feeling for each other's needs than they would for the members of a sports organization. At best they will have sympathetic understanding of the sports club's needs. Interrelating with each other or with the more largely conceived organizations in which they are embedded would be strictly determined by their own particular needs, interests, and goals. *Vereine* are of direct concern to each other only when they can conceive their interests to coincide. Their homeostatic range is a range which serves their narrowly conceived interests and is rather small. New values and goals are rarely important to such a *Verein*.

More largely conceived organizations which have greater internal cohesion and which place a far higher value on their own existence will find that the health of the various subgroups in their midst is critical to their own ability to thrive and develop. A *Gesellschaft,* constituted to pursue a wider range of values, options and goals, is more inclusive. It forms the seedbed on and in which *Vereine* can prosper or die. *Gesellschaften* are directly concerned with the health of their component parts and see the health of these component parts as essential to their own mission. So as to adapt to changing situations, so as to evolve, prosper, grow, and survive, such an organization must have a better capacity to enunciate, experiment with, and ultimately adopt or reject new values and ways of doing things. The ferment of individual difference presented by the various associations in its midst is necessary if such a task is to be successful. The homeostatic range is a range which serves more broadly conceived interests. New values and goals are of considerable but perhaps not of overriding importance if the *Gesellschaft* is to adapt to changes, is to evolve, and survive.

When a *Gemeinschaft*, as I have used the term, develops the task of formulating, experimenting with, and adopting or rejecting new values and goals a homeostatic system permitting stability while enabling evolution becomes far more critical. *Gesellschaften* value the persistence of the *Gesellschaft* largely but not entirely as an instrumental goal: a goal which serves the ends they wish to pursue but not yet a goal which is truly transcendent and a value in its own right. *Gesellschaften* find it necessary to adopt new values and goals along a much narrower range than will *Gemeinschaften* as defined here. The interest of a *Gemeinschaft* in the prosperity of its members as well as in its interrelationships with other associations is much deeper: since community itself has become a transcendent rather than a merely instrumental goal and since community depends upon external and internal relationships such considerations assume critical importance. The homeostatic range which must serve a far wider range of broadly conceived interests is consequently a more generous one. New values and goals, new ways of conceiving homeostatic balance and new ranges of operation are of critical importance. However, *Gemeinschaften* not only must experiment with the new and adapt to new events and learn to explore and adopt or reject new goals and values; they must, if they are to accomplish this task, do so within a stable setting which permits a peaceful territory on and in which to accomplish their task. When new set-points of homeostasis are slowly generated in a setting in which the transcendent value of community is clearly evident and in which peaceful stability is maintained, communities can grow, prosper, and survive.

When persons are without the basic necessities of life or lack fair access to those things necessary for developing their individual talents solidarity is shattered and community cannot long endure. Unless a community remedies such a situation by evolving new values and goals the solidarity of the community is threatened. Such communities are no longer *Gemeinschaften*, often are barely *Gesellschaften*, and are too large and interrelated to be *Vereine*. When persons in an association see the association as no longer supporting their interests, the transcendent value of the association not only is lost but becomes a negative value. Homeostasis in such a system cannot function: its ranges of value are inimical to its own survival and the organism will perish. When homeostasis fails, resort to other means (revolution of one sort or another) is not only probable but is justifiable and probably inevitable. It is difficult for a nation which started its life by declaring the legitimacy of revolution when all other redress fails to deny this.

Peace within a *Gemeinschaft* (or even a *Gesellschaft*) is, however, not by any means secured by merely fostering internal cohesion. The complex relationships among various associations demands general stability so that such external relationships can be fruitfully developed and worked out. This balance among external relationships can, I think, also be fruitfully conceived as a homeostatic balance. All associations share a common interest in their own prosperity, share at least a basic common way of reasoning and conceiving logical propositions, and share basic needs. A homeostatic balance mindful of such commonalities can provide the stability in and by which diverse associations can jointly formulate new values and goals. To be operative such a balance requires an acceptance by all concerned that cohesion is needed. Unless associations in interrelating with each other begin to see a transcendent value in such a larger association (a transcendent value at first largely instrumental but one which ultimately can be strengthened until it becomes a value in its own right) their cohesion will be sorely wanting and their relationship will approximate the relationship among *Vereine* with quite diverse interests and little that unites them. When different associations see the larger association as vital to their own interests (when, indeed, they recognize that to define their own interests outside of the context of the association is incoherent), the transcendent value of such an association is established.

I have claimed that to achieve the goal of community, solidarity, and individual flourishing is to hold suffering to a minimum. To achieve the goal of a world community in which nations may be, if not moral friends, at least moral acquaintances likewise requires that suffering be minimized. Accomplishing this on a worldwide basis is far more difficult and complex than achieving such a goal in a given community. But it is a goal which must be achieved if the health of all communities is to be safeguarded. Just as my peace and prosperity cannot endure when my neighbor starves, a nation's ultimate fate is inextricably linked with that of its neighbor. To achieve an enduring world community requires solidarity. Each must see their interest as linked to the interest of their neighbor. Achieving solidarity requires that (1) all individuals and nations must have equal access to first order necessities (those things needed to sustain biological existence) as well as to second order necessities (those things essential so that individuals can fully develop their talents in a given social setting); and that (2) the historically disadvantaged must, by some form of effective international "affirmative action," be advantaged until reasonable living conditions pertain. Achieving these goals may entail a burden on prosperous nations many of whom have gained and continue to gain advantage from their neighbor's disadvantage. Just as within communities in which taxing the wealthy to benefit the destitute may be a moral imperative, it is not unreasonable to expect that the wealthiest nations will have to reduce their own opulence so as to aid their neighbor. Peace in a community cannot long endure when destitute persons in one setting are daily confronted with those in other settings living an opulent lifestyle. International peace, likewise, cannot be hoped for as long as the crass inequities (especially since these are more often than not based on present and prior exploitation) persist. Prosperity for one bought at the price of destitution for another (whether that other be a nation or a person) is not prosperity which can evolve, grow, and survive.

When some associations are without the basic necessities of life or lack fair access to those things necessary for developing their individual talents solidarity is shattered and the larger association cannot long endure. Unless such a state of affairs is remedied by evolving new values and goals solidarity is threatened. When associations see the larger association as no longer supporting their own needs (when indeed they perceive it as inimical to such needs) the transcendent value not only is lost but becomes negative. Homeostasis in such a system cannot function: homeostasis requires a common goal toward which various forces in their own way strive. Without such a transcendent goal to which other interests are adjusted and at which these interests are aimed a common range of values will be difficult to define and adhere to. When homeostasis fails in promoting the interests of the weaker as well as that of the stronger, resort to other means (warfare or an uprising by the destitute against the prosperous) not only becomes probable but is justifiable and inevitable. It is difficult for nations that have persistently gone to war to preserve their own often narrow interests to deny the legitimacy of such an undertaking.

Different societies have different strengths and different vulnerabilities. As I have noted in previous chapters, the relationship among cultures as well as the relationship among individuals is based on and often defined by mutual and variable vulnerabilities: The vulnerability or weakness in one particular sphere is made up for by the strength of another in that particular sphere.[14] Since no one individual or nation is composed of all strengths or all weaknesses (and since today's strength may be tomorrow's weakness) the interrelationship between and among individuals and nations is complex, complicated and necessarily interwoven. No one individual or nation can entirely exist without the help of another.

The fact that individuals and associations are ultimately strengthened by fostering the peculiar talents and strengths of single or corporate individuals can be seen in many ways. I have mentioned that the health and survival of communities is intimately connected with the health and survival of their members. When such members are unable to develop their peculiar talents not only they but their community ultimately is the loser. A rich fabric of values and points of view within a framework which seeks to prevent and ameliorate suffering and which places emphasis on community as a value in its own right best allows growth and evolution through the development of new options. When communities suppress their individual members' ability to flourish (either by failing to provide them with basic necessities or by crushing their individuality) community shatters. This is as readily seen in the Capitalist United States in which talent is wasted by a lack of attention to the value of social justice as it was in the Bolshevik states of the Eastern bloc where individual talents were crushed. On the one hand, community in the United States is sorely wanting and solidarity is virtually nonexistent; on the other hand, recent events in the Soviet Union have equally pointed to the lack of community and solidarity in that nation.

Nations have different strengths and weaknesses, strengths and weaknesses which cannot be defined merely in material terms. Nations, whether because of natural resources or cultural history, have capacities and vulnerabilities peculiar to themselves. The obligation of others and of the world community to such nations and the obligation of such nations to others and to the world community is defined by these vulnerabilities and capacities. It is an obligation which, for the survival of all, must place a high value on sometimes idiosyncratic material possibilities as well as upon often quite unusual ways of pursuing a given cultural bent. Some nations may have a mineral or some other resource sorely needed by the rest of the world; others may engage in a particular form of dancing or making music handed down from generation to generation. The world is richer for all of this just as the community is richer for the talents of the merchant as well as for those of the poet. Allowing diverse talents to flourish, indeed nurturing such diversity, is in the best interest of all if best interest is defined as constituted of those things most likely to help experimentation, growth, evolution, and survival.

REFERENCES

1. Engelhardt HT: *The Foundations of Bioethics*. New York, NY: Oxford University Press; 1986.

2. Nozick R: *Anarchy, State and Utopia*. New York, NY: Basic Books; 1974.

3. Engelhardt HT: Health Care Allocation: Response to the Unjust, the Unfortunate and the Undesirable. In: *Justice and Health Care* (E. E. Shelp, ed.). Dordrecht, The Netherlands: D. Reidel; 1981.

4. Jonas H: *Das Prinzip Verantwortung*. Frankfurt a/M, Deutschland: Suhrkamp; 1984.

5. Kant I: *Grundlegung zur Metaphysik der Sitten*. In: *Immanuel Kant Kritik der Praktischen Vernunft, Grundlegung zur Metaphysik der Sitten*. Band VII (Wilhelm Weischedel, ed.). Frankfurt a/M, Deutschland: Suhrkamp Verlag; 1989.

6. Engelhardt HT: *Bioethics and Secular Humanism*. Philadelphia, PA: Trinity Press International; 1991.

7. Hampshire S: *Innocence and Experience*. Cambridge, MA: Harvard University Press; 1989.

8. Loewy EH: *Suffering and the Beneficent Community: Beyond Libertarianism*. Albany, NY: SUNY Press; 1991.

9. Kant I: *Zum Ewigen Frieden*. In: *Immanuel Kant's Werke*. Band XI (Wilhelm Weischedel, ed.). Frankfurt a/M, Deutschland: Suhrkamp Verlag; 1989.

10. Kant I: *Die Metaphysik der Sitten*. In: *Immanuel Kant's Werke*. Band VIII (Wilhelm Weischedel, ed.). Frankfurt a/M, Deutschland: Suhrkamp Verlag; 1989.

11. Kant I: *Kritik der Urteilskraft* In: *Immanuel Kant's Werke*. Band X (Wilhelm Weischedel, ed.). Frankfurt a/M, Deutschland: Suhrkamp Verlag; 1989.

12. Arendt H: *Lectures on Kant's Political Philosophy*. Chicago, IL: University of Chicago Press; 1982.

13. Engelhardt HT: Morality for the Medical Industrial Complex: A Code of Ethics for the Mass Marketing of Health Care. NEJM 1988; 319(16): 1086–1089.

14. Springer-Loewy RA: An Alternative to Traditional Models of Human Relationship. Cambridge Quarterly 1993 (in press).

CHAPTER 6

Suffering and Communities Today

In past chapters I have briefly reviewed the concept of suffering as a basis for ethical consideration and intertwined it with a notion of communal structure whose obligations are grounded in the inescapable experience of nurture and beneficence which all developing beings must experience to survive. I have argued that obligations can be justified by an appeal to such considerations as well as by appealing to deductive logic and have suggested that justification ultimately depends upon a "compost heap" of mutually re-enforcing considerations. Beyond this, I have examined the alleged conflict between the individual and the community and have suggested that a model of homeostasis was closer to the mark and more fruitful than was one of a dialectic struggle. Such homeostatic relationships pursue common goals much as do the homeostatic relationships observable throughout nature. In homeostatic relationships there is a balance between a multitude of forces. Although these forces can superficially be described as contending with each other, these forces, since they serve a common goal of survival, can be said to "contend" in only a limited sense. In communities the forces of homeostasis must serve to balance communal and personal interests so that both the community and the individuals within it may grow, evolve, and survive. The existence of community itself as well as the personal flourishing of individuals within the community are of vital interest to all.

In moving from a general statement about mutual obligations in a community to more specific problems one must balance and adjudicate the interests of all members as well as balancing these interests with the interest which the community has in its own existence and integrity. I have claimed that all sentient beings share a fundamental common interest in not suffering, that it is, in fact, this fundamental fact of life which allows us to determine when an object is and when it is not directly morally relevant (relevant, as it were, in itself). We have said that morally relevant objects are either (1) those which are directly morally relevant because of their capacity to suffer; or (2) those which are morally relevant by reflection: while they themselves cannot suffer, they are of value to those which can; and, in addition, (3) the future itself since it forms the grounds for all life plans, hopes and values is morally relevant. Community itself has such moral relevance as the necessary condition for valuing (that it has what I have called "prior worth") as well as because community makes individual fulfillment and life plans possible (that in that sense it has "secondary worth"). Beyond this, I have claimed that the interests of individuals in their own thriving cannot be separated from their interest in the thriving and success of their community. Success of the community and success of the individuals within it must be defined on each other's terms. In speaking about interests which communities and individuals have and pursue, in speaking about what interests must be safeguarded and balanced so that communities as well as individuals may thrive, one inevitably will encounter and have to deal with the language of "needs."

In this chapter I want to: (1) briefly define and discuss needs; (2) relate the concept of community with needs; and (3) discuss the relationship of needs and homeostasis. I will then go on to (4) and examine the consequences of a homeostatic relationship illustrating my point with examples from medicine, education, and affirmative action. I will claim that using an ethic in which the capacity to suffer is central necessitates a society which while far more egalitarian than what we have today is one which needs not be absolutely egalitarian when it comes to supplying some of these needs.

LOOKING AT NEEDS

The notion of needs is central to any discussion dealing with communal structure, obligation, and social justice. Without grappling with the concept of needs and arriving at some workable definition of needs, one cannot coherently discuss issues of allocation or justice. Communities even minimally concerned about beneficence will feel that crying needs must be met; the more seriously they take obligations of beneficence, the more seriously will they feel obligated to meet more than merely the most minimal needs. Beneficent communities devoted to preventing or ameliorating the suffering of their members will have to deal with such "needs."

In several prior works I have discussed the concept of "needs" as I shall use the concept in this work.[1,2] Here I will merely and very briefly summarize the argument and define the concept of "needs" in the way in which I have been and will be using the concept throughout the remainder of this work. To say that something is a "need" is to claim that a thing is necessary to attain a given goal. Saying that something is a "need" does little to denote how essential that something is. The value of the goal, not the fact that something is a "need" to reach a goal, makes that something important. I need to look in a shop window to satisfy my curiosity as to what the window contains: looking into the window is a "need" if my curiosity is to be satisfied. I also need to have shelter so that I may survive the blizzard or food so as not to starve to death: these are needs to the end of my survival. What makes the one need trivial and the other need important cannot be determined by acknowledging that each of them is a need. A "need," then, is somewhat like the "ought" in a hypothetical. It is an "ought" which must be fulfilled if the indicated goal is to be reached: if you want to reach x you ought (need) to do or have y. As such, and in and of itself, the term "need" (as the term "ought" when hypothetically used) is essentially value neutral. It can be applied equally to the despicable (if you want to kill Jones you need—ought—to use poison) as it can to the commendable (if you want to save that child you need—ought—to give it food).[1,2]

To claim that persons need certain things and that since they need them beneficent societies may have an obligation to provide them is, in such a definition, absurd. If we want to determine what needs communities like we have envisioned them are ethically compelled to supply and what needs communities may have no role in meeting, we must focus on which goals are and which are not essential to the way communities see themselves.

I shall speak of needs as "basic" when such needs are (1) necessary to a person's biological survival or (2) essential for having free access to "the fair opportunity range"—necessary, that is, to sustain an acceptable individual existence within a given social context so that reasonable individual goals can be met.³ "Basic" here is intended to denote something of fundamental importance, something which serves to support existence as well as allowing a socially determined sufficient ability to thrive. Basic needs, then, are those needs which allow "species normal function" (biological)³ as well as underwriting our nature as "men and specific persons" (social).⁴ Basic needs are those which in one or another significant way serve the goal of preventing or ameliorating suffering.

When needs underwrite the goal of biological survival, I shall term such needs "first order necessities": such things as air, food, warmth, and shelter are needed to permit "normal species function" and are examples. Though the particulars as to what counts as "first order necessities" (what, for example, is "adequate" as shelter or warmth) may differ in different societies and in different climes, "first order necessities" are things without some form of which no living organism can survive. When first order necessities are not met, a terrible amount of suffering is let loose in the world not only for those who go without and who, therefore, ultimately die, but for others who treasure and love them. Furthermore, if such needs are not met for some persons while other persons are allowed to enjoy opulent luxuries, the very idea of *Gemeinschaft* is called into question. How can we speak of *Gemeinschaft* or community (literally of common or united effort) when such conditions of crass inequity pertain? How can we speak of *Gemeinschaft* or community when some are allowed to starve or go homeless while others enjoy hundred-dollar meals or own million-dollar yachts? How, under such circumstances, can we even speak of more than a most primitive "Gesellschaft"?

I shall call a need which underwrites a person's capacity to make the most of his/her life within the setting a particular community provides a "second order necessity." "Second order necessities" can be aspired to and appreciated only when first order needs have been met. Persons who do not have access to adequate first order necessities necessarily must perish. Those for whom obtaining access to adequate first order necessities is an ongoing struggle will have little energy left to seek out personal fulfillment. Developing their talents generally will be impossible if all energy and time must be spent on the struggle for daily existence. In this sense, the meeting of first order necessities is the necessary condition for the existence of those of the second order. A second order necessity is one which allows us to fulfill our nature as "men and specific persons" and to attain a "fair opportunity range."[3,5] Such needs are still "basic" needs within the terms of our definition since persons who do not have such needs met will find their lives unnecessarily sterile and empty.

What counts and what does not count as a second order necessity is, however, not a universal. Engelhardt is undoubtedly quite correct when he remarks that the Ba Mbuti have no interest in health care.[6] What is not justifiable is to transpose such an insight as a meaningful insight in the context of a modern industrialized society. Among the Ba Mbuti, health care is not a second order necessity as, I shall continue to argue, health care in industrialized nations is. Second order necessities, however, undoubtedly do exist for the Ba Mbuti just as they exist for members of industrialized nations: necessities which by their nature and by the structure of their particular society would be incoherent in a modern industrialized one. A great deal of suffering is caused when persons with ability and talent, whether these persons are Americans or Ba Mbuti, are frustrated in achieving those goals legitimate in their particular society because the material (access to education or health care) or intellectual (freedom to think, speak, and write) conditions for accomplishing such goals are unavailable to or forbidden for them.

Poverty breeds suffering not only when it deprives people of the bare necessities to hold on to life itself but at least as much when biological existence fails to be coupled with social fulfillment. Communities which fail to provide access to a fair opportunity range to some of its most talented members while allowing others who perhaps have less talent access to opulence and wealth, underwrite a type of suffering which is not far less than the suffering of hunger. Frustration, an important part of suffering, results. Communities which allow such conditions to continue also call the very idea of community or *Gemeinschaft* into question. How can we speak of *Gemeinschaft* or community when persons of lesser talent live in luxury while those of greater talent remain deeply frustrated? How can we speak of *Gemeinschaft* when all who belong to the *Gemeinschaft* do not have the opportunity to fully participate in creating their common future? If communities fail to provide fair access to second order necessities they will find the idea of community betrayed and solidarity disrupted. What counts as a second order necessity and what counts as fair access in a given social setting is a calculation communities mindful of their material possibilities, structure, priorities, and values will have to decide for themselves.

What is and what is not a second order necessity may depend on the way persons envision their future. If a community sees becoming a violinist as being within a reasonable opportunity range, persons whose talents seriously point them in that direction may find a violin to be a reasonable second order necessity. Such decisions are a joint effort between individuals and their community: when persons have peculiar talents and abilities both they and their community may be well served to develop them. When communities define second order necessities or when they try to determine what constitutes a reasonable range of opportunities to which reasonable persons may aspire within their community, sufficient latitude to make such decisions will be needed. How much latitude will be allowed depends not only on a community's material resources but likewise on the particular world-view to which the community at that particular moment in history subscribes.

Even when needs are not basic they may still be very important to certain individuals or to certain associations of individuals. Here the goals which such "needs" serve are goals which associations or individuals define for themselves; They depend on their peculiar tastes, likes, and dislikes. I may feel a compelling need to go to concerts or to travel abroad but fulfilling such a need neither serves to underwrite my biological existence nor allows me access to a full and reasonable opportunity range in the context of our particular society. Some collectives as I have previously sketched them may be formed precisely to meet such "third order necessities." Such an association or *Verein* devoted to its member's need for playing chess or chamber music may see the need for chessboards or instruments to be basic needs for its members, may in fact consider them as second order necessities for itself. Without having such needs met, persons may find their lives to be rather sterile and empty. In a sense, such persons may be said to suffer. So as to meet a reasonable opportunity range within that association, members must have access to the things needed to play chess or to make music. But for the world outside its doors, such things are not basic needs and they feel no basic necessity to fulfill them. Such needs are what are often called "wants": a "want" in one social setting may be a need in another. The border between such "third order needs" or wants and "second order needs" is a negotiable border (negotiable between the *Verein* and the larger collectives of which it is a part) in the sense in which the border between first and second order necessities is not. It is a dynamic border, a border which is subject to political restructuring. The "third order need" of today may well become the "second order need" of tomorrow; or, at a time of shrinking resources, the opposite may be the case.

COMMUNITIES AND NEEDS

Collectives or associations which are devoted to a narrow goal (*Vereine* such as chess clubs or chamber music groups) are members of more complex societies. These more complex societies (or *Gesellschaften*)—they may be municipalities, for example—in turn, are members of even more complex societies and eventually of communities (*Gemeinschaften*). (See Chapter 5.) The *Gemeinschaft*, the *Gesellschaft*, and the *Verein* interrelate in part on the basis of their understanding of what are second and what are third order needs. Negotiations among members of communities determine the range of what the community will consider to be a "second order" and what a "third order" necessity. In turn, negotiations among the members of a given *Gesellschaft* or *Gemeinschaft* will determine this for their own constituents.

A *Gemeinschaft*, a *Gesellschaft*, and a *Verein* are, among other things, distinguished by their differing ranges of values and goals. The values and goals of a *Verein* are far less complex and its structure is therefore far simpler than are the values, goals, or structure of either a *Gemeinschaft* or a *Gesellschaft*. The interrelationship between these different types of collectives has been discussed in previous chapters and will continue to be important to the rest of this work.

A true community (or *Gemeinschaft*) as I have sketched it, beneficent and, therefore, dedicated at least to some extent to the welfare of its individual members, has certain ongoing and evident tasks when it comes to needs. Such tasks include (1) defining the specific nature of biological first order necessities (what are the minimal acceptable standards of air, food, water, and shelter, for example) and (2) determining what constitutes a fair opportunity range within its own conception of itself (what are minimal acceptable second order necessities). Beyond this, communities truly interested in the welfare of their members (and I have claimed that to be a true community means to be interested in the welfare of its members just as being a member of a community means being interested in the welfare of the community) will feel compelled: (1) to see that first order necessities for all are met before going on to worry about further needs; and once this task is accomplished (2) to attempt, as far as this is possible, to establish a system in which all members have fair access to what the community recognizes as second order necessities before allowing some others free access to opulent third order necessities. Such a task is, of course, a constant process of negotiation: a sorting and sifting of individual and communal values in which both individuals and communities pursue a common goal of growth, evolution, solidarity, and survival.

Consistent with my argument in previous chapters, there is another "need" which is not first, second, or third order and which, to be consistent in my language, I shall refer to as a "prior need." By this I mean the need for community itself. In more than the most primitive hunter-gatherer societies first order necessities cannot be met adequately for all without some sort of collective. When an association undertakes at the very least to assure access to first order necessities it binds its members into greater solidarity: to achieve the goal of living, individuals must support community. When an association further undertakes, as much as it can, to see to it that individuals have sufficient access to the second order necessities indispensable so that they can flourish and develop their individual talents (when, in other words, education and health care is supplied to all by virtue of being members of the community), solidarity becomes much firmer. To continue to exist as well as to develop their life plans, individuals now must hold community itself as a most important goal. The notion of community as an end in itself, as one of the goals common to all members of the association, is not far away. Solidarity not only enables personal survival and growth: solidarity assures the continuation of a future which without the community would be unattainable.

In practical terms, communities will find that the definition of needs and the definition of obligations to meet such needs is an ongoing process, not a task which is ever finished. Since first order necessities are biological needs, the need for them remains stable: all creatures need air, food, water, shelter, and warmth. But the particulars of such needs in any particular society change as that society evolves. Is it a communal obligation to supply clean air rather than merely air? Must food and water meet minimal standards of cleanliness and palatability or will merely access to food and water do? Is supplying mass shelters and minimal heat sufficient or must a certain living space and a certain range of temperatures be assured? Surely, it is not a communal obligation so supply filtered air, gourmet meals, fine wines, and beautiful temperature-modulated homes to all its members. Defining the range of the acceptable for all is an ongoing task.

The less communities envision themselves as "beneficent," the more narrowly will they define and meet both first and second order necessities; the more will they allow such needs to slip into being defined as third order necessities and, therefore, mere wants. Even when it comes to first order necessities communities which see "needs" narrowly defined will be disinclined to provide more than minimal soup-kitchen type nutrients or more than merely mass shelters. Wanting more than this will be defined as unnecessary and as a mere want, something persons "can easily do without." Often, in fact, communities will claim that not supplying more than the bare necessities is a virtue since it stimulates the poor to work harder, "make something of themselves," and thus acquire more. Poverty, in that philosophy (a philosophy generally not held by those who themselves are poor), is an excellent and quite desirable prod to self-improvement.

When communities only grudgingly accept the obligation of beneficence for themselves, they will generally supply a safety net for the destitute which narrowly defines and skimpily supplies first order needs. Second order necessities will be left to individuals who are now expected to "pull themselves up by their bootstraps." In such societies the underlying philosophy is what has been called a "poor law philosophy." Communities which take obligations of beneficence more seriously will move from such a "poor law" mentality to what has been called a "welfare" society.[7] A "poor law" mentality will supply a safety net supposed to allow the meeting of minimal critical needs: entitlement is by virtue of poverty.

The holes may be larger or smaller but a society based on a poor law mentality will, however grudgingly, supply some sort of net. A "welfare" type of community, on the other hand, will supply what it has defined as necessities to all its members: entitlement is by virtue of being a member of the community or *Gemeinschaft*. In the way it defines itself, a welfare type of community will accept such an obligation. A poor law society will, for example, supply medical care (Medicaid is an example) to a group narrowly defined by its income; a welfare state will supply such care to all its members. These differences and the difference between supplying basic necessities in a one or in a multitiered fashion will be discussed and elaborated later in this chapter.

Communities, furthermore, are limited by their own resources. They cannot be expected to supply what is not there to be supplied. Resources are not infinite and rationing decisions have to be made. Whether such rationing is explicitly done by communal action or whether rationing proceeds under the pretext prevalent in market economies that there is no rationing, rationing is a fact of life. Beyond this, resources, while not infinite, are often very badly distributed. Just as some individuals have access to far more resources than do others, some communities have much more than their neighbors. (In past chapters I have briefly examined the interrelationship of communities among themselves and analogized this relationship to the relationship which pertains between individuals and their community as well as between pre-communal associations and the community.)

NEEDS AND HOMEOSTASIS

Homeostasis in biology as well as in society serves the goal of stability. Stability, however, is hardly meant to denote a frozen state in which no change occurs and consequently, and however measured, in which no progress can take place. Progress by its very nature needs a framework of stability. When stability is not present and when instead turmoil or chaos exists eventual progress may be achieved, but it is progress achieved only after some stability (and usually despotically imposed stability) has again recurred. The history of chaotic revolutions bears witness to this fact: The indubitable long-range benefits of the French or Russian Revolution were hardly at once apparent. The social and legal

systems were entirely disrupted. Chaos and eventually te
lowed both these revolutions and only after some seml
stability (whose price was terror followed by despotism) was
achieved could the fruits of these revolutions be realized. The
American Revolution was not followed by terror for the very reason that, while very crucial changes were wrought, a framework
of social as well as legal stability remained. The grandeur of the
American Revolution resides in the very fact that it was not a
"real" revolution in the sense of totally destroying the existing
framework. What little was left of a homeostatic balance in the
case of the French or Russian Revolution (a balance which had
gone badly awry and which had become largely a- or dysfunctional) was totally and finally disrupted. To re-establish itself society had to pass slowly and with great difficulty, through the pur-
gatory of terror and the night of despotism. In the case of the
American Revolution, the parameters of homeostasis were shifted
somewhat but the social and legal parameters were not destroyed.
Terror never followed.

Homeostasis serves the needs of organisms whether such
organisms are individuals, members of a species, or social
groups. The forces homeostasis balances would, if allowed to be
out of control, destroy the organism and with it would destroy
themselves. When several species occupy a given living space, no
less than when individuals inhabit a commons, they cannot each
pursue their own narrow self-interests without destroying first
the balance and ultimately themselves.[8] Self-interest must, therefore, be seen as necessarily encompassing the interest of the commons without which such self-interest becomes counterproductive and ultimately dysfunctional. The needs of all members of a
commons must be considered not only in terms of individual
interests (or "rights") but in terms of how the pursuit of such
interests (or the insistence upon such "rights") would affect all
members. Since the survival of the commons is necessary for the
survival of its members, such a commons constitutes a true community (or *Gemeinschaft*) in which the stability of the commons
in itself necessarily is a unifying and essential goal.

One may, of course, argue that it is in an individual's rational
self-interest to be a "free rider": a person who contributes little
and takes much. Such an argument is based on an entirely individualistic notion of "self"—of a self which exists without social

moorings and without communal identity. Such a point of view commits the fallacy of believing that individuals exist outside a communal nexus, that they are asocial in the widest sense of the word: that is, not only bereft but independent of social moorings. It is akin to what Jonathan Moreno so aptly refers to as the "myth of the asocial individual."[9] A few persons may and do get away with such an attitude: an attitude which, in the long run, is not as much a- as anti-social. A few persons acting like this can be tolerated by the community: not all individuals will function as expected any more than all cells in an organ or all organ systems in an individual will function optimally. Communities are dependent for their survival on the proper functioning of most but hardly of all members. Narrow self-interest, however, becomes self-destructive when a critical number of persons assume (or are socialized to assume) such an attitude. "What's in it for me?" is, within bounds, a natural reaction: all individuals (just as all communities) have an understandable interest in their own particular good. Ultimately, however, "what's in it for me" can only be expressed, defined, and in the end accomplished within a social nexus. Destroying that social nexus, destroys the possibility of realizing one's alleged self-interest. Self-interest outside the embrace of the social nexus cannot even be imagined.

When Nozick and Engelhardt argue that, in order to be peaceful, communities must be founded on the sole requirement of respect for each other's autonomy and when they argue that, therefore, freedom can be restrained only in order to assure a like freedom for all, they deny the lesson of the commons. If the commons and the members which constitute it are to survive, their liberty must be limited by obligations which transcend leaving each other alone to pursue their own interests. Pursuing such interests may not technically restrain the like liberty of others to do the same. But pursuing such interests inevitably will lead to a competition which has been reduced to a zero-sum game. Losers who lose by no longer having the necessities for existence cannot pursue their own interests: Their like liberty to pursue these interests is, in fact, not only restrained but made quite impossible. Beneficence, which underpins communal action aimed at benefiting members of the community, is not only necessary for the survival and flourishing of individuals. Without beneficence and beneficent action (which is in the ultimate interest of all because the continuity of the community is of interest to all) the community, and the individuals of which it is composed, will perish. Even if one accepts a crass version of social Darwinism, unlimited competition within a commons results not only in the inability of some to survive; ultimately it must destroy the commons itself.

In this section I will present some examples of what I shall argue are "second order necessities" and show how by using the concept of homeostasis progress in societies can be made. I shall define "progress" as, among other things, accomplishing a change from a situation of social inequity to one of greater equity, albeit not one of absolute equality. By "equity" I shall not mean equality in terms of income or even of status but rather equity in terms of access to basic necessities as well as to fair opportunities within a society. Equity in terms of fairness can be said to exist when all within a society have the necessary means to sustain their life at a decent level as well as a fair opportunity to pursue a reasonable range of opportunities within their civilization. A decent quantity of first order necessities must be provided to all so that second order necessities can be realized. I shall argue that in a modern industrialized society, education, and health care are necessary to realize access to the fair opportunity range. Beyond this, in a society in which radical and traditional inequities have existed and do exist today (and until such a time as such traditional inequities are abolished) some sort of affirmative action will likewise be needed.

My definition of "progress" (which I have defined as, among other things accomplishing a change from a situation of social inequity to one of greater equity, albeit not one of absolute equality) may be challenged. Why, after all, is it progress to move from social inequity to greater equity? How and by whose definition and criteria do we measure progress? If an ethic based on a creature's capacity to suffer and a community based on more than minimal obligations (among other things by virtue of being necessarily founded on beneficence experienced in developing oneself) is accepted, then progress would seem to be moving toward a state in which unnecessary suffering is less rather than more and in which persons truly care about each other's weal and woe. It is progress toward a state of being in which fewer persons suffer and in which a larger number of persons are able to develop their talents to the fullest. Among other things, such a state constitutes progress because such a state of being best supports the growth, development, and survival of the community and, ultimately, of the future.

One may ask further why individuals should be concerned about fairness or justice? To libertarians such as Nozick or Engelhardt, freedom is the main consideration of ethics and moral judgments can occur only when individual freedom is the limiting condition of all judgments.[6,10] In their view peace in an inevitably pluralist world cannot be maintained without this limiting principle which, as they see it, assures sufficient solidarity to prevent conflict. Justice, in such a framework, is describable simply as allowing maximal freedom to all. Freely entered contracts and agreements must be punctually kept. Unless someone has a type of misfortune or illness directly caused by another individual or by the community, no one has an obligation to remedy such a state. The natural lottery (for which no one is responsible) has determined which of us will draw the short lot. It is certainly undesirable to draw the short lot (to be poor or ill or deformed) and those who draw the short lot may be considered to be unfortunate; but since no one has directly caused their misfortune, no obligation to remedy the misfortune exists. We cannot help the station of life into which we are born; we cannot usually help being ill or becoming crippled; some are fortunate, and others are not. But being fortunate is not unfair to anyone and being unfortunate is not an instance of injustice; therefore, society has no obligation to help the loser.[11]

In prior sections of this book as well as in previous works I have argued that the libertarian principles of stark individualism rest on a misconception of individuals as freestanding entities and upon communities as mere conglomerates of such freestanding individuals. I have tried to show not only that the libertarian system is flawed in theory and despicable in practice but also that it is inimical to societal progress. Such a system lacks homeostatic mechanisms of adjustment and sees individuals as the sole bearers of legitimate interests (or "rights") and communities as constituted merely to assure individuals of their liberty. Such associations are not truly communities or *Gemeinschaften* because community itself not only is not a value and a goal but because any firm and not entirely voluntary association beyond the most superficial form of association is conceived almost as an ethical misfortune: a misfortune which deepens as communities become more active and more entrenched. Communal solidarity is not only weak, it is painted as desirably weak. Persons are and properly should be devoted to their own private interests. Communities of this sort are founded and are properly founded on individual entrepreneurialism.[12] Entrepreneurialism can, and should to the benefit of all, form the proper basis of community.

This way of constructing the pyramid is peculiar. It is, in some ways, reminiscent of Locke's social contract which presupposes property and an economy before any coming together. To view community or morality as emerging from entrepreneurialism is to invert the pyramid. If my notion of a dynamic, evolving community into which all are born and through which all are shaped is even approximately correct, community may be seen as the foundation in and through which entrepreneurialism develops and is ultimately shaped: entrepreneurialism (however one may think of it) can perhaps emerge from community. But community must pre-exist and form the soil in and on which entrepreneurialism, shaped by the community, ultimately evolves. The way we look at ethics, at community, and at mutual obligation shapes our notion of entrepreneurialism. Entrepreneurialism is subsequent and not prior to community and to ethics.

Rawls's views as expressed in his *Theory of Justice* are critical to any contemporary analysis in the field. Rawls considers an initial contract between freely contracting persons as a crucial heuristic device. Persons, in what he terms "the original position," choose behind a "veil of ignorance" which hides the particulars of their own station from them but allows them to see the general goods and stations available in society. Behind such a veil of ignorance, prudent choosers who have no notion of their own station in life would, according to Rawls, make certain that (1) all persons had maximal freedom consistent with a like freedom of all others; (2) everyone of equal talent had equal access to offices and positions; (3) when differences in status or income exist such differences are justifiable as being of benefit to all; and (4) distribution would benefit the worst off maximally until all basic existent inequities were rectified.[13]

Rawls relied on a process he calls "reflective equilibrium" to establish the fairness of his principles. Rawls understands an intellectual process of weighing various conceptions of normative ethics and social theory with one's almost intuitive sense of justice as reflective equilibrium. Theory, observed practice, and reasoned judgment are mutually corrective.[13]

In Rawls's conceptions, individuals are still isolated beings, separate from community, and rational choosers are rational choosers because they choose for their own freestanding good. The original position, indisputably a most valuable heuristic device, fails to account for the fact that all prudent choosers have, and have always been, shaped and conditioned by their community. The very prudence of their choice reflects the fact that man as a social animal is a product of what Kant refers to as the "common structure of our mind" and of the way in which a particular culture or community has imprinted this common structure. The common structure of our mind adapts cultural and communal values, experiences, and conditioning to form the individual who cannot be conceived of as being "freestanding." Such individuals then are the product not only of their innate capacities, are not merely prudent choosers out to make the best choices for their starkly individualistic selves, but are as inseparable from their particular culture and community as their culture and community is incomprehensible without them. Reflective equilibrium is reflective in the way that the shape of our mind (its structure), and the shape of our culture and community and its values and precepts, has allowed it to be.

The Rawlsian conception of justice has provided many insights not only into what justice is but into the way we can fruitfully conceive of and ultimately shape justice. In my view, Rawls's point of view falters in its continuous insistence on the individualist notion of the self and in its basic conception of community as an association of contracting individuals. To Rawls, communities are less a *Gemeinschaft* than they are a *Gesellschaft* or, at times, even a *Verein*. For communities to hold community itself as a prime value more than merely freely contracting individuals are needed. The fair opportunity range which prudent choosers would want to be able to avail themselves of is one which individuals inevitably see through the kind of eyes their culture and their community has conditioned them to have.

In a proper homeostatic balance the balancing forces pursue not merely their own ends: Their ends inevitably must include the ends of the organism, species or ecosystem of which they are a part.

In true communities (*Gemeinschaften*) the end of community itself is one of the composite of interests which go into shaping the interest of every member. When community itself is no longer a vital part of each individual's interest, solidarity is lost and the community easily threatens to fall apart. Similarly, when communities no longer concern themselves with the individual interests of its members but see the collective as the single and overriding goal to which all else must be subordinated, solidarity and, therefore, community is lost. In such cases communities and their individuals, rather than seeing a collective common goal in which their personal interests find full expression, see their personal interests in competition with each other. The veil of ignorance prudent choosers for heuristic reasons wear as well as the persons prudent choosers are is conditioned, shaped, and expressed by and in community.

SOME PRACTICAL EXAMPLES AND CONSEQUENCES

In a modern, industrialized society as we know it today there are two main opportunities persons must have so as to be able to avail themselves of the fair opportunity range societies may have to offer. Without equity of access to at least education and medical care the opportunity range will be quite different for those with than it is for those without ample funds. Inequities will be institutionalized: those who are well-to-do will be able to achieve an adequate education and maintain an adequate level of "species function" so that they can develop their talents; those who are not equally well-off may not be able to achieve an adequate educational or health level and their talents will consequently whither and eventually die.

Modern society justifiably requires persons who wish to perform certain jobs to meet a predetermined standard of excellence. Persons who want to be automobile mechanics, attorneys, or physicians must acquire a knowledge of the principles of automobile engines, legal structure, or medicine in order to be given the opportunity to practice in their chosen field. The level of education or training required may be quite different but some education and training is a prerequisite for almost all jobs in the modern world. When education is available only to those who can pay for it, when the well-to-do can afford to become educated while the poor cannot, equity in the opportunity range is not present.

It is true that persons can often, even if not always, secure loans and pay for education by means of such loans. Sometimes, at least, the poor may be able to mortgage their future. Many, however, are unwilling to try. Taking out a loan means having to pay it back either after you succeed or even if you do not succeed. The person graduating from medical or law school not rarely has a loan of sixty to one-hundred thousand or more dollars to repay after graduation; usually, but not always, such a loan can be more or less readily paid back from future earnings. However, those who fail to graduate may easily have a similar loan to pay back without having the necessary future earnings to fall back on. Prudent choosers who must choose behind a veil of ignorance and who do not know whether they are destined to pass or fail (especially when they come out of a poor environment in which success is hardly the rule) may easily choose not to take the chance and, therefore, risk going into almost hopeless debt. Mortgaging a future one does not really think one has amounts to mortgaging one's soul. Talented, gifted, and highly motivated persons who would benefit their community are, therefore, lost; often their places are taken by those with more money but with far less talent and far less motivation. Not only does the individual lose: The community loses in many ways. The community loses talented, gifted, and motivated persons who instead of being fulfilled by their job and who, therefore, contribute to their community are disgruntled, frustrated, and unhappy. Solidarity with a community perceived as not only not facilitating their efforts but of actually frustrating it and standing in their way is weakened; the belief of the disadvantaged in a common goal and purpose no longer exists.

Some have argued that health care is what I have called a first order necessity since it is necessary to sustain species normal (i.e., biological) function.[3,4] I am willing to grant that health care, since under normal circumstances it is not strictly necessary to sustain normal life (one can live to a very ripe and healthy old age without ever needing health care), is not in that strict sense a first order necessity. Nevertheless, it is so often essential for proper function that it comes very close to being a first order necessity. Even, however, if one grants that it is not strictly speaking a necessity of the first order, health care at the very least is critical since it underwrites our nature as men and specific persons (our social functioning).[5]

Many persons are born more or less disabled and such persons can achieve access to the full opportunity range their society may provide only with the help of health care. They may have clubfeet, be diabetic, be mentally retarded, or may need eyeglasses. Without medical attention such persons cannot flourish to their fullest and their talents perforce will remain under- or undeveloped. Perhaps even more importantly preventive health care is vital if many of us are to be spared illness, disability, and unnecessary anxiety. Behind Rawls's veil and in reality, none of us can know what fate holds in store for our health and ability to function. Health care may hold little appeal to the Ba Mbuti living their particular existence; but health care is of overriding concern to those of us who live in an industrialized and modern community.

In the United States today, many (about 20 percent) have access to medical care only when medical care is supplied by charity. Many others are severely underinsured. When disaster strikes, such persons may be able to be hospitalized, but since they would have to pay for outpatient services out of their own pocket they are financially incapable of visiting their health-care providers on an outpatient basis. Illness for this group of patients is, therefore, much more likely to become serious illness before it can be checked.

The United States is a technically oriented as well as a crisis-oriented society. This in part may explain why even the most advanced technology is made available when those without previous access to medical care finally become critically and often irremediably ill. Patients who become extremely ill may find admission, albeit often grudging admission, to a hospital. Ultimately the often tremendous and sometimes quite unnecessary cost of such crisis care will be borne by someone. Such costs are often unnecessary both because on many occasions the condition could have been treated earlier (or could have been prevented entirely) and sometimes unnecessary because resources are used beyond all reason.

Examples of the avoidable and excessive use of resources in supplying futile therapy are frequently seen. When persons have no private means, are not eligible for Medicaid or Medicare, and carry no insurance they cannot visit their physician to receive services which often could indeed have prevented the crisis itself.

Premature infants just in excess of five hundred grams, infants whose chance of survival at best is remote, are regularly sustained even when, as is often the case, they have other deformities. Many have intercurrent severe hemorrhage into their central nervous system which almost certainly will at best leave them severely impaired and probably will leave them not far from insentience. Such infants are regularly sustained in America's neonatal ICU's. Often they are on ventilators. The cost for such care, I am told, has topped fifteen hundred dollars a day in most institutions. Many of these children are premature because their mothers lacked good prenatal care, proper food, and proper quarters. It would cost less to provide these mothers with proper care than it now costs to maintain such children only to have most of them die. On the other hand, billions of dollars are used annually to maintain permanently vegetative or comatose persons alive. Likewise, resources are often used in last-ditch efforts which are known to have almost no hope of success. Physicians are well acquainted with examples of both kinds of misuse. And yet little is done to correct either.

Once a crisis presents itself the American health-care system, no matter what the cost and no matter how remote the chances of success, seems willing to intervene. A story may help to illustrate this point. I was asked to see an eighty-six-year-old gentleman about three weeks after he had been brought from his poorly heated apartment to the emergency room with pneumonia. The patient lacked sufficient resources to eat a proper diet as well as lacking sufficient monies to supply more than the most minimal heat in what was a very cold February. In the emergency room his heart stopped. It was restarted, he was placed on a ventilator, taken to the intensive care unit, and vigorously treated but had never regained consciousness. A neurologist felt that the chance of this patient's ever regaining more than minimal consciousness was remote. The question of whether we were obligated to continue treatment was posed to me: a question which almost seemed to answer itself. If his medical condition had been such as to permit recovery, he would have been discharged to the very same milieu responsible for his problem in the first place. In the course of his treatment, tens of thousands of dollars were readily expended to achieve this dubious goal. At the same time, similar poor persons continued at risk for sharing his fate.

This case illustrates several important things: (1) poverty is central to many of these illnesses and taking care of illness without alleviating the causally implicated poverty is largely begging the question; (2) prevention (not only by alleviating poverty but by providing early access to medical care) could quite possibly have forestalled the problem at a fraction of the cost; (3) funds (even a very large amount of funds) for crisis intervention, even for crisis intervention beyond all reason, are far more readily available than are the modest funds needed for prevention. The problem lies not so much in the medical establishment as it resides in the social setting in which the medical establishment is embedded. The problem is far deeper than a merely medical one: if things are to change it is communal attitudes which must change.

Many if not most of the elderly in the United States are covered by Medicare and most of those over sixty-five are the recipients of social security or other retirement benefits. Such social measures are, however, not quite what they seem. Basic Medicare covers in-patient care and then covers such care only for a certain length of time, and with the understanding that a deductible is to be paid. A policy which covers out-patient visits is available at fairly reasonable cost: reasonable, that is, for those who can pay for it. Medicare, basic or not, pays neither for drugs nor, for any length of time, for extended-care facilities or nursing homes. When the elderly cannot afford the cost of such care, supplemental coverage will usually be given by the state but then only after the person has been entirely pauperized. Many of the elderly are caught in a situation in which they can consult their physician but, since they cannot afford to buy the drugs or appliances prescribed, cannot follow their physician's advice. Their social security, in many instances, will be barely sufficient for food and shelter. Not surprisingly, many elderly choose to eat and to have shelter rather than to buy often exorbitantly expensive drugs.

Motivated at least in part by the fact that Medicare for the elderly is expensive and that this expense is often resented, there has been discussion of stopping all but very basic comfort measures after an arbitrary age has been reached. This idea, if not indeed solely driven by economic concerns, is certainly often enthusiastically supported by those who may have to bear the financial burden. The arguments for providing no more than minimal medical care for the elderly have been based either on the notion of a "natural" life span,[14,15] or upon a Rawlsian argument of early in life choosing (behind a veil of ignorance) when and for how long to expend resources.[3,16] Furthermore, it has been suggested that resources for research to expand the life span should not be made available to researchers.

When it comes to limiting care because of the existence of a (discovered?) "natural life span," I have previously argued that (1) the notion of having discovered what is "natural" when it comes to life span makes little sense; (2) one cannot simultaneously claim to have "discovered" these limits and then pretend to set them; (3) what is "natural" is not really the issue since the "natural" course of many conditions would, but for medical care, lead to death; (4) setting an arbitrary individual "limit" on medical care, a limit which at best can be statistically derived, violates the fact that statistics are not meant to apply to individuals within the group but are meant to serve as guidelines; (5) all of human history consists of stretching our limits by learning to manipulate our environment and expand our possibilities; and (6) stopping research on expanding the supposedly "natural" lifespan creates a self-fulfilling prophecy which locks the future into the present.[1]

A rather Rawlsian argument, a much better one in my opinion, nevertheless suffers from problems concerned with the thickness of the veil (which, in fact, in the original position should be used not to distribute but merely to discern principles of distribution). Prudent choosers will find that choosing at an early age (say at age twenty) for a later age (say for age eighty) is difficult if not indeed impossible: values, hopes, expectations, and, therefore, choices, change significantly with age.[1] Arguing that persons by some arbitrarily set age have predictably had the opportunity to fulfill their life plans flies in the face of experience which teaches us that very many persons lead fulfilling and productive (productive for themselves and their community) lives at an often quite advanced and certainly at an unpredictable age. Some elderly people may have had a most difficult earlier life. Their early life may have been full of hardships, disappointments, and suffering and only in later life may comfort and moderate happiness have been possible. Their best years may yet be in front of them. We cannot at age twenty predict what life holds in store for us at age eighty.

This is not the place to repeat these arguments in detail. The suggested solutions to the perceived problem of medical care for the aged is illustrative of a neglect for community and a disregard for solidarity. Setting limits on the rights of all members of a community to share in equal access to those basic things needed to sustain existence (first order necessities) does not jibe with the definition of justice in communities accepting beneficent obligations. There is, however, more to life than meeting first order necessities. Even if we may grant that medical care and education are not first order necessities (and not all would grant this), arbitrarily limiting second order necessities to persons capable of enjoying such benefits does not accord with a sense of justice true communities must have. Defining membership so that the entitlements of membership regardless of function are lost at an arbitrary age makes a mockery out of the notion of membership as well as out of the concept of community. Knowing that my community may decide to stop medical care or that it may no longer recognize my legitimate membership at an arbitrary age without caring whether I am working on another book or, on the other hand, vegetating in a nursing home does not incline me to feel secure and cared for. If true communities care about their member's weal and woe—if caring about their member's weal and woe is, in fact, one of the hallmarks of beneficent communities—then arbitrarily making services unavailable to some who might benefit while continuing them for others (even for others in a permanent vegetative state or those born severely premature and with severe brain hemorrhages) is ultimately inimical to solidarity. It is logically peculiar to on the one hand use resources for those unable to knowingly benefit (severely damaged premature infants or permanently vegetative or comatose persons) and on the other hand contemplate saving resources by denying them to persons who could knowingly and enjoyably profit by their use.

One cannot examine specific social policy or, for that matter, specific medical treatment or education outside the social context in which such health care or education takes place. When not even first order necessities are assured, providing second order necessities in a desperate attempt to make up for our deficiencies seems irrational. The social context in the United States is one in which millions go hungry and homeless while others enjoy the most incredible luxuries. The failure to supply first or second order necessities is not one which can rationally be based on limited resources. Higher taxes, especially higher taxes for the very wealthy, as well as a reordering of priorities giving more priority to social concerns and lower priority to things like defense, could easily overcome such a limit.

I will take it as a given and not further argue extensively for the proposition that just communities who can afford it must see that first and second order necessities for all are met before allowing some to enjoy incredible luxury. I will assume this in the face of the argument that producing such luxuries creates industries which help the economy and, therefore, serves to prevent poverty. While such an argument has at least superficial merit, the amount of good done locally by building, for example, yachts for the wealthy begs the question: meeting basic needs by sufficient taxation and redistribution of wealth before allowing opulence meets the basic needs of all rather than merely of a few local members. Just communities, in the sense of a concept of justice I have argued for, will prefer to limit the economic freedom of some (if necessary by taxing those who can best afford to be taxed) rather than to allow others to go without access to basic needs. The question of following a poor law or a welfare model, however, remains.[7] Societies which follow a poor law model will be likely to have two or multitiered rather than single-tiered access to second order needs whereas those subscribing more closely to a welfare type of system are apt to introduce single-tiered systems of distribution.

With the notable, and regrettable, exception of the United States, most industrialized countries (and many who are not industrialized) have systems of health care providing access to at least health-care services to all inhabitants.[17] Even in the United States where no system assuring access to at least basic services exists for all, some services are provided by the community to certain population groups. The argument has not concerned itself as much with the question is health care a basic need[2,3] (most countries tacitly or explicitly have come to recognize health care as a basic need) as with two other questions: (1) are communities obligated to provide for the basic needs of their members? and (2) if basic needs are to be provided, should provision be single- or multitiered?

I will spend little further time on the first question. Its answer

depends on the way social contract is envisioned and, consequently, on the way community is defined.[1] When only obligations of mutual non-harm are accepted by individuals and by
their community, when in other words, a libertarian minimalist
ethic holds sway, no obligation to provide for basic human needs
will be recognized; when obligations are seen more broadly and
obligations of benefiting others are accepted, obligations to provide for basic human needs are apt to be acknowledged.
Although libertarians will, in theory, argue for a starkly minimalist ethic,[6,10] purely minimalist communities cannot and in fact do
not exist. In practice, the question is not "shall communities be
built on a minimalist model?" Rather the question becomes
"how can a balance between the minimalist philosophy (which is
predominantly concerned with individual rights) and a communitarian one (which is mainly concerned with social justice) be
best and most equitably achieved?"

Throughout this book I have argued that communities must
concern themselves with the basic needs of their members, that
those needs include education as well as health care and that,
therefore, the provision of some level of both education and health
care to those within the community is a legitimate communal concern. The fact that certain basic needs are basic because they provide access to a fair opportunity range (defined as those opportunities supporting an "array of life plans reasonable persons may
construct for themselves" [p. 33]) forms the basic ground for this
assumption.[3] There is no question that any system, be it single- or
multitiered, which enables all persons to have at least some level of
access to health care is preferable to a system in which, as is the
case in the United States today, large numbers of persons have no
access at all.[18] The question of single- or multitiered health care
systems is, however, a question which is hardly limited to the
United States today. It is a question actively debated in many if not
all countries of the world which in justice feel themselves compelled to provide at least some basic health-care services but which
also have had to face the grim facts of limited resources.

In a single-tiered system (be it a system of education or health
care) all members of the community receive equal services and
none can buy more. In multitiered systems various possibilities of
buying "more" exist for those capable of doing so. There is a
marked philosophical difference between those subscribing to one

or the other system. In general, those who are more inclined to be egalitarians will hold that basic services must be equally distributed while those inclined not to be egalitarians will be comfortable with having more or less crass differences even when it comes to access to basic needs. In general single-tiered systems are more apt to exist in communities like Denmark which accept a "welfare" philosophy: a philosophy which makes entitlement, at least when it comes to basic services, a function of being a member of the community rather than a function of being a member of some definable class.[7] Contrasted to this is a "poor law" philosophy in which entitlement is by virtue of belonging to a particular arbitrarily defined economic class.[7] It is, of course, possible to have a welfare state which equally supplies a basic set of commodities to all but permits the purchase of more by those who can afford it and thus welfare states can, in principle, accommodate two-tiered systems. Such states may give entitlement for a broad range of services as an implicit benefit of membership in the community and still permit what they consider to be less essential services to be bought by those who want and can afford them. States in which a "poor law" philosophy underpins communal decisions, however, will be more apt to have multitiered systems. Welfare states, in other words, need not be strictly egalitarian, albeit that welfare states are far more apt to be egalitarian when it comes to what they define as essential services. Consequently they are apt to have single-tiered systems.

Even in states such as Canada or the Scandinavian nations which have predominantly single-tiered systems there is frequently a small private component in which particular medical procedures (or quicker access) can be bought. In such states, however, the amount of such care and its influence on the public sector is negligible (less than 5 percent).[18] Such states feel obligated to grant all citizens free access to what are defined as essential services. It has been shown that the citizens of these states are quite comfortable with free access to all and basically are satisfied with their health care and educational systems.

In states whose philosophy is more individualistic, two-tiered models are more apt to exist and their influence on the public sector can be expected to be high. Individuals and institutions can earn far more by working in the private than by working for the public sector. Since people are human, the attraction of a better wage is considerable and there may well be a tendency for the best trained individuals as well as for the best equipped institutions to devote themselves largely if not completely to private care. Not too many actual studies are available. In one important study between 1979 and 1988 investigators in the United Kingdom found significant differences in waiting time and outcome between National Health Service (NHS) and private patients in both waiting and ultimate outcome. Private patients waited 17.2 days for catheterization and 22.8 days for surgery; NHS patients 115.8 days for catheterization and 305.9 days for surgery. During the ten years of the study the waiting time increased significantly for the NHS and not at all for the private patients. It is of note that of 619 NHS patients 15 died, while there were no deaths among 204 private patients.[19] As more facilities and talents are devoted to private care, the public sector and the patients in it inevitably loses out. Multitiered systems disadvantage patients in the public sector at the outset (fewer services are available) as well as at the end (because of the private sector the waiting period of patients in the public sector is unduly and artificially prolonged). One can, of course, argue that these figures speak against the concept of a National Health Service: after all, patients in the private sector did so much better; why not switch to an all-private sector and give up the NHS? Such a move can advantage only those with sufficient money (by insurance or otherwise) to avail themselves of services. Inevitably such a move would end up with a market system similar to the one experienced in the United States, a system which ultimately results in a much larger wastage of health and lives.

In multitiered systems, furthermore, what will and what will not be counted as "basic" and, therefore, furnished to all will inevitably be defined by those most powerful. Those most powerful unavoidably are those most well off: the very ones who by insurance or private means could avail themselves of a higher tier. Defining what is "basic" generously is not in their interest.

Communities in which a strongly individualist philosophy holds sway are united by the belief that the community will assure private liberty although they realize that little may be done for individuals falling upon hard times. Some persons may flourish and others languish in such communities; that is largely, if not altogether, a matter of luck. Communities in which an overwhelming communitarian philosophy predominates, are united by the belief that basic needs will be met but realize that their personal ability to flourish may be seriously limited. Homeostasis, a non-competitive balance for a common goal rather than a competitive striving after purely private ends, is more apt to assure measured growth. When either extreme predominates solidarity, if it exists at all, lacks strength.

I have argued that societies which accept beneficent obligations must do at least two things for all their members: (1) they must see that all members of the community have access to the basic necessities needed to sustain life; and (2) they must provide fair access to the fair opportunity range for all. Education and health care are both critical for attaining a fair opportunity range. When a minimum of either is supplied to all but some can buy more there is a tendency to institutionalize basic inequality and perpetuate a sharply divided class system. When, as is the case in multitiered systems of education or health care, some persons are denied certain types of education or health care available to others, their opportunities for developing and utilizing their talents to the fullest are severely impaired.

To argue that those who save money for education or health care are simply expressing their own values and ought to be free to do so lacks force when it is applied to critical illness in individuals and especially when one tries to apply this argument to their children. A person's value for acutely needed health care is quite different than is the value such persons may have given to the same health care prior to realizing their need. Will a society be willing to let someone either unable to save or improvident enough not to do so (or someone whose income is poor) die because of a lack of money while another whose resources are better lives? Will a society deny education (or health care) to the children of the improvident (or, what is far more often the case, to those who do not have the means to be provident since they live a hand-to-mouth existence) simply on account of their parents? And if that is truly the case, can one expect much solidarity from such an association?

A frequent comparison (one made at the Private Sector Conference in Medicine at Duke University) between multitiered systems and classes on airplanes[20] is unconvincing. As was pointed out by Fletcher, all passengers on an airplane, no matter what the class, have the same pilot, the same destination, the same safety standards as well as the same likelihood of getting there.[21] And if they crash, they crash together. Their solidarity is not greatly disturbed by one having to buy his/her own drinks while another gets a gourmet meal or champagne. Education and health care can hardly be compared to gourmet meals or champagne. If we truly believe that all within a society must have basic biological needs met and must be afforded similar opportunities to develop their own talents we cannot be satisfied with supplying such commodities in an unequal fashion. If societies as well as individuals are to flourish, evolve, and ultimately survive they must foster their own solidarity and support each other's goals.

We do not find societies in an original condition. As useful a heuristic device as pre-social humankind or the concept of an original position may be in examining the issue, we must go beyond to analyze societies as they exist today and then move on to create what we define and ultimately create as progress. Societies, if they are to do this, must draw upon the expertise of many disciplines and ultimately if they are to pretend to believe in the democratic process must move in the direction determined by a well-educated and informed electorate. This proposition is, of course, another argument for supplying "second order" necessities such as education to all in an equal manner. An uneducated electorate may be able to operate the machinery of the democratic process: it can be trained to go to the polls and to pull levers. Such an electorate records choices it cannot comprehend and makes a sham out of the political process. Having a highly educated electorate certainly does not guarantee democracy's process. The example of Hitler Germany would certainly invalidate such a claim! Many more factors enter into it. An educated electorate far from guarantees democracy: but an educated electorate is the necessary condition for a democracy's success. A lack of education makes persons vulnerable to slick and dangerous demagogues hawking easy solutions to complex problems. A democratic community if it is to be a *Gemeinschaft* and work together for the common good requires an educated electorate for its own ends as much as individuals require education for their own ends.

If society is to be shaped by the will of those within it, all must have access to first as well as second order necessities. Since meeting these necessities is ultimately essential for the community as well as for the individual, first as well as second order needs for individuals are first and second order needs for the community as well. Communities, if they are to survive and grow, are just as dependent upon the meeting of basic necessities for all as are those individuals for whom such necessities are met.

Even if a system which allows either single- or mutliple-tiered access to first and second order needs is established, access has been far from assured. There is more to access either to health care or education than mere availability on an even footing. Conditions in the United States and perhaps in some other industrialized nations (South Africa, for example) have a tradition of racial, sexual and other injustice which has rendered certain groups far less likely to avail themselves successfully of such opportunities. Prejudice abounds and admission and later hiring policies often reflect such prejudice. It is unlikely that persons who already before they start working hard know that their hard work is unlikely to give them the same opportunities that others enjoy, are apt to avail themselves of the opportunity to work hard only to bat their head against the wall of prejudice. To succeed in producing a just society the issue of racism as well as the issue of sexism and other forms of severe prejudice need to be examined.

In today's world societies have many traditional inequities which must be corrected if a fair opportunity range for all is to be established. In this chapter, I shall use conditions as they historically and in fact exist in the United States today to illustrate what I mean. I shall argue that a process which has been called "affirmative action" is, if properly applied, not only ethically justifiable but in the view presented here an ethically necessary condition for the building of a just society. "Affirmative action," as the term will be used here, is a process whose aim is to maximally advantage groups which have been historically disadvantaged until equal access to the fair opportunity range exists. By fair access I mean more than merely access on paper; providing legal possibilities, while essential if the process is to come about at all and inequities are to be addressed, is an insufficient condition for gaining truly fair access for those who have been traditionally disadvantaged.

A fair opportunity range is often denied persons as a result of

prejudice or racism. Racism (as well as sexism and similar prejudices) often serve as the convenient excuse behind which economic issues hide. The issue of prejudice, racism, and disadvantaging might well be examined by considering a passage from the
introduction to Primo Levi's *Survival at Auschwitz*.

> Many people—many nations—find themselves holding, more or
> less wittingly, that "every stranger is an enemy." For the most
> part, this conviction lies deep down like some latent infection; it
> betrays itself only in random, disconnected acts and does not lie
> at the base of a system of reason. But when this does come
> about, when the unspoken dogma becomes the major premise in
> a syllogism, then at the end of the chain there is the Lager. Here
> is the product of a conception of the world carried rigorously to
> its logical conclusion; so long as the conception subsists, the
> conclusion inevitably remains to threaten us.

It is a mistake to reduce Auschwitz or the Nazi experience to
a curious and unique series of events pitting a few Germans
against some Jews. Reducing the experience in this fashion loses
its meaning as a transcendent and human one. The experience is
neither uniquely German nor uniquely Jewish. Rather the experience is, as Primo Levi says, an experience analogous to that of a
latent infection: the latent infection of "other-ism" which infects
no specific group and does not occur at a specific time. It is an
experience which has occurred throughout history and which
continues to occur. Inevitably, wherever it is allowed to occur, its
logical outcome leads from antagonism, to discrimination, and
eventually to Auschwitz, or Capetown, or Jerusalem, Birming-
ham, Alabama, or a detention camp for Japanese.

The problem with "other-ism" is perhaps most easily exemplified by the way in which racism in the United States has been
aimed at Afro-Americans. The struggle for civil rights in the
United States is representative of the problem. The African slave
trade robbed individuals of more than their freedom: it robbed
them of their language, their faith, their cultural roots, and their
families. It depersonalized slaves by robbing them of their cultural
selfness much as the Nazis later depersonalized Jewish inmates in
the camps by systematically robbing them of their identity.

The civil rights struggle dates back to the time when slaves
were first brought here in the early 1600s. Often such slaves had
been sold to white slave traders by African tribes who had cap-

tured them in war; at other times slave traders themselves abducted Africans. Those who survived the trip (a trip which has many remarkable similarities to the trip Jews and others took four hundred years later on their way to the camps) were separated from the others and completely lost all connections with their previous families and cultures. It is amazing that despite this separation and disconnectedness attempts to escape and overt resistance, even from the first, continued. A history which reduces the civil rights struggle to an active struggle by whites for the sake of blacks (a popular way of looking at history in the United States today) is simply an historical fiction. This historical error is often an act of unconscious and subconscious condescension which has its roots in the very same racist attitudes that it set out to destroy. From the time of slavery onward and today, blacks have fully participated in the struggle. Interestingly enough, the stories of Jewish resistance to the Nazis likewise have received little publicity although participation by Jews in partisan forces and Jewish resistance were not rare.

Slavery, the forebear of much American racism, was initially built on an economic basis. It maintained itself because it was of great profit to some who held power and, ultimately, fell because economically speaking keeping slaves was a less profitable venture than exploiting labor. Slavery as well as keeping the newly freed slaves in a system of economic instead of personal slavery, was done largely by promulgating the myth of inferiority and by forcing a separation which helped sustain that myth. The reason supplied the myth and the myth fortified the reason. The economic issue lies at the root of racism as well as sexism.

The modern struggle for civil rights became particularly intense during and after World War II when Japanese, whose parents were incarcerated in concentration camps, and blacks, many of whose parents lived in a South in which they could not walk on the same sidewalk or drink from the same drinking fountain as whites or in a North which likewise insisted on their "inferiority," repeatedly distinguished themselves: The Nisei in a Japanese regiment in Europe, blacks in many places including in a well-known black fighter squadron. It is interesting that the same blacks who as officers distinguished themselves piloting fighter planes were not allowed when back "home" to enter the officer's club on their base and Japanese soldiers home on leave went "home" to their parent's camp. Persons home from active and successful participation in a war are unlikely to allow themselves to be disparaged, belittled, and disadvantaged. Nor are they likely to feel much solidarity with those they hold responsible for causing their condition.

It is curious that almost all the violence until the ghetto riots in the 1960s was violence committed by whites against those, black or white, who refrained from violence. Non-violence took place in a setting of extreme violence on the part of the Ku Klux Klan and its allied groups. Lynchings, other murders, beatings, bombings, cattle prods, whips, and clubs were the order of the day. To be successful, non-violence requires a certain soil. Non-violence requires at least one of several conditions: (1) those who are violent or brutal ultimately are sickened by their own violence or brutality; (2) those who are violent are surrounded by a community in which brutality is not long tolerated; or (3) non-violent resisters overwhelm the machinery of those who are committing violence or brutality.

In India, Gandhi had found that (1) most British soldiers forced to club, beat, and shoot at defenseless Indians who simply presented themselves to be beaten, clubbed and shot, soon sickened; (2) the people back home in England largely disapproved of such tactics and had not brought up the soldiers in this way; and (3) jails and other places of confinement could not cope with the volume of resisters. Violence and brutality backfired on the British raj.

In America most members of the KKK, just like good Nazis everywhere, were certainly not sickened by their brutality; indeed, like good Nazis everywhere, they seemed to enjoy it. However, even in the South and more so in the North, many people were sickened by the outrages taking place before their eyes, even when these same persons were terrorized by both the perpetrators of the violence and the legal machinery which largely supported the violence. The claim that one could turn to local or federal police for protection (a claim even at times still made today) is fictitious: during those days turning to the local police was madness and turning to the FBI was largely naive folly. Police (local, state, and federal) ultimately, however, are part of the community and the community was less than enthusiastic about the grosser outrages committed. This was not because the community did not share the racist attitudes of the KKK: more often than not, a large number of Americans did. The statement that "they" wanted "too much," the presumption, in other words, that wanting equality was "too much," was and in many ways is today an ingrained American presumption. Community opposition came about because the community, by and large, could not stomach the brutality of the methods used. Furthermore, the machinery of the state was simply overwhelmed. When one went to a small southern town, or even to a fair-sized city with a group of marchers or freedom riders which exceeded the capacity of the jails, arresting them proved to be almost impossible. Building concentration camps for this mass of persons, and with the recent Nazi experience, was not possible in the time available.

Today, civil rights has seen many setbacks. In saying this one must acknowledge that the America of today is not the America of the World War II or post–World War II era. Thanks to the struggles of the 1960s undeniable progress has been made. Thirty-five years ago the number of blacks in professional schools was few. A quota system for Jews, women, and blacks was largely still in place. Progress has been made even though severe backsliding has occurred and progress is severely threatened by a wave of reactionary feeling and reactionary policy and action. Hate groups proliferate and women's rights and affirmative action are being dismantled. After all of yesterday's hopes and plans, racism and sexism has again begun to seriously infect America. Primo Levi was quite right when he spoke of a "latent infection" which betrays itself in an unspoken dogma and becomes the major premise in a syllogism. Passive resistance no longer seems to be as effective and the passive resisters are losing their patience. Many, although they were at least aesthetically or emotionally horrified by brutality, are far from ready to accept true equality. Basically this unwillingness to accept equality has economic roots: if a group of persons can be kept in slavery, or traditionally underpaid and exploited, enormous, even if very temporary and, therefore, short-sighted, benefit accrues to others.

The economic benefit which the exploiter reaps by exploiting others is, from a communal perspective and especially in today's society, a very temporary one. Like a Pyrrhic victory, it is a Pyrrhic benefit. The United States can no longer survive if it continues to subscribe to the racist or sexist myth. Racial and other stereotypes perpetuate economic and class differences for which racism and sexism are only markers. The United States is faced with a well-educated, economically strong, and intellectually progressive Europe and Japan which do not waste their human resources. Becoming doctors, engineers, or teachers does not take an almost superhuman effort for many as it does in the United States today. The ghettos—enclaves of hopelessness and of traditional despair—as they exist in all American cities, are unknown; social justice not only guarantees to most their basic necessities but includes in those necessities the opportunity for health care and education. Eliminating racism is not merely ethically necessary; it is imperative if the United States is not to become a backwater, let alone a laughing stock. Unless the conditions as they exist in the United States today are ameliorated what little solidarity there is cannot be maintained.

I shall claim that what is called "affirmative action" in the United States today can legitimately be considered to be a basic second order necessity until such a time as equity not only in educational and health opportunities but also in life-plan opportunities has been established and confirmed by ongoing practice: until, in other words, it has become part of normal communal behavior. Affirmative action is needed if all members of the community are to have their rightful station and place as "men and specific persons."[5] One need not worry that persons will be disadvantaged in the market place because their hair color is different; hair color is not considered a relevant feature when it comes to access to educational, health-care, or life-plan opportunities. The aim of affirmative action is to have race, sex, ethnic origin, or disability (and whatever other arbitrary states of being serve as excuses for various forms of discrimination) likewise become irrelevant conditions in gaining access to the various opportunities society may offer. Class or economic status often serves as a similar excuse at first to stereotype and then to disadvantage groups of people.

Certainly differences of race or sex may be most relevant in a specific context and applying them in that context is, therefore, justifiable. Persons from certain ethnic or racial backgrounds are more prone to develop certain diseases which may make them unfit for given occupations and testing for such diseases is not unreasonable; men cannot bear or nurse infants; and certain physical or intellectual disabilities disqualify one for particular offices or occupations.

My claim that affirmative action in the United States, and undoubtedly in many other parts of the world today, is a critically necessary and ethically not only justifiable but ethically mandatory second order need rests on the fact that without affirmative action certain groups cannot hope to have full and fair access to the opportunity range offered by their society. Such a claim is further strengthened by arguing that societies which do not rectify social injustice are inevitably societies on their way to fragmentation: a *Gemeinschaft* in the sense of its members seeing the *Gemeinschaft* itself as a value in its own right, cannot develop. Solidarity is at best weak and at times entirely nonexistent. A war of all against all may not be the order of the day but a war of one group against another may become almost inevitable. Such a war may be a "war" in the true meaning of the word instead of merely, as it has been so far, being a series of skirmishes, skirmishes in which individuals and small groups of individuals strike at each other.

Opportunities for Afro-Americans as well as for Hispanics, women, and other disadvantaged groups are sorely lacking. I do not claim that affirmative action is needed merely on the basis of race; rather I shall claim that affirmative action is needed by persons who have been historically disadvantaged for whatever reason. Race is an excuse and often a marker for such disadvantaging but it is not a root cause. I firmly believe that such disadvantaging not only plays itself out economically but that it has largely, if not exclusively, economic roots. Those who are advantaged inevitably, and whether they want to or not, profit from the fact that others are disadvantaged: since there are fewer contenders their chance of success in what they aim for is better. When persons can be kept as slaves (or, which is quite similar, when employers can grossly exploit employees making them into what has been called "wage slaves"), slave keepers, employers, and many of those whose livelihood ultimately depends on them profit. It is to the benefit of the exploiting class to have access to a class of persons who can be readily exploited. In the market where profit is enshrined as at least one of the greatest goods (indeed, where some would have it as a proper ethical principle) it is obvious that selling a product at the lowest price and at the highest profit is desirable; and the highest profit depends on the cost of raw materials and labor. Paying one's employees as little as possible, just as buying raw materials at the lowest cost, is certainly one way of increasing one's profit.

Race, sex, or other attributes which are not relevant in terms of the person's talents or capacity to "do the job" serve as convenient markers for economic disadvantaging. Ghettoization, the exploitation of women, and unfulfilled lives for the disabled inevitably result. The exploited are now seen as strangers and strangers are seen as enemies. The "other-ism" of some in the service of profit has been employed to its fullest advantage.

When a certain number of persons seek access to certain offices, desirable occupations, or stations in life and some are arbitrarily excluded, those not excluded are reciprocally advantaged. When two persons seek admission to the same institution or seek to be employed in a certain position, and unless the choice is an entirely arbitrary one, the one ultimately chosen is chosen because he/she had some attribute or quality which the other lacked and which gained them an advantage. The particular advantage was seen as a relevant difference between the two; the person chosen was advantaged by it, the person not chosen was reciprocally and inevitably disadvantaged. Such an advantage may be a genuine, very relevant, and entirely justifiable difference for the institution or employer: it may be higher scores (on fairly constructed and administered) aptitude tests, more experience, or any one of a number of things readily acknowledged to be relevant. Persons with attributes which are truly relevant can be expected to perform better.

Affirmative action rests on an almost Rawlsian philosophy that justice as fairness must maximally advantage those who have been traditionally disadvantaged until as full as possible equity is achieved. Availing oneself of second order needs is truly possible only when true access to a fair opportunity range exists. As I have pointed out previously, there is a multitude of historical problems to be dealt with and overcome. Racial disadvantaging on the basis of color or sex (or the disadvantaging of traditionally poor groups among whites) is not simply a matter of offering equal access. There is a lot more to success than the ability to enter certain schools or the possibility of having certain jobs. To have parity requires parity from the very start: families with certain attitudes, traditions, and values are more likely to have children whose attitudes, values, and traditions are similar.

Some of these attitudes, values, and traditions are helpful; others may be a hindrance. A tradition of poverty, a tradition of hopelessness, a disbelief in the value of education and, at times, just a certain way rather than another way of looking at things can spell failure whereas another might spell success.

Parity implies much more than merely the opportunity to be educated or the opportunity to live wherever one may want to. Persons who have been traditionally disadvantaged and disparaged will find comfort in living with those whose experiences are similar. They feel protected and appreciated rather than unsheltered and derided. When this occurs the traditional attitudes and values of a traditionally "failing" group are apt to perpetuate themselves and grow. Educational opportunities will not be taken and consequently certain jobs will remain out of reach. The cycle of disadvantaging is apt to be perpetuated and to perpetuate itself. Some by dint of exceptional luck and great talent may, with the expenditure of often almost superhuman effort, escape such a setting; but it is only a few and it leaves a vast number of others behind to continue the same cycle.

Affirmative action seeks to advantage those who have been historically disadvantaged. In so doing and inevitably it will confer a certain disadvantaging on those who prior to this have been advantaged. When two persons apply for one position which only one can fill and when a certain number of "Points" are given to one, the chances of the other decrease. That is inevitable and is, in fact, what has traditionally been happening to minority groups. Belonging to such a minority decreased the chance for employment, admission to certain schools and colleges, or getting (as it still does today) bank loans. Affirmative action, among other things, seeks to create a more just situation by advantaging the formerly disadvantaged until parity has been achieved.

Objections to affirmative action are consistently raised on the grounds that all affirmative action does is to reverse discrimination: in a zero-sum game in which only a finite number can win (admittance to school or a coveted position, for example) advantaging group A automatically disadvantages group B and reversing the matter, while making things different, does not in itself make them more just. It is often claimed that individuals living today and competing for various life chances cannot be held responsible for having created the inequities that exist. Since individuals living today have, for the most part, played no role in causing the inequities that exist they, therefore, ought not to be penalized; they ought not to be forced to sacrifice in order to remedy a situation not of their own making.

Responsibility and culpability are two quite different things. One is often recognized for being responsible for things without being directly culpable for them.[23] As Hans Jonas mentions, the old story about the missing nail in the horseshoe which (ultimately) caused the loss of the kingdom illustrates the point. Direct causal responsibility for the misplacement of the nail falls on the employee of a smith charged with shoeing the horse. Responsibility for redress, however, falls on the employer who while not blameworthy directly for his worker's negligence, can be held responsible for the consequences. To be causally responsible for something, furthermore, does not entail culpability: aside from the obvious fact that mindless forces of nature or mechanical devices which are responsible for causing a given event are not culpable, a person may have causal responsibility without being culpable. I may, for example, skid on a patch of ice and hit your car but unless I drove in a reckless manner I am not culpable.

One may be responsible for something or someone by virtue of many things: professional or other roles, experience, capacity, as well as many other circumstances may create responsibility. One does not have to be culpable or causally responsible for something in order to be responsible for helping to redress a situation. The term "responsibility" can be used in several ways. Responsibility may denote causal implication in a chain of causes eventuating in a given effect. Such responsibility may or may not denote culpability. If I lose consciousness because I have a stroke while driving and my car kills a pedestrian, I am causally implicated in something for which I cannot be held morally responsible or culpable. If I deliberately kill an enemy who chances to walk in front of my car, I am causally as well as ethically responsible. I am culpable. I may not be directly causally responsible (even though I most certainly am involved in the causal chain) and yet be culpable, as when I hire someone to drive the car which kills my enemy. When I know that someone is about to kill my enemy and fail to warn my enemy of the danger, I am even less causally responsible even though I certainly cannot be absolved from culpability. Not killing my enemy (whether directly by hitting him with my car or indirectly by having someone else drive) can, in Kantian terms, be conceived as a perfect duty: one which would be seen as binding under all (or, at least when prima facie, under most) circumstances. Allowing something I could prevent from happening by failing to warn would, in Kantian terms, be a more imperfect duty. In a past chapter I have argued that the difference between such obligations depends, among other things, on circumstances and context. Trying to avoid killing my enemy who happens to stray in front of my car and risking a head-on collision may arguably be much less of an obligation than warning my enemy that someone is about to kill him.

If I have the capacity to stop a course of action and fail to do so I become, to a greater or lesser degree, involved in the action. If I have the capacity to stop a course of action from which I derive benefit but fail to do so, I am implicated in its results. When I allow something to continue that I could stop or have a part in stopping and I fail to do so I partake of causal responsibility; when the reason for my failure to do so is that I profit from such a course of action, I become ethically involved and culpable. Stopping a train of events which harms another and which I could stop (or assist in stopping) but which I have not brought about and which does not benefit me is an act of beneficence; an obligation to stop such a train of events when I am one of the persons who profits from the harm done is beyond mere beneficence. If one has traditionally gained advantage from the unfair disadvantaging of another (even when one had no part in that disadvantaging) one may have responsibility to partake in an action to redress an injustice from which one has benefited and continues to benefit. The continued disadvantaging of the historically disadvantaged inevitably profits the same group (even if not the same individuals) who were those originally responsible. Individuals who continue to derive profit from the disadvantaging of another (even when they themselves were not responsible for initiating the process) become causally implicated in the continued disadvantaging of others when they refuse to participate in remedying the situation.

White, middle-class, largely Christian, and native-born American males belong to a group which have traditionally been the beneficiaries of the disadvantaging of other groups. Much of the country's wealth and power has been amassed by this group and the best opportunities have traditionally been open to them. Many white middle-class American males have not only themselves not wished to be the beneficiaries but sometimes have resented their role as beneficiaries. Some have actively participated in society's attempt to remedy the situation. Nevertheless and despite everything they might do, they have continued to profit from this situation and they inevitably continue to profit today. When such persons, because of a valid claim not to be personally responsible for initiating the process, refuse to remedy a situation from which they continue to profit, they arguably become not only involved but culpable: culpable not for initiating but for continuing it. White male native-born Americans cannot be held ethically responsible (or culpable) for having created the inequities that exist; but when they oppose measures designed to correct a situation from which they continue to profit, even when such measures would cause them some disadvantage, they become morally responsible (culpable) for continuing the process.

The best chance for access to the opportunity range offered by American society is held by those who are white middle-class males. Beyond this, however, tradition in such families has tended to foster success: when persons grow up with a tradition of plenty (or, at least, of enough), have never had to scramble for food, shelter, or warmth, and have had ready access to good schools and jobs, and when all of their friends and acquaintances come from a like background, inevitable and justifiable expectations express themselves in hope. Surrounded by success, failure becomes only a remote option. When persons grow up with a tradition of want, have often had to go hungry, have been poorly housed, inadequately clothed, and have had little access to good schools or jobs, and when all except a very few of their friends and acquaintances share a similar background, inevitable and justifiable hopelessness will result in giving up before even trying. Surrounded by failure, success becomes a remote and almost unthinkable option. It is the stuff dreams but not realities are made of. When limited resources and opportunities exist, those from a tradition of hope are inevitably advantaged before the game even starts. The cycle of hopelessness cannot (except with great slowness and uncertainly) be remedied without visibly rectifying conditions. To remedy the cycle of hopelessness, the traditionally disadvantaged need to be surrounded by others like themselves, others who are able to develop their talents and others who, when they are encouraged to avail themselves of the opportunities a given society has to offer, succeed. When this happens the cycle of hopelessness can be broken and the traditionally disadvantaged will develop new hope and with it new attitudes, values, and ultimately traditions.

The objection to affirmative action that it is simply "reverse discrimination" and that just like discrimination it results in conferring an advantage on some at the cost of disadvantaging others is, superficially and in part, correct. I hope to show that such temporary disadvantaging is (1) not as truly a disadvantaging as it may seem and that (2) to the extent that it is disadvantaging it is a justifiable form of disadvantage based on relevant distinctions and criteria.

The claim that affirmative action is not as truly disadvantaging to those who have been traditionally advantaged as it may, at first blush, seem, rests on the fact that persons who because of a tradition and an environment of success (or at least of failure as unusual) have an enormous advantage vis-à-vis others who come from an environment of failure. Persons who come from an environment in which success is the norm almost invariably have easier access to better schools and even when in the same schools as those more traditionally disadvantaged generally live in a social setting more conducive to study. It is not surprising, therefore, that such persons often will do better on tests and that they often present a better appearance when applying for jobs.

Women, while they may grow up in a family environment like that of the advantaged group, are often disadvantaged in more subtle ways. Tradition in such groups sometimes either opposes higher education for women or puts a lower priority on such education than it does on similar education for males. While females in such families have the same access to first order needs as do their brothers, their chances to avail themselves of a full opportunity range is often less. Since their ability to derive optimal advantage of the full opportunity range is limited, their capacity later in life to have even adequate first order needs met is considerably lower. In the United States, single women, often among the elderly, live in much greater poverty than do men.[24,25]

Temporarily disadvantaging those who have been traditionally advantaged may be somewhat like placing a handicap on the experienced golfer when he/she plays with one of lesser experience. A fair game demands parity from the outset.

Undoubtedly affirmative action results in some temporary disadvantaging of formerly advantaged persons. When a certain number of points are given for belonging to an historically disadvantaged group, the person who is not given these points feels unfairly treated and resents being disadvantaged. There is merit in such an argument. In building a more equitable society in which equity of opportunity is the rule out of a society in which traditional exploitation has been the rule, hard choices have to be made. One must choose between merely paying lip service, regretting one's history but continuing to exploit and profiting (and being morally responsible for continuing a patently unfair state of affairs) or one may have to choose to redress a greater historical wrong with a temporary and lesser one.

At the very least, those who have been historically advantaged and who continue to gain advantage from their history have, if beneficence is to have any meaning, an obligation to see that an injustice from which they continue to profit (whether they want to profit or not), is remedied even when remedying such a situation places them at what may actually be a slight disadvantage. But beyond this, those who have been historically advantaged and who continue to gain advantage from their history are morally implicated in continuing this historical injustice. They, therefore, arguably have an obligation beyond beneficence: being causally implicated not in initiating but in continuing a morally unacceptable state of affairs makes them culpable and therefore obligated to remedy that which they have caused and otherwise would continue to cause. Because of the continuing traditional advantaging from which the historically advantaged continue to benefit, their disadvantage is relatively slight. When those from traditionally deprived areas are given some extra points and because of these points are accepted into schools or jobs with lower test scores the theory of handicapping those who have had a better opportunity to become proficient so as to create a fairer game is followed. Better test scores for the advantaged group may not be a marker of greater ability but merely one of greater traditional opportunity.

Many are afraid (or at least many raise the objection) that affirmative action will simply continue until conditions are reversed and the exploited become the exploiters. Such an objection, while it has theoretical merit, has little practical application. It is another form of the "slippery slope" argument. Slippery slopes, as I have mentioned previously, are unavoidable. They counsel caution rather than suggesting that a given course of action necessarily be abandoned. When the slope is slippery, one puts down sand: that is, one proceeds with due caution; when it becomes too steep, one wisely erects a barrier and stops. The slope of affirmative action is as yet neither very slippery nor very steep; we are far from the point at which serious anxiety about having a society in which native-born white males are cruelly disadvantaged is in order. Obviously such a state of affairs would be no more just (even if some would argue that it might be well deserved!) than what is the case today. But just saying that having everything destroyed by water is just as bad as having it destroyed by fire does not suggest that the fire department should not spray water on one's burning house: it merely says that one ought to be careful so that one can reasonably choose a point at which to stop putting water on the fire. The fact that extinguishing a fire will often and almost inevitably produce some water damage is no argument against calling the fire department.

Homeostatic forces within a society tend to allow progress within a slowly shifting framework. Homeostasis seeks stability not as a frozen and unchanging state but as the framework which enables evolution and allows progress to a condition of greater equity. Solidarity enables a smooth working together for the common good in which all share. Solidarity, in turn, is enabled and fostered by the sense of equal opportunities for and participation by all. To be a community (a true *Gemeinschaft*) means accepting and internalizing community itself as one of the values and goals. Communities which enjoy solidarity will be able to grow, survive, evolve, and endure. In truth, communities without solidarity cannot be communities (*Gemeinschaften*) in the sense that the term is used here. Homeostatic forces tend to seek stability through a dynamic equilibrium operating within a framework changed by external as well as by internal forces. Its goal or telos is the survival of the organism, species, eco-, or social system in which it operates. Solidarity and true community are means to such an end. Affirmative action, which seeks to enfranchise the previously disenfranchised, in every sense of the word supports the concept of community and solidarity and is, therefore, supportive of homeostasis.

I have argued that by virtue of being the necessary condition for meeting first as well as second order needs, communities themselves have prior necessity. If societies are to become communities, to have solidarity, and to progress they must, to the extend possible, meet the first and second order needs of their members. In a world in which no historically disadvantaged group exists, needs of the second order are, at the very least, those of education and health care. When traditional disadvantage has historically disabled a group of persons, affirmative action must be added to these second order necessities. Unless this is done, the prior value which community has is destroyed and the society ultimately stops developing and must perish.

The suffering brought about for some when their needs go unmet is especially severe when their needs go unmet while others live in luxury. Such suffering is produced not only in those whose stark poverty cries out for relief but also in those incapable of developing their talents and pursuing their life plans. Those living in luxury, on the other hand, may undergo a more subtle sense of suffering. When they encounter the poor, the hungry, and the disadvantaged, their primitive sense of pity and compassion is aroused. Living with feelings of guilt or, at the very least, with feelings of dis-ease in such circumstances is the price any compassionate person pays in such a situation. One of the drawbacks of living in a middle-class setting in America is waking up feeling vaguely guilty and quite helpless each morning.

The middle and upper class in America has often met this feeling of guilt by denying the existence of poverty or lack of opportunity. Poverty areas and ghettos lock away those that others would rather not see. Often when the poor and those without homes or hope are encountered on the street, they are simply not consciously acknowledged, or are ignored or dismissed with some excuse as to why what is the case is in fact not the case. Examples of such attempts to evade or deny reality are numerous. They range from persons simply denying the existence of poverty (claiming that while incomes may be low, sufficient opportunities for having access to the necessities of life as well as access to opportunities exist) to victim blaming in which the victims of social injustice are described as its causes. The suffering about them is either rationalized out of existence, denied or blamed on the sufferers themselves.

Associations of people not united by a strong sense of common purpose lack solidarity and cannot evolve successfully. Sufferers look, sometimes desperately, for solutions to their suffering and may see such solutions in turning against the very association of which they are a part but which they feel, with a good deal of justice, has turned against them. When that is the case societies cannot long endure.

In true communities members share a common belief in community itself as a uniting value, are ready and equipped by education and equal opportunity to participate fully, and are united by a common sense of purpose. In such communities suffering is held to a minimum, solidarity is firm and purpose strong. Such communities have a homeostatic framework which permits the working out of problems and the common quest for solutions to proceed so that all eventually benefit. Communities of this sort are best equipped to evolve, grow, and survive.

REFERENCES

1. Loewy EH: *Suffering and the Beneficent Community: Beyond Libertarianism.* Albany, NY: SUNY Press; 1991.

2. Loewy EH: Commodities, Needs and Health Care: A Communal Perspective. In: *Changing Values in Medical and Health Care Decision Making* (U. J. Jensen and G. Mooney, eds.). London, England: John Wiley and Sons, Ltd.; 1990.

3. Daniels N: *Just Health Care.* New York, NY: Cambridge University Press; 1985.

4. Braybrooke D: Let Needs Diminish that Preferences May Prosper. In: *Studies in Moral Philosophy.* American Philosophical Quarterly Monograph Series, No. 1. Oxford, England: Blackwells; 1968.

5. McCloskey HJ: Human Needs, Rights and Political Values. American Philosophical Quarterly 1976; 13: 1–11.

6. Engelhardt HT: *The Foundations of Bioethics.* New York, NY: Oxford University Press; 1986.

7. Barry B: The Welfare State vs the Relief of Poverty. Ethics 1990; 100: 503–529.

8. Hardin G: The Tragedy of the Commons. Science 1968; 162: 1245–1248.

9. Moreno JD: The Social Individual in Clinical Ethics. J Clinical Ethics 1992; 3(1): 53–55.

10. Nozick RH: *Anarchy, State and Utopia.* New York, NY: Basic Books; 1974.

11. Engelhardt HT: Health Care Allocations: Response to the Unjust, the Unfortunate and the Undesirable. In: *Justice and Health Care* (E. E. Shelp, ed.). Dordrecht, The Netherlands: D. Reidel; 1981.

12. Engelhardt HT: Morality for the Medical Industrial Complex: A Code of Ethics for the Mass Marketing of Health Care. NEJM 1988; 319(16): 1086–1089.

13. Rawls J: *A Theory of Justice.* Cambridge, MA: Harvard University Press; 1971.

14. Callahan D: *Setting Limits: Medical Goals in an Aging Society.* New York, NY: Simon and Schuster; 1987.

15. Callahan D: *Health and the Good Society.* New York, NY: Simon and Schuster; 1990.

16. Daniels N: *Am I My Parent's Keeper?* New York, NY: Oxford University Press; 1988.

17. Navarro V: Why Some Countries Have National Health-Insurance, Others Have a National Health Service and the U.S. Has Neither. Soc Sci Med 1989; 28(9): 887–898.

18. Reinhardt UE: Future Trends in the Economics of Medical Practice and Care. Am J Cardiol 1985; 56: 50C–59C

19. Marber M, MacRae C and Joy M: Delay to invasive investigation and revascularization for coronary heart disease in South West Thames region: a two-tier system? BMJ 1991; 302: 1189–1191.

20. Iglehart JK: Report on the Duke University Medical Center Private Sector Conference. NEJM 1982; 307(1): 68–71.

21. Fletcher RH and Fletcher SW: Multi-Class Health Care. NEJM 1982; 307(24): 1530–1531 (letter).

22. Levi P: *Survival in Auschwitz: The Nazi Assault on Humanity* (Stuart Woolf, trans.). New York, NY: Collier Macmillan Publishers; 1986.

23. Jonas H: *Das Prinzip Verantwortung.* Frankfurt a/M, Deutschland: Suhrkamp; 1984.

24. O'Neill J: Women and Wages: Gender Pay Ratios. Current 1991; 331: 10–16.

25. Bureau of the Census: Statistical Abstracts of the United States. Washington, DC: US Government Printing Office; 1990.

CHAPTER 7

A *Summing Up:*
Groping towards Tomorrow

This book has been an attempt to sketch out a theory of social and individual ethics and to relate them into a workable model. I have argued that the way individuals relate to each other and to their community and the way communities relate to the individuals of which they are composed in many respects mirrors the way collectives in general must interrelate with other collectives and ultimately with a world collective on the inevitable way to becoming a world community.

Throughout this work I have used and adapted Rousseau's notion of "pity": an innate sense which gives *l'impulsion intérieure de la compassion* (the internal impulse of compassion). I have argued that this innate sense is what Schopenhauer already called the driving force or *Triebfeder* of ethics: The force which provides the fuel for initiating the entire enterprise. It is this primitive sense of pity or compassion which raises the initial question of ethics. This sense of pity or compassion, I have argued, has preserved itself because it has survival value for the individual as well as for the species. Caring about each other's weal and woe, accepting obligations of beneficence instead of accepting merely obligations of not harming each other, is what lends cohesion, and therefore solidarity to communities. It is this cohesion which allows communities to proceed together so as to cope with internal as well as with external problems and, therefore, which allows them to evolve, grow, and survive.

My claim has been that what makes of mere objects objects of moral concern ultimately relates to suffering. What arouses our feeling of revulsion at seeing not just our own but the suffering of others is our innate and virtually reflexive feeling of pity. If we did not have this primitive sense of pity the suffering of

229

another would leave us cold. Without such a sense of pity, empathy (which allows us to feel ourselves in the shoes of another) or sympathetic understanding (which at least allows us to sympathize with another's experience even if we cannot imagine ourselves in his/her place) could not come about. Being aware that an ethical problem exists and then grappling with it would, at best, be predicated and predicable on pure and largely self-protective logic.

I have called entities which have the capacity to suffer (whether they be non-human or human animals) objects of primary worth. Their capacity to suffer gives them prima-facie protection against being made to suffer, prima facie because it does not give them absolute protection but, so to speak, gives them standing at court. To legitimately cause the suffering of such another being which has primary worth at the least requires one to show an overriding justification. Objects or ideas, which in themselves lack the capacity to suffer, are still of moral concern. They are of moral concern because the way they are treated is important to those capable of suffering. I have called such objects objects of secondary worth and have divided such worth into "material" and "symbolic." Objects of "material" or "symbolic" worth can have positive or negative value. The value of beings of primary worth is inevitably positive, albeit that such primary worth is not, therefore, equal worth. Fundamental to both primary and secondary worth (fundamental to being able to think about ethics or relationships at all) is the community. I have, therefore, called the moral worth of community "prior worth": prior, that is, to any other considerations. Without a community in which we act, without others with which to work, build or contend there can be no "us." It is community which enables our existence and allows our flourishing; in turn, our individual actions and talents are what fashion and shape our community.

I have argued that communities and their members have more than the minimal obligation of non-interference with each other. I have grounded beneficent obligations in the inevitable nurture which all infants must experience before developing a sense of self as well as in the beneficence essential to any person's further ability to thrive. Such obligations are only in part purely deductively justifiable. As important and even vital as deductive logical justification certainly is, deductive logical justification does not suffice to describe the various sources from which our obligations are derived. (For a more extensive treatment of the problem of justification, see chapter 3.)

The obligations individuals have toward each other and to their community and the obligations communities have toward their members (and ultimately toward each other) are beyond the merely minimal ones of mutual non-harm. Unless beneficent obligations are accepted and acted upon, collectives will have little cohesion. They will lack solidarity. Collectives which lack solidarity cannot serve the prior worth communities must have: that is they cannot serve to underwrite the existence of their composite parts. Beyond this, the future which today we have the capacity to destroy not only for our particular polis but for all mankind requires a peaceful and cohesive community. If the obligation to strive for the survival of our species (and, for that matter, so that the species can survive to strive for the survival of the ecosystem) is acknowledged as an obligation we all have (an obligation which we have by logic and by deeply ingrained biological need) then obligations cannot be simply reduced to the barest minimum of mutual non-harm but inevitably must include obligations of beneficence and caring.

Some will claim that using ingrained biological needs to argue for an obligation is committing the naturalistic fallacy. It is deducing an "ought" from an "is" and thereby reduces philosophy to biology. In prior chapters I have pointed out that the is-ought distinction as well as the naturalistic fallacy argument rides piggyback on the alleged distinction between "facts" (supposedly empirical) and "values" (assumed to be metaphysically a priori). Such distinctions constitute a dualistic way of looking at things: "facts" can be understood only in the embrace of values and "values" are not isolated entities from the facts to which they must necessarily address themselves. Doing philosophy in any meaningful sense outside the physical reality which sooner or later even philosophy at its most abstract must deal with is not realistically possible. As humans (or as any other biological organisms capable of reasoning) we cannot reason outside the framework of our reasoning, a framework which, inevitably, is biological. Ingrained biological drives, innate feelings (like the primitive sense of pity) are facts of life: not "facts" in the immutable sense but "facts" which we use to manipulate our daily existence and which must shape our thoughts. An "is" of this sort, of course, is not ethically normative: our sex drive is very much a drive but no one could argue that it, therefore, not only excuses but somehow hallows seduction, let alone, rape. But an "is" of this sort sets the stage for our grappling with an "ought." Without such "facts" the question of an "ought" would not truly come up: without the sex drive, the thought of rape would be incoherent. Our biology necessarily forms the framework of our very thinking about all human endeavors. It is best not to ignore its role. Saying that a natural drive is "good" or "evil" is in a sense incoherent. The sex drive can lead to happy union or to rape; the sense of pity can be used to make action impossible (imagine a physician so sorry for the patient that he/she could not amputate a gangrenous leg) or it can be used to add compassion to logic, to, as it were, temper justice with mercy. Such "facts" about our biological (or psycho-biological) being are necessary not in an immutable, let alone in a normative, sense but are things which we ultimately use to shape our ethical judgments.

Since, among many other things, we share a common biological and even to some extent a common bio-psycho-social framework, we are not, as some would have it, complete moral strangers who lack a common frame of interest and moral reference. Our common interests of survival, our common interest in preventing our, and by inference our fellows', suffering, our fundamentally similar way of arranging our perceptions of the external world by virtue of our common structure of the mind, hardly makes us moral friends; but these commonplaces make us, at the least, moral acquaintances: persons who share a basic frame of reasoning and who understand some of the fundamental interests and drives the other has.

Individuals, necessarily social creatures, cannot (especially in today's world) develop their individual talents and lead their individual lives outside the support their community affords. On the other hand, communities, cannot develop and thrive as communities, without developing the unique talents their members possess. A regard for community as well as a respect for the uniqueness of individuals are both essential if one is to support the other so that both may survive. When seen in this way a homeostatic balance between communal and private ends in which ultimately both must be reconciled within the context of common goals and ends seems inevitable. In such a balance community in its own right becomes a value and a goal for the individual and fostering individuality becomes a value and goal for the community.

Rather than the model of a dialectic in which communal interests (interests in social justice) clash and compete with individual interests (interests in autonomy), a model of homeostatic balance in which both pursue their own interests only within the context of their joint common goal is far more realistic and fruitful. Such a model, I have argued, lends itself far better to the analysis of such relationships. Homeostasis provides the stability so that interests, values, and goals can be pursued and reconciled. The stability provided by homeostasis is not one which is inimical to change but rather is stability necessary so that evolution and with it change can occur. Evolutionary change is itself involved with changing the set-points of homeostasis. Homeostasis provides the stability which allows experimentation with new values, goals, and ways of doing things so that the framework itself can slowly change.

Obligations, I have argued, depend among other things on relationships, capacities, and vulnerabilities. It is our universal vulnerability and our inevitably different strengths and weaknesses (different and differing over time and in complex arrangements and ways) which relate us and which cause us to assume ongoing obligations toward each other.[1] It is our primitive sense of pity (not merely our common sense of basic logic or our personal self-interest) which urges us to care about others, even about others who are social (albeit not moral) strangers. Because it fosters social cohesion, such a sense of pity has survival value for persons as well as for species. A sense of pity inevitably leads us to care. This mutual caring, inevitably (if it is considered to be innate in normal human beings) also vitiates the notion of moral strangers. Persons who care about one another, or even if they do not care in a more complex sense persons who are by nature affected by the suffering of another, cannot be said to be total moral strangers: persons who share no common values and no moral framework.

Social arrangements are necessary for individual existence. Social existence takes place in a variety of collectives or associations. I have examined these collectives and divided them, using Tönnies's language and adapting Tönnies's basic definitions, into *Vereine, Gesellschaften* (loosely translatable as "societies"), and *Gemeinschaften* or communities in their deeper sense.[2] Briefly put, the more collectives approach being a community the more do such associations share a large cluster of common goals, interests, and values, and the more they are united by the transcendental value of community as a goal in its own right. As such collectives approach true communities in the sense used here, they begin to generate and experiment with new values, goals, and interests so that their homeostatic framework can slowly evolve. Such a process allows adaptation to changing external and internal circumstances and is conducive to evolution and, therefore, ultimately to survival.

I have contrasted true communities to what I have, for want of a better term, called "cloistered" communities. Cloistered communities often are (but do not have to be) religious. Such communities are not communities in the sense used here. They are collectives firmly united by a more or less unchangeable ethos, usually devoted to a narrow set of tasks; they are collectives in which individuality tends to be discouraged or swamped. In such collectives community itself is more than a uniting transcendental value and goal: community is its own raison d'être. It is only by means of a rigid set of beliefs and by complete subjugation of individual interests and values that such communities can maintain themselves. This is as true of monastaries as it is of entities like the Bolshevik party. Discipline in such communities is generally rather rigid and deviation from a narrow set of rules is generally not tolerated. Such collectives, though they are often considered an "idealized" version of community, are rather community's caricature. Such communities lack a true homeostatic balance: The set-points are narrowly conceived, basically unchangeable, and there is little latitude and little room for experimentation with new values and goals. Such communities are not well able to adapt to internal or external changes and consume their energies battling outside forces rather than learning to adapt to and work with them. Communities of this sort, lacking the capacity to evolve in a meaningful fashion, are apt to perish. Cloistered communities are not the sort of community I have in mind when using the term community.

I have sketched the relationships of collectives and the obligations they have to one another and have suggested that the relationship and the kinds of obligations envisioned are arguably similar to the relationship and obligation which individuals have toward one another and toward community. Just as is the case when it comes to obligations individuals have toward one another and to their community, obligations various collectives have to each other cannot be exhausted merely by those of mutual non-harm. More broadly based obligations must be included. In previous chapters I have argued that unless collectives assume such obligations toward each other, they cannot create a cohesive larger world community and will be subject to periodic strife. Our current capacities make clear that continued strife will not only ultimately harm all but will ultimately destroy the future itself. This capacity to destroy the future has done much to shape the kinds of obligations we must assume today.[3]

In this chapter (largely one of summing up) I am briefly drawing together the threads of this book. I will try to sketch some of the problems faced by mankind today. These problems have, in one sense, been aggravated by the recent disappearance of the Soviet state. The Soviet state with its caricature of social justice balanced the United States with its caricature of individual rights. This was hardly a world one could wish to inhabit: The danger of mutual extinction (whether brought about by deliberate action or by accident) was ever present. It was a world in which both sides devastated their economies in an effort to maintain a vast military establishment. Not surprisingly, such competition could not endure. Not unexpectedly the Soviet Union, more rigid, less flexible and above all recently devastated by World War II, collapsed first, leaving the United States as the dubious victor. The "victorious" United States, firmly devoted to a capitalist market economy appeared to the rest of the world as something to be admired and emulated. Even in countries such as Denmark or Sweden, not to speak of the countries emerging from Soviet tyranny, the idea of modeling themselves after the United States and its market became popular. In good part this admiration and desire to emulate the state of affairs in the United States was due to a false perception of that state of affairs. Persons who visit the United States rarely are shown ghettos, poverty areas, or the real nature of the problems. In truth, most middle-class Americans have never visited true ghettos and poverty areas and are totally unfamiliar not only with the actual state of affairs in such areas but with the hopelessness and therefore the mindset which pervades it. What these persons as well as their visitors see of problems in the United States is largely filtered through the media which are hardly entirely outside the control of the very same power groups in whose interest it is to minimize the problems rampant in Capitalist societies.

In what follows, I want to sketch some of the problems as they exist in America today and compare the relationship of the American community to its individuals and the relationship of affluent and more powerful collectives or states to poorer and weaker ones. And, ultimately, I want to suggest an analogy between the homeostatic relationship of individuals and their community with a similar relationship between the several states and the world community. From this parallel emerges an obligation not only to structure an American society (a society which sees its goals as minimizing suffering, sustaining itself, and fostering solidarity) internally but likewise and of equal importance an obligation to structure a world community based on such a model. Such a restructuring, in my view, cannot be successfully done unless a homeostatic balance mindful of the need for common goals and interests can be established. This restructuring, to be meaningful, has to be a restructuring in which all participate: a restructuring achieved by a communal democratic process.

The market has not produced what most of us would call an equitable solution to many of the problems in the United States today. A nation founded as a republic which, at least in theory, evolved into a fully participatory democracy, predicates its existence and further function as a democracy on, among other things, an equitable distribution of power. If power is to be equitably distributed among all members of a community, all members must have fair access to certain material and non-material commodities of the community. Persons cannot be said to be empowered (even when they are empowered on paper by, for example, being given the franchise) when they are uninformed, poorly educated, ignorant, ill, hungry, cold, or homeless.

Having power in a democratic society means more than having one's basic needs assured or having fair access to education and one's health needs attended to. Ultimately it means making choices through the ballot: it means not only being able to choose but having an array of options to choose from. When the power to choose the options themselves is exercised by a prior power structure whose vested interest is in perpetuating itself and its own narrowly conceived advantage, persons may be empowered to choose but in reality have nothing or only little to choose from. Operating a democracy (and I have steadily predicated my vision of community on a collective in which choices are made in pursuit of a set of evolving common goals and values by all members of the collective) is not possible unless all members have the freedom to choose from an array of meaningful and not previously and arbitrarily limited options.

Persons derive their knowledge, values, and opinions in the home, in the schoolroom, and increasingly more through the media. The pulpit, once an important source for most, has receded (some of us would argue luckily) in importance. The home reflects the knowledge, values, and opinions parents picked up in a similar manner. Schools in the United States have been acknowledged to be less than what one would want them to be and, if anything, have been shown to be getting worse. Inequalities in what schools are available to the wealthy (who, of course, to a large part are the children of those in control) and what schools are available to the mass of people (from whom most of the electorate inevitably is derived) are profound.[4] Illiteracy, raw as well as functional, when compared to other industrialized countries, is a national disgrace. In the United States gross illiteracy (the total incapacity to read or write) is, at the last count, 13 percent; functional illiteracy (the inability to make any meaningful sense out of simple written instructions) stands at 19.5%; and "bare literacy" (the ability to read and write but not the ability to, for example, fill out a work application) is 33.3 percent[5] Even when students leave high school literate (and graduation from high school far from guarantees their functional literacy), their ignorance of the world about them has been repeatedly shown to be profound: many Americans are not able to find their own country on a world map and do not know key actors in recent (not to speak of more remote) history. What is taught, since those in power obviously also control the schools, is to a large extent what those in power want taught. The media, largely controlled by the power structure, pander to the lowest denominator; often they see their proper function more as one of amusing than one of informing a public conditioned to be avid for amusements. The media's ability to survive depends on advertisers who with the money they pay for advertisements largely fund (and, therefore, control) the media and the programming offered. And advertisers, in general, are those who control industries. The power structure, therefore, is controlled by big business and directly as well as indirectly controls not only what information the public is given but also how such information is supplied to it. The media, controlled by their advertisers, bring to the public whatever a public conditioned to want to be amused wants to hear. By doing this, they readily distract an electorate all too willing to be distracted from real issues and real problems. It is true that the media do offer some intelligent discussion of real problems and real issues: but, except for those in the intelligentsia who with notable exceptions have never played a large role in American public life, most people are neither equipped to be or are, in fact, interested. The real or fancied sexual exploits of a candidate receive much more attention and are given much greater importance than are the candidates substantive qualifications.

In the Soviet Union as it existed prior to its collapse, an almighty party first determined its own options and only then offered these options to the general electorate which, in theory if not in actual practice, was educated and had its basic needs met. The electorate had no options to choose from and elections were, on that account, a farce. The difficulties which the Soviet system faced and which ultimately destroyed it are the difficulties of a system which in theory is communitarian and which in praxis is an autocracy controlled by those in power.

Beyond the fact that many in the United States today lack proper education or fair access to essential needs, there are few real options to choose from. The ability to run for office or to present meaningful options is controlled by the need to fund ever more expensive campaigns. Even the very wealthy cannot run for office or present meaningful options without drawing on heavy financial support from outside their own means. The effective means to fund elections ultimately lies with those who have the money to contribute and most of the money directly or indirectly is derived from the existing moneyed power structure. A capitalist power structure is unlikely to fund (nor can it be expected to fund) candidates so that these candidates can present options and offer choices seen as disadvantageous to the power structure's own (unfortunately narrowly conceived) interests. Throughout this work it has been my thesis that the true long-term interests even of those in power are ill-served by pursuing narrow and immediate interests. The collapse of society inevitably would also entail the collapse of those in power. Ignoring homeostatic balance which counsels a context in which inevitable common goals are realized and worked toward, is destructive to the oppressor and the oppressed alike.

The electorate, even when they vote, have little to choose from and elections, therefore, have largely become a farce. The difficulties which the system in the United States faces are the difficulties of a system which in theory is democratic and which in praxis has led to control by and for those in power. To argue that parties change and that the electorate is free to vote as they please is specious when (1) the electorate is often ill-informed, frequently deprived of basic necessities, and feels desperate and powerless and when (2) who runs for office in either party is ultimately controlled by the virtually identical power structure. In the United States today much of the electorate is effectively disenfranchised by virtue of poverty or ignorance and the options offered are options effectively limited by those capable of exerting power. Democracy, to operate as democracy (that is, to operate through the effectively expressed wishes of a majority of its citizens) must meet at least two conditions. It must, first of all, have an electorate which is interested, well-informed and, therefore, able to make choices; and secondly it must present meaningful options to choose from. When the electorate is indolent, hungry or ill-informed, or when the choices given are not real options among which a meaningful choice can be made, democracy in its true sense cannot exist. Furthermore, these two unmet conditions constitute a vicious cycle: an electorate which is offered no meaningful choices has little incentive to become participatory; an electorate which is uninformed cannot truly participate; and those in the electorate who are hungry or homeless worry (as unfortunate as that may be) about more immediate things than the making of political choices. Persons who are not participatory cannot press the political system to offer meaningful choices and a lack of meaningful choices discourages participation. Thus the electorate is given election as a form of sport or amusement, a circus instead of a meaningful way of charting their own destiny. The difficulties which the American system faces and which ultimately threaten to destroy it are the difficulties of a system which pays lip service to the dignity and importance of the individual but which in praxis is an ill-concealed autocracy controlled by those in power. It is a system in which individuals are shaped to become the willing puppets of the power structure.

When a powerful group controls the community and the individuals within it so that their personal expression is rendered meaningless, a homeostatic balance cannot function. Such a collective begins to resemble a monastic type of community, in which goals become predetermined, monolithic, and unchanging. In monastic groups internal harmony is achieved by limiting membership to those willing to subject themselves to this discipline and either ejecting others or allowing them to go their own way. In collectives in which a powerful group controls and manipulates its members for its own private ends, members have little choice but to accept such discipline. Having only the information allowed them, educated to consider such information complete and even "free," distracted by issues contrived to appeal to their prurient interest rather than allowed to grapple with more substantive issues, such persons are much worse off than those in a truly monastic community. Monastic communities, when they exist in the context of wider communities, are only internally totalitarian. Ready (even if at times emotionally difficult) exit is available. A ready wider community to receive the expatriate exists. A homeostatic balance in a community in which a powerful group controls is no longer a homeostatic balance. It is a rigid collective controlled and manipulated by the few for their own benefit and heedless of the group. Totalitarian collectives, when they are states, make exit much more difficult. There is no ready wider community willing or ready to receive the expatriate.

Such a state of affairs has been the case in most autocracies whether they be of the extreme left or the extreme right. Thought is controlled by propaganda, by distracting the citizenry and, ultimately, by terror. Nazi Germany's propaganda machine, as an example, effectively controlled all by controlling the schoolroom and all that the people could hear, read, or ulti-mately, think. It distracted the citizenry by producing pageants, providing spectacles, and sponsoring events calculated to deflect dissatisfaction and it played on latent prejudice to create the myth of racial threat. And, when that failed, it instituted concen-tration camps. Nazi Germany, it is evident, ruled by far more than merely terror. Stalin's Soviet Union, likewise, was operated in a similar manner. In neither state could a meaningful homeo-static balance in which the needs of the community and the needs of the individual harmoniously adapt themselves to a com-mon goal develop. History has shown such a state of affairs to be self-defeating.

When capitalist policy sacrifices the interests of the many to the interests of a powerful few a similar state of affairs pertains. There may well be theoretical freedom of speech. But it is a free-dom of speech hedged by the conditions in which it takes place. Many are in traditional poverty and feel powerless; most have been educated in a way calculated to inculcate them with the kinds of information, values, and aims the group in power wants them to have. The media, controlled by the power group, play their role: They provide information within the framework set by the power group (who control the media by controlling the purse strings) and deflect the public's attention from substantive issues by raising prurient ones as well as by providing ready access to amusements as a smokescreen. Latent prejudices and fears are played upon when, subtly and not so subtly, racial and economic minority groups are held up as threats or when the danger from communists or external enemies (real or fancied) is appealed to. And when all else fails, the secret service of the state is not above blackmailing, harassing, maligning, or sometimes apparently even killing those it considers to be a threat or to be its enemies. When capitalist interests control affairs, as they increasingly have done in the United States and as they are attempting to do inter-nationally, a meaningful homeostatic balance in which the needs of the community and the needs of the individual harmoniously adapt themselves to a common goal cannot develop. Such a state of affairs eventually is self-defeating.

The social problems in the United States, while they cannot be reduced to poverty, are so intimately linked to it as to make every attempt at rectifying these problems which does not take account of the central role of poverty non- or even dysfunctional. Racism, another of the problems pervasive in American society, has economic roots and would, except for poverty, largely disappear. Feeling superior because of race, color, or nationality might to some extent persist if all were assured essential commodities and access to those things necessary to avail oneself of the fair opportunity range a society had to offer.[6] But racism would not have the same compelling interest were it not for the struggle waged for bare existence. Once true equity of opportunity is established, a belief in ethnic, racial, sexual, or national superiority would soon be seen to defeat itself. Likewise the drug problem is inevitably linked to poverty and frustration. Combating the drug problem by ever more severe punishments and legal strictures has very obviously not worked. Much as the power structure ostensibly deplores both, the power structure derives a certain amount of profit from continuing racism as it does from the continuing drug traffic. One need look no farther than the use of racially charged issues in various political campaigns (Mr. Bush's use of Willy Horton in his campaign is only one of many examples) or the repeated involvement of the CIA with drug trafficking to recognize the truth of this statement. The poor standards of education likewise are linked with poverty and cannot be meaningfully and truly improved without addressing the problem of poverty. Children cannot learn on an empty stomach, or learn when they are cold or frightened. Schools cannot function in their prescribed educational function when poverty induced violence stalks the halls and erupts in the classrooms. Without addressing the problem of poverty, these other problems cannot be meaningfully addressed.

Social problems within the United States are not that different from worldwide social problems. In recent history, the Western powers have relentlessly and successfully exploited and devastated lesser-developed nations. Such nations have been exploited for their cheap labor as well as for their raw materials. In return (analogous to the relationship between owners and slaves during slavery or to the relationship between the advantaged and the disadvantaged in America today) the Western nations have provided minimal resources so that lesser-developed nations could, even if barely, survive and be further exploited. Slave keepers were "kind" to their slaves, not because they cared very much for them as fellow creatures but because their survival was economically of benefit to the owner. Industrialized nations were "kind" to their colonies not because they really cared about their well-being or about their culture but because their survival was necessary to permit their exploitation. Likewise the poor of whatever race, as long as they are readily exploited, have made for a convenient source of exploitable labor. The problem is basically economic: it is the exploitation of the weak for the benefit of the strong. Race, gender, or nationality are merely excuses provided for the benefit of the gullible by the cynical.

The Capitalist system as it is constituted today has as its first order of interest the continued prosperity of those who are already more than prosperous. It is, therefore, in the narrowly conceived interest (and I shall argue most certainly not in the more widely conceived interest) of the capitalist system, operated largely by agreements among the few who win in a competitive zero-sum game, to seek not only to control the means of production and the market place but to control the framework within which the market place and means of production operates. While Capitalism is an economic and democracy a political system, capitalism is essentially and basically inimical to true democracy in that it seeks to place power in the hands of a relatively few who control the economic resources, whereas democracy seeks to place such control in the hands of the many. Democracy, seeking to diffuse power, and capitalism, seeking to concentrate it, cannot well coexist. Education of the masses is not in the interest of those who seek to maintain power.

Capitalist power, while best exemplified by and in the United States, is hardly limited to the United States. Today much of this power is vested in international cartels and power structures. Decisions and long-term planning for the world are apt to originate in the board rooms of Washington, Bonn, or Tokyo. As an example, the proceedings of the trilateral commission which unites the main Capitalist interests of Japan, the United States, and Western Europe bears witness to this.[7,8] As a report of the trilateral commission so succinctly stated:

> The vulnerabilty of democratic government in the United States comes not primarily from external threats, though such threats are real, nor from internal subversion from the left or the right, although both possibilities could exist, but rather from the

internal dynamics of democracy itself in a highly educated, mobilized and participant society. (p.3)[7,8]

The trilateral commission, founded in 1973 under the chairmanship of David Rockefeller of the Chase Manhattan Bank, united the business interests of Japan, the United States, and Western Europe in a powerful coalition aimed at perpetuating Capitalism. Members are drawn from the international business community, government, and conservative labor.[8] In the United States members come from both parties: members such as Cyrus Vance, Walter Mondale, Andrew Young, Jimmy Carter, and George Bush, just to mention a few. The interest of the commission is not the interest of any particular party; the interests of the commission are in the maintainance of the Capitalist system.

It is evident that the education of the masses is not high on the agenda of the trilateral commission. Keeping persons brainwashed and impotent while allowing them the trappings of democracy is more to their taste. Together they represent the industrialized world whose interest in exploiting the rest of the world as well as using the population of the industrialized one for its own ends is high on their agenda. When one keeps this in mind, the deterioration of the educational system, the mockery of the democratic process (which consistently presents candidates with little substantive difference between them, consistently supports right wing causes and opposes left wing proposals and progressive governments in third world nations) should come as no surprise.

If one sees interrelationships as working on a basically homeostatic system exploitation is ultimately counterproductive. When individuals fail to acknowledge the necessity of and their role in collectives, they ultimately will perish because individual existence outside a social nexus cannot long endure. When collectives exploit their members, the collective ultimately perishes because it is individuals which permit the growth of the association. The exploited, incapable of developing talents eventually needed by the exploiters, stop being of value to their exploiters and in desperation will seek to destroy them and, with this, often themselves. The ends of both must be reconciled and jointly pursued. Without common values, goals, and interests individuals as well as the collectives of which they are a part cannot thrive, evolve, and ultimately survive.

Interrelationships among various collectives bear a certain similarity to such a model. When more powerful collectives exploit weaker ones, the stronger ultimately cannot endure. Exploited nations have resources and talents which ultimately are needed by the exploiter. Unless the exploiter fosters these resources and nourishes these individual talents both will be exhausted. Exploitation often is comingled with a form of cultural condescension, an attitude which is one of bestowing the largesse of the exploiter (who, because richer, considers himself worthier) upon the now fortunate exploited. This adds humiliation to exploitation and further breeds resentment and perhaps even hatred. The exploited nation not only eventually becomes unexploitable, its members bitterly resentful not only because they are exploited but because they are also condescended to, but in desperation will seek to bring down the exploiter and with it itself.

Some will argue that this point of view is an oversimplified, even a simplistic view. I do not argue its oversimplification. I make no claim that this point of view accurately paints all or even most of reality. I do claim that as long as individuals relate with their community or as long as the less powerful relate with the more powerful collectives merely in a minimalist and predominantly competitive framework exploitation by the stronger of the weaker (instead of cooperation) is inevitable and that just as inevitably both must loose. If we are to have any regard for the future and are to, as I have claimed, attach a moral value to its preservation and fashioning, we cannot reduce our relationships (whether our private or our corporate ones) to competition limited only by a mutual respect for explicit contract and freedom.

Explicit contract and the freedom to choose imply at least a level of parity between the contracting parties. When one is weak and the other strong, when one is coercible by virtue of this weakness and the other holds all the cards, competition inevitably becomes exploitation. Workers desperate to feed their families are easily coerced into signing contracts promising at least minimal conditions of survival; poverty-stricken nations, likewise, are apt to enter into contracts which allow their survival at the price of their continued subjugations. Such a state of affairs can continue for some time until the exploited, with little to lose and much to gain (whether they be individuals or nations), will not be restrained by a theoretical minimal obligation of not harming their exploiter who they very much see as harming them. In justified wrath such individuals or such nations will rise up and revolt. History, unfortunately, has shown that such revolutions are unlikely to simply seek redress for an evil. They will not and indeed almost cannot stop when their justified grievances have been met: in destroying a system, they will cause grievances of their own. A terror once unleashed may take generations to rectify.

In the past the exploited were often pacified by playing on their latent fears and hatreds. In medieval times and in some regions antisemitism served to turn the wrath of poor peasants and other exploited groups against Jews who were handy whipping boys. In Nazi Germany the frustration of many of the impoverished was likewise channeled against the Jews as well as against other outside enemies. The hostility between minority groups as it is regrettably found in the United States today serves much the same purpose. When tempers flare between Hispanics and blacks or when the justifiable frustration of the black community vents its anger by attacking Jews, energy which could have been used to deal with the exploiter is consumed and the danger of revolt is, for the time, deflected. Splintering the disadvantaged, stimulating them to fight against instead of alongside one another, is a time-honored method used by a power structure which feels itself threatened.

Underdeveloped nations are often similarly dealt with. In the last few decades the United States and most of the other trilateral powers have persistently opposed progressive and supported repressive right wing governments in underdeveloped nations. Heads of other states have been found to be in the pay of the American secret service. Often the government has been selected and empowered by overt or clandestine activities conducted by the secret service of the United States. When bribery was ineffective, coercion could always be used. In fulfilling that task, heads of state seen as successfully opposing exploitation have been blackmailed or assassinated; governments have been destabilized and attacks against the harbors and territory of nations not at war with the United States have been carried out. Foreign aid as often as not has consisted of weapons, uniforms, and other military supplies.

Capitalism has been short-sighted. The stupendous wealth

and the incredible income of the wealthy ruling class today is bought at the price of tomorrow. Ultimately it is in the interest of the ruling class to ameliorate the conditions of social injustice as they exist today even if that were to mean redistributing some of the wealth so that all could at least share in the fruits of common labors. To forget that we are a community, to insist on merely minimalist obligations toward each other, invites violence and eventually makes revolution and its attendant and subsequent terror inevitable. A cursory examination of history will make that point rather clearly.

Just as it is in the interest of individuals within a community to safeguard the health of the community which is the condition for an individual's existence and prosperity, it is in the interest of individual communities to assure the health and prosperity of the larger community of which, inevitably, they are a part. Likewise, it is in the interest of the larger community to support the individual flourishing of its component parts. Strengths and weaknesses of each are different and it is these strengths and weaknesses which are ultimately complementary and which provide the conditions of their relationship. The fear that in a united world individuality will be suppressed and flat homogeneity produced is not a legitimate fear if such a world wishes to survive. Fostering the individual talents and differences of its members is necessary if a community wishes to evolve, grow, and survive; likewise fostering the particular talents and differences of specific communities is necessary if the world community is not to perish.

Powerful communities need to be concerned about poorer and less powerful ones for a number of reasons. Obligations of beneficence, first of all, demand that communities which are more powerful care about those which are not; an individual primitive sense of pity which makes us look with horror at the picture of a starving Ethiopian child counsels us to translate such stirrings into action. Beyond this, powerful communities which have played their part in disenfranchising weaker ones have a causal obligation to come to their help. Even when they were not themselves directly implicated in disadvantaging such countries, they continue to derive benefit from such exploitation by virtue of belonging to the historically more powerful group. Such nations may not be responsible for causing such disadvantage but, unless they partake of action calculated to remedy this situation, they are culpable for perpetuating an injustice. Affirmative action on an international scale is just as called for as it is on a more local and individual one.

There are other reasons why caring about the misery of humans in foreign lands is critical if one is to seriously propose a system based on at least a minimal appreciation of ethics. When we deny the very obvious contemporary fact that all of us in this world are ultimately interconnected and that "our" individual (or corporate communal) prosperity is enmeshed with that of all others we are likely to invite disaster. Persons denied just access to basic needs when such fair access could be provided or associations of people denied their rightful place in the sun will disturb and ultimately destroy the peace of their community. Desperate, given no satisfactory ways of redress or recourse, they are liable to take to more violent and more destructive ways of seeking recourse and redress.

Solidarity in a community (be it a smaller, larger, or world community) is necessary if peace is to reign and if persons are to be capable of leading at least acceptably satisfactory and fulfilling lives. Solidarity depends on a community's recognizing that community itself must be a transcendent goal. To maintain community means to do those things which help individuals within the community to flourish and grow; to maintain the flourishing of individuals means to do those things which maintain, strengthen, and solidify community and ultimately allow it to evolve and thrive.

The world today is radically different from the world of former years. It is a world in which not only the destructive possibilities for the entire world have become so realistic that morality itself has to be viewed differently: *fiat justitia, pereat mundus* (let justice be done even if the heavens fall) may, once upon a time, have been a justifiable precept. The heavens then fell upon only a small part of our planet: The heavens might have fallen upon and destroyed our polis but the rest of creation would have been unimpaired by such a manifestation of justice done. Even then, such a proposition was at best questionable. Doing justice at the price of the destruction of many others always and at best necessitated a peculiar or at least a questionable definition of justice.

Today, our technical possibilities have made *fiat justitia, pereat mundis* into an extravagant (an almost "prissy") expression of our private virtue and have rendered it indefensible: what is and what is not justice done must be measured not only locally but has far more world-ranging dimensions.[3] If being or the future possibility of being is itself destroyed when justice is done, the concept of what is and what is not just must be seriously re-evaluated. Justice, when doing it may preclude the existence of all there is or ever may be, can no longer be argued to be justice.

The world is also radically different in another aspect. We live in a world in which the future has taken on quite different dimensions than it had in the past. As Hans Jonas has pointed out, we live in a world in which we know both a great deal more and a great deal less about the future than we did in the past. In former times the world (while not, as Hans Jonas would have it, static) was, nevertheless, relatively static from generation to generation. Our conventions, manners, ways of looking at things, political structures, and technical possibilities remained pretty well unchanged or, better said, changed so slowly that adaptation was much more comfortably possible. Individuals, families, collectives, and, indeed the whole world, could expect that a world in which one went to sleep only to wake up in fifty years would be somewhat but not radically, changed. Rip van Winkle may have been confused but he was hardly entirely disoriented or felt himself to be on another planet. When radical change occurred it was largely social. Revolutions and cataclysmic natural events brought about radical change, change which caused severe societal disruption. The plague of the fourteenth century radically changed the world: it brought with it devastating social and even geographical changes. But these changes, radical as they were, did not encompass the technical possibilities of today's world. The French and Russian revolutions, brought on by intolerable social conditions (conditions which at least in some important ways are reminiscent of conditions in the United States today) occurred in a setting in which technical possibilities were far less profound than they were but a few short years later. Today, radical changes due to technological "advances" have become commonplace. People today must adapt on a routine basis to revolutionary changes which heretofore where seen to be momentous.

Today the only certainty is that things tomorrow will be quite different from things today. The difference will not only be social but it will be social brought about by and reinforced by devastating technical possibilities. These possibilities, furthermore, are possibilities which are difficult to anticipate and prepare for. We can ill afford a laissez-faire attitude toward technology and "progress." Knowing itself has assumed moral dimensions. As a result of tomorrow's uncertainty and of the inevitable rapid changes, not only is there a widening generational knowledge gap but generational alienation is far more frequent and devastating. We live in a dynamic society in which both technical and social changes are and predictably will continue to be profound. And while our ways of predicting future events are better, these drastic changes make reliable prediction unlikely.[3] Today changes and technical possibilities have united to produce a world in which responsibility for tomorrow has rightfully assumed a central place. Ethics has had to go far beyond the basically individualistic emphasis it has heretofore enjoyed.

In such a world, collectives need to be stronger rather than weaker. The exterior forces (the *milieu extérieur*) which are apt to impinge on us requires greater adaptive capacities than ever before. Constructive dialogue has become essential if survival is to be made possible. We cannot afford to live in a collective in which solidarity is wanting or weak: to meet the challenges of tomorrow, our collective must, at the very least, be a *Gesellschaft* well on the way to becoming a *Gemeinschaft*. This is true not only for our small even if expanded national polis but likewise and with equal force is true for the world community. We need to integrate our collective into other collectives and to mesh our goals with theirs. We need to engage in continuous dialogue not only within our particular collective but among all collectives. Collectives who have little respect for other collectives or who have little regard for their future but believe that their future can be dissociated from the culture and future of all others cannot long endure. The goals of our polis and the goals of others, as well as the goals of the world polis, must to some significant degree coalesce and mutually support each other. If we fail in this, if we continue to pursue our individual (or our nation's individual) existence mindless of the needs of others and heedless of the responsibilities we all share, we will not be able to adapt. When homeostasis fails, destruction is not far behind.

I have repeatedly claimed that the problems in the United States (as well, at least in good measure, in the world at large) are largely those of poverty. Such problems are not due to a lack of sufficient resources but rather to a totally and progressively more inequitable way of distributing the resources we have. There is no doubt that there are not sufficient resources so that everyone can live an opulent life or have access to unlimited baubles; but there is also little doubt that all could have access to basic biological (first order) as well as basic social (second order) needs. Such access by all would be bought at the price of a smaller vision of opulence by many others. But such a point of view does not necessitate the absolute equity of all. There is, in the way I have conceived justice, no reason why, once basic needs are determined and met for all, some would not earn more and consequently live, at least materially, better than others. Such a point of view, however, does necessitate a willingness on the part of the well-off to limit their wealth so as to benefit others who are in poverty. I have argued that doing so, ultimately, will benefit those who are well-off and that not doing so would, ultimately, destroy them. A community lacking solidarity inevitably will splinter and cease being a community. Collectives in which members are deprived of basic needs while others live in incredible luxury inevitably lacks solidarity. Unless those in power (those who control what we continue to call, innocently or cynically, "the democratic process") begin to rectify this situation, justifiable and justified attempts to rectify it for them are inevitable. Such attempts, when no meaningful peaceful options to gain justice are believed to be present and when desperate people are therefore frustrated, will become increasingly more violent. Such violence, while possibly and very likely ultimately destroying the system, will, in the process and at least for many years to come, extinguish the prosperity and well-being of all.

Likewise, the problems in the world (inevitably far more complex) are largely those of poverty. These too are not due to a lack of sufficient resources but rather to an inequitable way of distributing the resources we have. There is no doubt that there are not sufficient resources so that all nations can live in luxury, can (as the United States does) consume half the world's energy and earn a large part of the world's income. But there is also little doubt that much could be done to see to it that all nations could have far better access to basic biological (first order) as well as basic social (second order) needs. Just as in the American microcosm, such access by all nations would be bought at the price of a reduction of opulence by others. This, however, does not necessitate absolute parity. There is, in the way I have conceived justice, no reason why, once basic needs are determined and met for all, differences could not legitimately exist. National differences, just like individual ones, imply a rich diversity of values and goals. I speak here merely of supplying basic biological and social necessities, allowing fair access (including rectifying historical evils) and living peaceably together so that each may flourish for the sake of all. Such a vision does necessitate a willingness on the part of the very well-off to limit their wealth so as to benefit others who are in poverty. Unless such a willingness is demonstrated in meaningful action, solidarity among nations cannot exist. A world in which some nations are deprived of basic needs while other nations continue not only to live in luxury but continue to do so at the expense of those in poverty cannot be a community. Unless those nations who are powerful begin to rectify this inequity, justifiable and justified violent attempts to rectify it for them are inevitable. War, uprisings, and rebellions will inevitably follow and, with today's capacities for harm and destruction, will ravish the earth and attenuate if not indeed eliminate the future itself.

Our hope lies in instituting a democratic process not only throughout the United States (which I have claimed lacks effective democratic process) but ultimately throughout the world. Doing so either implies deliberate effort by those who now hold power to seek to bring about such a state of affairs for the common (and ultimately for their own) good; or, absent such expeditious and meaningful efforts, it implies revolution which, in the end, will spread misery for many years before, if ever, realizing its goals. I have argued that such deliberate effort toward the end of meaningful democratic process necessitates a redistribution of goods and services so that the poorest have basic biological and social necessities met. Only then can a truly informed electorate participate in exercising their democratic right to choose between meaningful options. An attempt to allow a homeostatic process, which recognizes individual goals only within the context of common ones, to function and to right itself must be made. The vicious cycle of poverty, indolence, lack of participation, and consequent lack of options must be broken: either broken with the help of those in power or broken despite and against them. This is as true for the nation as it is for the world.

This book is not intended to offer specific concrete solutions to very real problems. It is written to point at one way of conceptualizing and analyzing the problems, our obligations, and our interrelationships not only as individuals or as Americans, Europeans, Japanese, Indonesians, or Nicaraguans, but as human beings whose fate is inevitably and intrinsically linked with one another. It is written to point out the danger and, in my view, the error of certain philosophical positions which insist that peace in a pluralistic world can only be maintained by reducing our obligations to a bare minimum, which would see us as moral strangers lacking any common frame of reference and which would allow competition and market forces to take care of solving our problems. If this book starts a dialogue, if it introduces another viewpoint into a controversy, if it stirs some to think and perhaps and hopefully even to act, it will have achieved its purpose.

REFERENCES

1. Springer-Loewy R: An Alternative to Traditional Models of Human Relationships. Cambridge Quarterly 1993 (in press).

2. Tönnies F: *Gemeinschaft und Gesellschaft.* Darmstadt, Deutschland: Wissenschaftliche Buchgesellschaft; 1963.

3. Jonas H: *Das Prinzip Verantwortung.* Frankfurt a/M, Deutschland: Suhrkamp; 1984.

4. Kozol J: *Savage Inequalities: Children in America's Schools.* New York, NY: Crown Publishers; 1991.

5. US Department of Education: *Adult Learning and Literacy Clearinghouse, Fact Sheet Number 4.* Washington, DC: US Government Printing Office; 1990.

6. Daniels N: *Just Health Care.* New York, NY: Cambridge University Press; 1985.

7. Crozier M, Huntington SP, and Watanuki J: *The Crisis of Democracy: Trilateral Task Force on the Governability of Democracies.* New York, NY: New York University Press; 1975.

8. Sklar H: *Trilateralism.* Boston, MA: South End Press; 1980.

INDEX